Illustrations

Good Friday procession past the White House 15
Delivering the statement in Lafayette Park...........16
Participants in the dialogue 37
Meeting with the press in Moscow........................51
Greeting Bishop Desmond Tutu at "475"................60
Being arrested for demonstrating against the
    South African apartheid system.........................77
Praying for peace in St. Pierre Cathedral,
    Geneva, Switzerland...78
Displaying a Crayola Brigade birthday card.........117
Signing the Williamsburg Charter 125
Delivering the homily at the inauguration
    of Robert Neff...179
A meeting of the steering committee at
    the ecumenical consultation............................233

The Historical Series of the Reformed Church in America

This series has been inaugurated by the General Synod of the Reformed Church in America, acting through its Commission on History, for the purpose of encouraging historical research and providing a medium wherein this knowledge may be shared with the academic community and with the members of the denomination in order that a knowledge of the past may contribute to right action in the present.

General Editor

The Rev. Donald J. Bruggink, Ph.D.
Western Theological Seminary

Foreword

Ecumenical Testimony is compelling because it is a story, and story has the power to draw one into its movement. This is the story of a pilgrim, a servant of Jesus Christ, who has become a significant shaper of the ecumenical movement of the Christian church.

Even in his college days it was evident that Arie Brouwer was a leader. We met at Hope College in 1954, he a junior, I a sophomore. His intellectual acumen, his ready grasp of the big picture, his capacity for concise articulation of issues, his exceptional gifts of administration, organization, and management marked him as formidable. Add to his giftedness his stature (6'7") and one did not need to be a prophet to know that this man would make a difference. And he has.

Throughout the years of his executive leadership in the RCA, the WCC, and the NCCC, I was proud of him and, because he was in the center of the fray for the imperatives of the gospel, the struggle for justice and peace, I felt part of the action. As I have had opportunity to read through this collection of his sermons, addresses, and writings of the past dozen years, I am prouder still and thank God for the work and witness of this servant of the gospel.

The work is divided into three sections focusing on the world, the church, and the tradition. With great clarity that comes to expression again and again, Arie Brouwer understood that the church is not an end in itself, but must give its life for the life of the world. His involvement on the international political scene was not a betrayal of the gospel, but for the sake of the gospel. Reading the record, that fact cannot be denied. The significant relationships developed with the churches of the USSR, his testimony on behalf of the South African Council of Churches, his involvement in the protest against U.S. Latin American policy, and much more, constitute a consistent vision and commitment shaped by the biblical vision of creation, peace, and justice and the contours of God's Rule.

No matter what the platform or where the arena, Arie Brouwer knew who he was and whom he served. Rising above personality, parochialism, and vested interest, he spoke and wrote with clarity and courage, often engendering conflict but never flinching, never yielding to expediency.

Rooted deeply in the Reformed tradition, formed in the Dutch Calvinism of his home and nurture, he consistently brought an informed biblical-theological perspective to his leadership responsibilities. He thinks, first of all, theologically. Because of his passion for the renewal of the church, he has wrestled intensely with the tradition. Because of his worldwide ecumenical experience, he has been exposed to the whole range of Christian traditions and the dialogue with other world religions.

Ecumenical Testimony is a rich mine of reflection. Brouwer's solid rootage in his own tradition as well as his broad exposure have resulted in a clear-eyed view of the promise and peril of tradition. Recognizing the historical conditionedness of church structures freed Arie Brouwer as a church executive from the numbing paralysis that immobilizes lesser leaders who expend their energy in shoring up outworn structures. In an article published in the *Christian Century*, he indicated a decade ago that he was already aware of the dwindling away of national denominational program bureaucracies and knew the trend was irreversible. Not happy about it, he nevertheless neither went on the defensive nor threw up his hands, but rather sought for a new future into which the respective denominational families might flow. That future, he felt then and still is convinced, lies in ecumenical relationship. The churches need more than a new way of acting; they need a new way of thinking, a new self-understanding. "Only thus," he contends, "can they be set free from cultural captivity, ecclesiastical enchantment, institutional survivalism, traditional confessionalism, and the other isms that bind them."

Such far-sighted and daring leadership is all too rare in the church. To that, no one can attest more poignantly than Arie Brouwer, whose courage and visionary leadership, which had put him in a prophetic posture over against governments and world leaders, finally brought him face to face with the vested interests of the churches in the establishment of the National Council of Churches of Christ. Seeking to implement the restructuring that had been mandated by the council's own executive committee which brought him to the task, Arie Brouwer spoke "truth to power" and paid the price of having the courage to act on his best insight. He resigned his executive position when it became clear that the future to which he was calling the churches had brought the NCCC to an impasse.

Ecumenical Testimony is an important document, providing a window through which to view the universal questions and challenges with which the church in any age must be engaged if it would be faithful to the gospel and serve obediently the Lord of the Church, being in its day a concretization of the Kingdom amidst the kingdoms of this world.

> Richard A. Rhem
> Minister of Preaching
> Christ Community Church
> Spring Lake, Michigan
> Lent, 1991

Debts

My original indebtedness for these testimonies I have already stated in the dedication of this volume. There are many more along the way. The title of this volume, for example, springs from its longest chapter (10), my testimony before the Eloff Commission of the Government of South Africa. Above and beyond all others, that seminal experience interpreted for me the meaning of ecumenical solidarity which is the leit-motif of this volume.

For the invitation to testify before the commission I am indebted to Desmond Tutu and Willis Logan (NCC Africa Secretary) and, in an unintended way, to the State President of South Africa who launched the Commission of Inquiry. But that is only the tip of the iceberg. Underlying that particular testimony are the decades, even centuries, of relationship between the Dutch Reformed Church in South Africa and the Reformed Church in America—to which I am heir and out of which I was privileged to witness at a moment of crisis.

The primary task of leadership, I have long held, is to discern and give voice to the hopes, dreams, faith, and aspirations of the people. Those for whom I have been privileged to speak are a mighty company and to them all I am deeply grateful for these experiences which have been among the richest of my life.

Hovering around each of these testimonies then is a cloud of witnesses. Some have provided occasion for these testimonies, or helped me to write them, to edit them, or to publish them—or even to speak them as their listening spirits drew from me what I was trying to say but could not have articulated without them. Others have created the time and space in which to write the testimonies and to speak them. In the office, this was true especially of Jeanette Doyle, my colleague in the Reformed Church in America, and of many others as well. At home, and above all, it is true of Harriet, my wife and too-often single parent of our four children—to each of whom I am also indebted and for whom, in the end, all of these testimonies were offered.

The Reformed Church testimonies took form most often in the typewriter of Raisa Nemikin. The NCC testimonies were shaped and reshaped in the word processor of Denise Morgan-Davis, as were the introductions to them all, which Dorothy Galbraith carried back and forth across the Hudson as I wrote in New Jersey and Denise typed in New York. The compilation of the testimonies in this volume and the challenge of writing the introductions I owe to Donald Bruggink's encouragement and advice.

Publication of the texts in their entirety was possible through the generosity of several friends, including especially N. Jan and Carol Wagner, Bruce and Susie Neckers, Carl and Sandy Ver Beek, and Harry and Joan De Bruyn, to all of whom I was already indebted for many years of friendship as well as active support and leadership in fulfilling more than a few of our shared dreams—especially for the Reformed Church in America. An even longer friend, Richard Rhem has also again put me in his debt by his glowing foreword—which I am almost embarrassed to acknowledge on the one hand and which on the other hand stimulates me to write another book so he can write another foreword.

I shall of course be indebted as well to any and all who find these testimonies useful to strengthen their own witness to the unity and renewal of the Christian community as sign, instrument, and foretaste of the unity and renewal of the community of humankind and the whole creation.

Introduction:
Patterns of Testimony

Reflecting on what I am doing, mulling it over, exploring backgrounds, probing for patterns, looking for trends—these have been my habits for as long as I can remember. Invitations to give a speech or write an article often stimulated me to give form to those reflections. This was especially true during the 1980s while I served as general secretary of the Reformed Church in America (RCA)(1977-1983) and then, after an interlude at the World Council of Churches (WCC), of the National Council of the Churches of Christ in the United States of America (NCCCUSA or NCC)(1985-1989).

Cast in many forms, given expression in many settings and spilling over both ends of the decade, these testimonies are nevertheless not random. There are patterns to them—which patterns are themselves fruits of the reflection and inherent parts of the testimony.

First in importance is the general pattern of the parts of this book itself: The world, the church, the tradition—and in that order. The significance of that pattern is discussed in the penultimate chapter (number 49), so it is enough here to identify and underscore it—and perhaps to encourage the reader to leap ahead for a moment to read that chapter first. (Some of you will want to begin at the end anyway. Now you can do so with a clear conscience!)

By mid-decade, or even earlier, I was well aware of this overall pattern and firmly committed to it. Some of the smaller patterns within the parts were more elusive, and the press of daily activity left little time to search them out. Following my resignation from the NCCCUSA in 1989, I resolved, therefore, to take some time to reflect on my ecumenical experience thus far. I was interested particularly in any possible patterns in the problems of the ecumenical movement and even more in patterns for potential renewal. The first results of that reflective search are sketched in the closing chapter of Part II (chapter 35)—and best read as the ending of that part rather than as part of this introduction!

After writing that article on mainline renewal, I prepared a talk in which the elements of renewal delineated in it were distilled to three:

A life-celebrating liturgy (worship and faith)
A community-building structure (order and life and work)
A Spirit-seeking tradition (theology, doctrine and dogma)

It was fascinating then to find, some weeks later while sorting out my papers for this volume, that all three of those critical elements were prominent among those papers—and again, in that order. They are focused particularly in Part III, chapters 36, 45, and 50 respectively, and once again best read in place.

The documents in Part III have been selected as well to show at least some of the elements of yet another pattern—the various interrelated strategies for ecumenical renewal available to persons in official denominational leadership such as I enjoyed as general secretary of the Reformed Church in America from 1977 to 1983. These strategies include consultations, priority setting, information sharing, interpretation, advocacy, celebration, critique, and others. All these have served me well to increase the traffic and accelerate the movement on the ecumenical way. I hope that others in similar positions critical for the future of the movement will find them useful.

All these moldable patterns are conditioned of course by unfolding patterns of place and time and position and circumstance, of providence. Part I, for example, is much concerned with relations between the churches, peoples, and nations of the United States and the Soviet Union. That is due not so much to my deliberate choice, but rather to my having been an American church leader present at the Central Committee meeting of the World Council of Churches in Jamaica in January, 1979, and at a later meeting in Geneva in March of that same year—a meeting which moved me profoundly. More of that in chapter 1.

Invitations to give a speech or write an article always received top priority attention and I accepted them whenever I could. I did so as a way of requiring myself to do what I wanted to do. Moreover, I considered such community relationship building an integral and important part of my responsibilities—enough to warrant a third of my time, although I rarely reached that goal.

Further, I enjoyed giving the speeches, as will be evident in a number of the chapters that follow. Writing them, and the articles too, was harder work, but usually enjoyable as well—except when time pressed in on every side, which, as we again shall see, was often the case. Even then, or better particularly then, I wrote to keep my perspective in a milieu often badly out of balance. I have longed treasured James Reston's lament during a long strike at the New York *Times* in the 1970s. "How will I know what I think," he asked, "if I cannot read what I write?"

Most of all, however, I wanted the people to know. This compelling motivation was deeply rooted in my personal experience. Reared in a conservative evangelical and scholastic Reformed tradition, my first introduction to the larger world was mostly negative. That changed dramatically for me when I had a chance to see the world and experience the larger church for myself, of which I have already written in the dedication of this volume and of which I will be writing again in the chapters that follow. The joy of that journey I wanted to share with as many people as possible.

Writing for "the people to know" of course affected the form, the style, and the substance of these testimonies—and tempted me mightily to rewrite some of them, not merely to remove an infelicitous expression here or clarify a thought there (which I have sometimes done), but to recast them wholly and entirely. I have resisted the temptation. Not only because of the time and energy required, but more importantly because the testimonies would then lose their spirit—their particularity, their link to the various communities to which they were addressed, their essence as markers on the ecumenical way, their implied invitation to join the journey. So, here and there, I have fixed the grammar, unpacked an allusion or reordered the syntax and otherwise accommodated spoken style to written. My afterthoughts I have, however, put in the introductions.

And what of repetition? Speaking to many different audiences on related themes, of course I used the same or related ideas many times. But not in this volume. Such repetition has been selected or edited out, except for one favorite story from my own life experience that appears twice because it is integral to two very different texts. My prime sermon on the ecumenical movement also crops up more than once, as does my attempt to deal with the full text of that ecumenical locus classicus, John 17. These exceptions are noted in the introductions to the chapters in which they appear. I excused them at last because I did not intend these testimonies to be read straight through from start to finish. They are offered as pericopes for pilgrims on the ecumenical way through the wilderness of schism—as bread and water, and perhaps now and then even as milk and honey, to refresh weary travelers—and I hope to enlarge the company.

Sometimes these pericopes offer a personal testimony (America the Beautiful), or a glimpse into an important milestone (A Millennial Greeting to the Russian Orthodox Church), or a reflection on a common pilgrimage (Mission in the USA), or the summation of a community experience (Jesus Christ—the Life of the World), or a challenge to the powers (The Race of Death), or a return to the sources (On Being Reformed in the Ecumenical Movement). Drawn from my own continuing pilgrimage toward wholeness, I offer them as testimonies both to the ecumenical way I have walked and to the path that stretches toward the far horizon— the way through to God's future.

I

For the Healing
of the
Nations

1
Choose Life

A joint statement by representatives of the churches in the USSR and the USA meeting in Geneva, Switzerland, March 27-29, 1979

In 1984, the National Council of Churches was expanding its program of relationships with the churches in the Soviet Union. It decided to publish a collection of background articles. Since I had chaired the NCC's special committee on those relationships from its creation in 1981 until I left for Geneva in 1983, I was asked to describe my involvement. I called my contribution "Together on the Way" (p. 6). That title was an English translation of the Dutch "Samen Op Weg," then being used as a slogan for a movement toward union by the two leading Reformed churches in the Netherlands, which were also leaders in the movement for world peace.

In addition to thus drawing on my own particular heritage, I hoped that readers would link that slogan with the very earliest designation of Christians as "followers of the Way" (before they were called Christians) and thus catch a glimpse of the radical nature of this commitment between the churches in the United States and those in the Soviet Union. I was pleased then to see that my friends at the NCC changed their plans and co-opted my title for the entire collection.

The first section of my article described the background for the Choose Life statement, for which purpose it is reproduced below. Since that piece was written primarily for promotional purposes, it may be informative to add a few between-the-line notes.

The first impediment in my suggested approach to drafting the Choose Life (p. 9) statement was the fact that the Soviets needed such "communiques" in those days to deliver to their government as proof of their ecumenical contacts. Unknown to me, in this my first such experience, the Soviets usually came to meetings carrying a draft that reported the outcome of the meeting! So great were the pressures on the Soviet churches that sometimes the Americans could do little more than edit or rehash this precooked bureaucratese. No wonder most were so deadly dull!

At this meeting, too, the Soviet's commitment to their prepared (lengthy, detailed, and technical) text was high. At first it seemed to them that I was proposing to undercut one of their main purposes for the meeting. It took a bit ot talking, but we made it through—and as a result were more prepared for the discussion to follow— all through the night and the next day. Most of the Soviet church leaders' specific concerns we managed to incorporate in the closing "action" section of the statement—hence its very different style.

Word by word, we labored over the document. Even the punctuation was problematic. Not long before this meeting I had discovered the interrobang(!?), but no other American present knew of it. The next day in plenary session, the Russians saved it. Archbishop Kirill said that there was indeed precisely such a punctuation mark in Russian and even if it did not exist in English, a few traces of Russian in the English text would enhance its ecumenical quality! In the end, everyone liked the statement so much, they all wanted to sign it personally and have their signatures reproduced on the distributed document.

The statement was promulgated first at the Ecumenical Center in Geneva on the last day of our meeting. I was immensely pleased when its "different quality" was immediately recognized by those who heard it read out. Six weeks later, on May 10 in San Antonio, Texas, the statement was received with acclaim at the NCC's Governing Board meeting. Wondrously stimulated by the presentation of the inimitable Protopresbyter Professor Vitaly Borovy of the Russian Orthodox Church, who had been present at the Geneva meeting as well, the board celebrated one of the high moments in its history. At least that was the publicly expressed opinion of veteran board member Grover Hartman, seconded by many others.

The great favor with which this statement was greeted in the Soviet Union as well (also described below) was often remarked upon in the years that followed (endangering new efforts I sometimes thought) as we conducted a series of talks which the Soviets insisted on calling the "Choose Life" meetings.

For me personally, this meeting, like the globe-circling journey described in the dedication, proved to be a life-changing event, as will be seen in several of the chapters that follow. Evident as well in some of the following chapters will be the theological method employed in the Choose Life statement—moving from worship to a life situation to reflection to action to reflection and back again to worship.

Together on the Way

"The Russians want to meet with the Americans." That was the word passed around among the Americans at the World Council of Churches Central Committee in Kingston, Jamaica, in January 1979. To veteran Central Committee members it was nothing new. Such meetings happened at almost every gathering of the Central Committee, usually at the initiative of the Soviet Church leaders. But this Central Committee member, attending his first meeting, was both interested and curious.

Over the next few days, even the old hands began to show considerable interest. Presidents Carter and Brezhnev had met—and embraced—shortly before in Vienna. They had publicly committed themselves to SALT II. For the Soviet Union that meant approval. But the treaty was in trouble in the United States Senate. The Soviet Union wanted the treaty badly. So did most of the peace movements in the United States and Western Europe. Would a highly public meeting between the church leaders in the U.S. and the Soviet Union help? In the Carter era, it was generally agreed that it might.

A few weeks later I was invited to join the delegation. We were to meet in Geneva for three days in March. By then, I was embroiled in three highly public and demanding controversies in the Reformed Church in America, all of them focused directly on my office, which I had occupied for less than 18 months, and all of them ecumenical. One controversy was related to a distortion of the Reformed Church's response to a statement by the National Council of Churches on the Israeli invasion of Lebanon. Another was sparked by the World Council of Churches' grant to the Patriotic Front of Zimbabwe in the summer of 1978. The grant had elicited a flood of overtures (petitions) to our General Synod demanding withdrawal from the World Council. A third controversy involved several allegedly illegal ordinations of women as ministers of the Word. All this was, of course, in addition to the usual—and not so usual—difficulties of denominational and bureaucratic life.

My staff colleagues advised me that I had quite enough trouble already on hand. Participation in such a meeting would certainly lead to more trouble in a church on the conservative end of the spectrum in both the National Council and the World Council.

At dinner that evening, I reported that conversation to my family along with my feelings of not knowing how I could find the time to attend the meeting, much less prepare for it. My 15-year-old daughter disagreed strongly: "Dad, this is too important not to do! I ordinarily would encourage you to stay home and would be glad for you not to go. This time I want you to go!"

I found time to go but not to prepare. For most of the previous decade I had focused my attention on justice issues, trying to stimulate social action in the Reformed Church in America by harnessing it to the growing public awareness of political and economic issues related to world hunger. My personal time for "movement work" had been given to Bread for the World. I had only a general knowledge of arms race issues.

The meeting began very formally. Most of us hardly knew one another personally. We were "the Americans." They were "the Soviets." That feeling was reinforced by our two delegations being seated along opposite sides of the U-shaped table and by needing to listen to one another across that open space—through interpreters— and across the barriers of culture, creed, tradition, politics, life-style, personal histories, etc.

The main paper "for our side" was read by Professor Bruce Rigdon of McCormick Theological Seminary. Metropolitan Juvenaly read the paper for "their side." The papers were factual, theological, frightening. Metropolitan Juvenaly declared that "the most urgent problem of the contemporary world is the problem of disarmament." Professor Rigdon called us "to look biblically and theologically at the greatest threat to human existence in the history of the world."

We also heard brief statements from the Soviet and United States ambassadors to the Committee on Disarmament in Geneva. The presence of Ambassador Victor Israelian of the USSR constituted an unprecedented recognition of the church in the Soviet Union by the officially atheistic government. The presence of the two ambassadors was in that respect positive. But it also had the negative effect of strengthening the elusive and important—albeit unfounded—feeling that in some way we Soviets and Americans "represented" the positions of our respective governments. In the ensuing statements and discussions, persons on each "side" made and scored their points.

Already at the beginning of the meeting, a committee had been appointed and charged to prepare a joint statement for our consideration on the last day. Together with the other members of that committee, I gave careful attention to the unfolding discussion, wondering what we could say together. Give all the impediments, I at first felt that we were boxed into three days of talk that could not be brought together in so short a time across so great a gulf.

But, by noon on the second day, there were signs of hope. Nothing of substance had taken shape, but the signs were unmistakable. Our different and sometimes conflicting points of view were becoming commonly understood and to some degree accepted. The "labels" were coming off the "sides." Personal relationships were being established or renewed. Our common faith and our common commitment to the human family were emerging as leit-motifs in the statements from both "sides" of the table. Perhaps they could now be woven together. Feeling still my heavy investment in coming to the meeting, and having been deeply moved by what I had heard and experienced in the meeting, I urgently wanted something more than just another committee statement. By the end of the afternoon, when the drafting committee met, I thought it might be possble. I volunteered to do a first draft.

We gathered at 9 p.m. to review and edit the draft. Together we tested words and nuances, researched biblical texts, and probed the minds of our specialist consultants to identify specific actions to recommend to the churches. By 4 a.m. we had forged and agreed upon a text both in English and in Russian—as well as forging a half dozen enduring friendships.

The text of the statement which emerged from our meeting the next day was published in *Isvestia* and disseminated throughout the Soviet Union. In May, it was adopted unanimously by the NCC Governing Board and subsequently by a number of denominational synods and assemblies in the United States. It was also used by various peace movements in their attempts to secure ratification of Salt II.

We failed in that struggle. We have failed many times since. But the bonds of commitment and friendship developed around that meeting, March 27-29, 1979, continue. At each meeting of the Central Committee, and at occasional other meetings, we have celebrated and deepened our friendships. The churches in both countries have developed formal structures to facilitate the growing relationship between the churches and peoples of our two nations.

Choose Life

I call heaven and earth to witness against you this day, that I have set before you life and death, blessing and curse. Therefore, choose life, that you and your descendants may live.
(Deuteronomy 30:19)

We make this appeal as servants of Christ gathered from among the churches of the USA and the USSR. We have been drawn together across the differences of language and culture by our common Christian calling to foster life in the midst of a race towards death. We affirm our unity in confessing Christ as Lord and Saviour.

Gathered in Geneva during the season of Lent we have been especially conscious of the sufferings of our Lord who offered Himself that we might have life and have it abundantly (John 10:10). From our faith in Christ, the All Powerful, the Conqueror of Death, we have drawn strength to choose life in spite of the spreading power of death.

Our three day session was marked by acts of worship and included presentation and discussion of theological and technical papers as well as dialogue on issues of peace and disarmament. During this time we heard and considered reports from Ambassador Victor Israelian, USSR, and Ambassador Adrian Fisher, USA, the heads of our two delegations in the Committee on Disarmament in Geneva.

We have been encouraged by the engagement of our two governments in an unprecedented range of disarmament negotiations; by the strengthening of the more significant measures taken by the United Nations for disarmament; by the renewed vitality of non-governmental organizations in the disarmament field; and by the indications that the peoples of the world are calling for disarmament. But our ambassadors' presentations and other information set before us have also filled us with profound anxiety for the future of our own and all peoples.

The Arms Race

We are convinced that the arms race cannot be won; it can only be lost. All of us have long been aware of the nuclear terror. Many people have accepted it as an inescapable part of our contemporary world. Numerous voices in the church have been raised against it in both our countries. Our experience in this consultation now compels us to cry out against it with one voice. The existence of forces having the capacity to devastate our planet not once or twice, but many times, is absurd and cannot be tolerated. It must be confronted and overcome in the name of the Christ who lives and reigns forever.

We express profound concern about the danger of a precarious balancing of humanity on the brink of nuclear catastrophe. We know that still more terrible weapons are being developed which can only lead to greater fear and suspicion and thus to a still more feverish arms race. Against this we say with one voice—NO! In the name of God—NO!

We are opposed to the arms race not only because of the danger that we will all lose it in the future, but also because we are in fact losing the race now. Already in 1978, the nations of the world were spending more than one billion dollars per day—400 billion per year—on armaments, a sum which is increasing every day. We were informed that the World Health Organization required a mere 83 million dollars to wipe out smallpox. What could be done with the other thousands of millions!? Could the hungry be fed!? Could the sick be made whole!?

Nor can the cost be measured in money alone. The gifts of God given to his people for the service of the new creation in Christ are everywhere diverted to the destruction of peace and order. Peoples are forced by economic and political pressure to offer up their lives in the manufacture of death. Nations already ravaged are wounded again as their irreplaceable natural resources are consumed in the arms race rather than being employed in the development of just, sustainable and participatory societies for their own people. Widespread moral devastation, cynicism and hopelessness are the only rewards.

Theological Reflections

To address the danger of these fantasies of destruction being acted out in our history on a global scale, we have sought to renew our vision. We have listened again to the ancient words of the prophet Isaiah:

He shall judge between the nations, and shall decide for many peoples; and they shall beat their swords into plowshares and their

> spears into pruning hooks; nation shall not lift up sword against nation, neither shall they learn war any more. (Isaiah 2:4)

We confess that the nations which, with the help of God, can transform swords, can also disarm missiles. We bear witness that the Lord our God is a God of peace who wills the well-being of the whole of His creation. He has granted us and all His People a vision of *shalom* for the present time and for the ages to come in which all peoples and nations will dwell together in security.

Yet we acknowledge that this, the very longing for security on the part of the nations, is often used to justify the arms race. The possession of arms by some breeds fear and suspicion among others which they seek to quell by acquiring their own arms. This in turn breeds more fear and suspicion, which results in an escalation of terror rather than the establishment of full security.

We recognize that we ourselves and the peoples of our two nations, and indeed, every man, woman and child in all the world, are caught in this spiral of terror. We perceived that the threat of this escalation is slipping beyond human control. We were then reminded of the Apostle Paul's exclamation that "we wrestle, not against flesh and blood, but against principalities, against powers" (Ephesians 6:12). We confessed that seeking our security through arms is in fact a false and idolatrous hope and that true security can be found only in relationships of trust. These relationships we believe to be possible, for Christ has overcome the principalities and powers (Colossians 2:15).

JESUS IS LORD!

Call to Action

We therefore pledge ourselves and encourage our brothers and sisters:

—to press for the earliest possible approval of the SALT II accords. While we understand that SALT II does not provide for more substantial arms reduction, it does provide a new and essential framework (of parity) for negotiating substantial and equal reductions in SALT III, and further steps in the direction of general and complete disarmament. It promises a new opportunity to consolidate institutions for halting the spread of nuclear weapons. The success of SALT II would open the way to decisive progress on other critical disarmament issues. It would enable our two goverments to share more fully in the constructive works of peace in economic, technical and cultural affairs. It would help to promote a new climate of international relations in general.

—to call for a full and general prohibition of: nuclear arms testing; the development and deployment of new nuclear weapon systems; and the production and accumulation of chemical and radiological arms as well as other weapons of mass destruction.

—to support the role of the UN in disarmament negotiations and such international forums as the Special Session on Disarmament and other initiatives in this field. The arms race produces hardships, and lethal dangers, not only for our two countries, but for all nations of the world, especially those having nuclear capability. Therefore, all governments have the right and the duty to participate constructively in the process of disarmament.

—to support ecumenical programmes concerned with disarmament, especially the World Council of Churches Programme for Disarmament and Against Militarism and the Arms Race; and to cooperate with other non-governmental programmes for disarmament.

—to express readiness to unite our efforts for peace and disarmament with the followers of all religions and all persons of goodwill.

—to call upon our churches to make available staff persons and financial resources for disarmament programmes.

—to urge our churches in their teaching and preaching programmes to emphasize the Biblical vision of peace; and also to stress the devastating social and personal consequences of the arms race.

—to give special attention to strengthening and enlarging the community which has been nurtured among the Christians in the USSR and the USA for more than twenty years, and which we have again experienced here, including the possibility of further consultations on disarmament and other visitations of a general nature, as well as joint days of prayer for peace using the Ecumenical Prayer Cycle (World Council of Churches) and respective liturgical materials of the churches involved.

Finally, our sisters and brothers, we call to your attention the authoritative predictions that nuclear war by the 1990's is an increasing probability. In that decade of high risks we will be approaching the end of our millenium. Even now, only twenty years separate us from the moment when we will be called upon to mark prayerfully the bi-millenary anniversary of the coming to the world of our Lord and Saviour, Jesus Christ, the Prince of Peace. How shall we meet that day!? In what state shall we present our planet to the Creator: shall it be a blooming garden or a lifeless, burnt out, devastated land?

Thus the Lord has set before us again life and death, blessing and curse: therefore choose life that you and your descendants may live.

2
Siding With the Suffering

A Church Herald *column and a witness outside the White House,* *Good Friday, April 17, 1981*

My experience at the talks with the Soviets in Geneva stimulated me to find out more about them and about the Soviet/American relationship. That led to a sharply increased awareness of the artificial but dangerous place of "the Soviet threat" in American politics. In late February, 1981, only a few weeks before the first anniversary of the assassination of Archbishop Romero, the newly inaugurated Reagan administration announced an increase in military aid and advisors for El Salvador. Administration officials justified it by casting El Salvador in the role of prime battleground between democracy and totalitarianism; between East and West; between the United States and the Soviet Union.

I was appalled and outraged at this callous abuse of the Salvadoran people for ideological ends. Something had to be done. With the NCC and its member churches newly disempowered by the Reagan election, the situation seemed to call for a public protest. I launched one with the support of other heads of communions and with the aid of resource materials and organizational expertise from the Inter-Religious Task Force on El Salvador (at 475) as well as from the Sojourners (in Washington).

Doctor Brouwer leads the Good Friday procession past the White House. Others shown are Dr. Robert Neff, general secretary, Church of the Brethren; Dr. Kenneth Taegarten, president, the Christian Church (Disciples of Christ); Dr. Avery Post, president, the United Church of Christ. This photo appeared on the front page of the Los Angeles Times, *Saturday, April 18, 1981. (Credit: Wide World Photos)*

The culminating event of the protest was scheduled for Good Friday, April 17, 1981, in Washington, D.C. The offices of various branches of the United States government participating in the oppression of the

Salvadoran people had been designated as "stations" on a contemporary way of the cross. Along that way, the assembled church leaders were to carry a cross, pausing at each station for prayer and brief statements of protest related to the work of that agency. The last "station" was the White House itself, where we were to gather in Lafayette Park for prayers and songs and several more comprehensive, but still brief, concluding statements. My statement was made on behalf of the church leaders.

Delivering the statement in Lafayette Park, April 17, 1981.

The *Church Herald* column, which precedes the statement below, was an explanation to the RCA in advance of the criticism I expected to receive—and did, along with a surprising amount of support and appreciation. (The ecumenical consultation referred to in the opening paragraph is explained in Part III, chapter 37.)

Siding With the Suffering

During the Reformed Church's Ecumenical Consultation last April, several overseas guests described the suffering of their people in various parts of the world. In response, the consultation participants declared themselves willing "to bear the burdens of our sisters and brothers who groan under economic exploitation and political oppression." A few hours later, in the closing moments of the consultation, we were suddenly informed that Dr. C. M. Kao, general secretary of the Presbyterian Church in Taiwan, had been taken prisoner by his government. Dr. Kao and the Presbyterian Church had long opposed the government's oppression of the Taiwanese. Now the government was exacting from him the cost of his convictions.

The consultation was also affected by the assassination only a few weeks earlier of Archbishop Oscar Romero. This spiritual leader of the Roman Catholic Church in El Salvador had been gunned down in the small hospital chapel where he was conducting worship. Under his leadership, the Roman Catholic Church in El Salvador had been in the front of the struggle for freedom and justice. Archbishop Romero had dared to speak up for the poor; he had called upon the government to stop its slaughter of the people and he himself had been slain.

A few months later, our newspapers and television screens carried the grisly pictures of the bodies of four American women exhumed from shallow graves in El Salvador where they had been hidden after being slain for serving the poor—for siding with the suffering. Two of the slain women were Maryknoll sisters, trained at the same mission institute where our Ecumenical Consultation had gathered. During the consultation, we had many times taken note of the gentle graciousness of these sisters and of the atmosphere of commitment to world mission with which they surrounded us. It was almost incomprehensible that two of their sisters, who seemed now to be our sisters, lay dead in El Salvador.

These four American women were accompanied in death by more than 10,000 Salvadorans during 1980 alone. Most of the dead were from among the peasants, who have long been under the control of the few wealthy landowners and repressed by military governments. After the revolution in neighboring Nicaragua, reforms were initiated which outraged many of El Salvador's wealthy families. Some emigrated to Miami or Gautemala from where they continue to finance "death squads" that kill agrarian reformers, politicians, trade unionists, priests, and other innocent people. The army and government security forces have frequently cooperated in these matters.

As I now write, on Ash Wednesday, the United States government has announced that it is adding another $25 million to the $10 million already given in military aid by the Carter administration and adding about 30 military advisors to the 20 already in El Salvador. Our Department of State argues that this military aid is necessary to counter the activities of the Soviets.

The root of the crisis is not in Soviet arms. It is in a long history of governmental injustice—an opinion expressed both by Salvadoran President Duarte and by Archbishop Rivera Damas and shared by an overwhelming majority of Salvadorans. Our government's attempt to prop up the military by providing it with guns and grenades to be used against its own people only adds to the injustice. In fact, it drives the people to desperation and may make communism appear to be their only hope.

The best hope for El Salvador lies neither with the Soviets nor with the Americans but with the people of El Salvador themselves. They must be given a voice—a controlling voice—in their own destinies. Our government should support international initiatives to seek such a voice for the people through negotiation. It should abandon our military involvement, which will only prolong the repression and killing.

The leading role played by the churches in El Salvador places a particular responsibility upon us as Christians in the United States. The voice of the people of El Salvador cries out through the priests who have baptized, and now must bury, the peasants and their children. It was this cry of the people which Archbishop Oscar Romero heard and lifted up and for which he died. It is this voice of the people—this voice of our brothers and sisters in Christ who cry out to us—that we must also hear and then ourselves lift up in our land against the policies of our government which crush out the life and hope of this people, violate our own national heritage, and eventually bring down upon us all the judgment of God, as did our involvements in Vietnam and in Iran.

The struggle over El Salvador promises to be long and hard; yet, it is not an isolated case of suffering. The suffering in Taiwan, in South Africa, and in the Middle East, which so moved participants in the Ecumenical Consultation last April...is no less severe now. Through the testimonies of these suffering brothers and sisters, I have come to believe that siding with the suffering across international boundaries may well be the most important function of the ecumenical movement in the '80s and '90s. The unity of the church is, after all, most significant as a sign of God's plan to unite all things in Christ. That plan cannot be fulfilled while our sisters and brothers are being murdered.

To side with the suffering will no doubt put considerable strain upon our Reformed Church fellowship in the future as it has in the past. The larger church represented in the ecumenical movement includes many more poor and suffering Christians than we are accustomed to in our denomination. When their voices are raised up, we may hear unfamiliar and even painful sounds. Since these voices are often heard through the World Council of Churches and the National Council of Churches, the storm and stress they evoke often swirls around these institutions.

Yet without such solidarity with the suffering, the church cannot—any more than the nation—escape the judgment of God. Perhaps the most dramatic example of such judgment may be found in the church of the Soviet Union. In the days before the revolution, the church seemed often to sanction the suffering of the people imposed upon them by their rulers. The resulting disappointment and anger helped to feed the fires of persecution kindled after the the revolution. Many expected that pattern to be repeated in a black-ruled Zimbabwe. That it has not may be partly due to governmental policies and partly due to the fact that much of the church, including the Lutheran World Federation and the World Council of Churches, was on the side of the suffering— where, as we must surely know on this Good Friday, we will also find Christ the Lord

Statement in Lafayette Park

For more than 19 centuries, Christians have gathered on Good Friday to commemorate the death of our Lord. Through the sufferings of Christ, they have sought to find hope and meaning in their own suffering.

We have come here on this Good Friday to witness to the sufferings of Christ in the sufferings of the people of El Salvador. We remember our brother and father in God, Archbishop Oscar Romero, who during last year's Lenten season was martyred for his ministry to the people of El Salvador. In the midst of these memories, and in the face of violent death rampaging across El Salvador, we are drawn together in the communion of Christ's suffering. We gather to pray to God and to petition the government.

We have come first to protest the sufferings and crucifixion of the Salvadoran people. For decades, the people of El Salvador have endured all manner of injustice, cruelty, and barbarism. In this very week we call Holy, they are under the cross. Daily, mothers see their sons stripped, beaten, and murdered. Just as the powerful in Jerusalem were prepared to crucify our Lord in order to maintain their positions, so the powerful in El Slavador are prepared to crucify a whole people in order to maintain their power.

We have carried our protest to Washington because our government is increasing the power of the persecutors through new and larger grants of military aid and through military advisers. The crucifixion of our Lord depended finally upon the imperial power of Rome. The crucifixion of the Salvadoran people depends finally upon the imperial power of the United States. We are gathered here to say to our government—Stop the crucifixion.

We protest the policy of seeking military solutions to human problems. We join hands with those who oppose military aid. We project the vision of a negotiated peace grounded in justice.

We are gathered as well to protest the violation of our national heritage. We are concerned not only for the Salvadorans, but also for ourselves, our fellow Americans, and our children. The American Revolution has for two centuries been an inspiration to free peoples everywhere. In the decades after World War II, the people of Africa and Asia found strength in the story of our struggle for independence as they themselves threw off colonial yokes to become free peoples and independent nations. Yet during the last few decades our government has apparently itself lost confidence in our own heritage of freedom. Again and again it has acted as if our primary value was anti-communism. In the name of resisting communism, our government has aligned itself with all manner of bloody and oppressive tyranny. Sometimes this has been done quietly, and we, the citizens, have not known. But we know of El Salvador. Our Secretary of State has trumpeted this terrible policy across the land and around the world. Faithfulness to the best in our national heritage requires us to protest.

Finally, we are gathered to protest the dehumanization of our foreign policy. In Jerusalem long ago it was said, "It is expedient for you that one man should die for the people and that the whole nation should not perish." Our Lord was crucified in fulfillment of that policy. Something like that was said last year in El Salvador and Archbishop Oscar Romero was assassinated. Now the Reagan administration is saying that it is expedient for one nation to die—in order to preserve its anti-communist ideology. Against this callous indifference to the people of El Salvador—this callous crucifixion— we have come to protest.

Above all else we would—if we could—stay the continuing crucifixion of the Salvadoran people. Neither ideological triumph over communism nor political advantage over the Soviet Union, nor renewed national self-confidence, nor any other cause can justify our government's support of the systematic slaughter of the Salvadoran people.

Twice we have sought to convey these concerns to President Reagan. Our written appeals have passed before blinded eyes; our requests for meetings have fallen on deafened ears. Today we address to our government the closing words of Oscar Romero's last homily addressed to his government:

The Church is the defender of the Law of God and of the dignity of the human person, and cannot remain silent before such an abomination.

Therefore, in the name of God, and in the name of this long-suffering people, whose laments rise to heaven every day more tumultuous, I beseech you, I beg you, I command you in the name of God: Stop the repression!

3

Impressions of the Soviet Union and Re-entry

Two Church Herald *columns, August 21 and September 18, 1981*

In 1981, my wife, Harriet, and I received an invitation from the Baptist Union to be their guests for a two-week stay in the Soviet Union. We brought greetings to their congregations in and around Moscow, Volgograd, Yalta, Kiev, and Leningrad. Both of us will always remember the kerchief-framed faces of the babushkas (Russian grandmothers) pressed together row upon row in the Moscow church, overflowing pews and aisles and balconies and porches. Many of the faces testified to lives of poverty and suffering as well as to deep and abiding faith.

We remember as well the young people who gathered around us in Simpheropol longing to hear a little news about youth in the United States, practice their English, and learn an American song. And we remember the farewells as the congregation became a sea of waving white handkerchiefs as the people lifted their voices in a song of farewell, "God be with you 'til we meet again." And we carry with us a thousand other memories and impressions, a few of which were shared in these columns, two of several such reports.

In the titles of these two columns, I should have referred to the Soviet Union rather than to Russia. No longer recalling the reason for this lapse, I can do no more here than regret and correct it.

Impressions of the Soviet Union

The devotion of the Russian people to their "motherland" was by far my deepest impression. In the United States, we may have almost forgotten World War II. In the Soviet Union, it sometimes seemed as if the war were fought only yesterday. "Unknown soldiers" and "heroes of the Soviet Union" are honored everywhere with eternal flames, massive monuments, and heroic statuary. Honor guards at the memorials include uniformed school children who compete for the privilege of standing one 15-minute watch. Newly married couples come directly from their weddings to place flowers before the memorials. Whole museums are dedicated to the great battles.

In Kiev, the mother city of Russia, a great monument commemorating the heroic defense of the motherland was completed only this May—40 years after the invasion! Newspapers still carry advertisements of children seeking parents—or parents seeking children—lost in what Soviet citizens call the Great Patriotic War. And there is still an occasional and much-publicized reunion.

I encountered all this first and most powerfully at Volgograd. In this city, called Stalingrad during the war, the Soviet army fought the Nazis to a standstill by clinging to a narrow strip of land along the river Volga. Soviet soldiers fought to the death during three months of hand-to-hand and house-to-house combat until finally only one building was left standing. On November 23, 1942, the Nazis were finally encircled, and on February 2, 1943, 300,000 German soldiers were taken prisoner. Among the tributes displayed in the city museum is a memorial tablet presented by President Franklin Delano Roosevelt in which he hails the battle of Stalingrad as the decisive turning point of the war.

Mamayev Hill, the focal point of the battle, is now the site of a massive complex of heroic statuary glorifying the defenders of Stalingrad. As visitors climb the hill, they pass between these giant statues and finally into an enclosed passageway. Emerging from its semi-darkness, they are suddenly surrounded by the glittering golden Hall of Valor. Against the far walls are red funeral banners bearing the names of 7,200 of the honored dead. The only sound is the mournful sadness of Schumann's "Reverie."

After spiraling around the inside of this hall, the pilgrim pathway leads to the gigantic, 160-foot statue of Rodina, the Motherland— sword upraised, concrete skirts streaming in the wind, fiercely calling the Soviet soldiers to repulse the invading army.

The shrine at Volgograd tells a terrible story. Other cities have similar stories. Four hundred thousand unknown dead were buried in one cemetery at Leningrad—and they were only half of the people who died from war, starvation, and cold during the 900-day siege of that city. One-third of the people of Kiev were destroyed. Altogether 20,000,000 people died. (The U.S. lost 407,316.) One-half of all Soviet families suffered at least one loss. The survivors have not forgotten. Their passion for peace is deep and strong.

Against the background of these powerful memories and emotions, the political leaders of the Soviet Union routinely cloak their military competition with the United States in the robes of self-defense. Our political leaders have for decades unwittingly encouraged that approach by proclaiming loudly that we are the most powerful nation in the world, by placing nuclear missiles on the very soil from which the Soviet Union was last assaulted, and by talking of neutron bombs or even a limited nuclear war in Europe. This political posturing of our leaders may reassure some folks here at home. In the Soviet Union, it is seen as a threat and as confirmation of party propaganda—and that's dangerous for us all.

Devotion to the motherland was my deepest impression. The most surprising impression is that communism was only skin-deep. It's a tough skin, to be sure, but the soul of the people bears the unmistakable imprint of their ancient national traditions. The party, after all, numbers in its membership only about one Soviet citizen in 10. For many, membership is a matter of convenience rather than conviction. With at least 40 to 50 million believers, the Orthodox Church outnumbers the party two to one. For a thousand years, this church has shaped and nurtured the Russian spirit and calmed the torments of soul and body. It is the enduring and unmatched symbol of the Russian spirit. Its art and architecture, music and pageantry are flashes of light in an otherwise drab and dull Soviet society. Keeper of an ancient tradition, the Russian Orthodox Church is a giant reservoir of life and hope for the future.

Finally, there is the all-pervasive authoritarianism of Soviet society. We Americans generally think of this authoritarianism as a fruit of Communism. Not so: it is a thousand years old and more. The czars repressed the people and sent political prisoners off to Siberia long before Communism existed. Authoritarianism in the Soviet Union is Communist only in its present form.

With very few exceptions, it seems that nearly everyone in Soviet society exercises to the full what control and power is available. The spirit of regimentation affects home, church, government, business—all of life. Women are subjected to men nearly always in practice and frequently in principle. News is written and doled out as the government wishes. Foreigners are sealed off from the people. What can be controlled is controlled.

Yet, with all these societal differences, one often feels that we Americans may have more in common with the Russians than we might think. Behind the passive, sometimes sullen, public face, there is an open heart and ready spirit that permits the easy formation of friendships. This openness, typically Russian and typically American, offers hope for building people-to-people relationships. And people-to-people relationships offer hope for getting around the posturing and propaganda of their political leaders and ours in order that we may live in peace. And peace belongs to the essence of Christ's mission and ours.

Re-entry from the Soviet Union

We've all had the experience. After a vacation or a business trip or a few days away, we re-enter the relationships and responsibilities of our day-to-day lives. Often we return to see the familiar and the routine in new perspective.

For denominational staff executives, re-entry is a routine fact of life. Most of us spend between one-third and one-half of our time away from home and office, meeting with congregations, consistories, classes, pastors, lay leaders, and other groups. I've been doing that for more than a dozen years now, and my re-entries have become fairly predictable: happiness, hugs, and handshakes; news from family and friends at home and at work; newspapers, magazines, journals, and mail to plow through; bills to pay; unexpected crises and problems—some solved, some unsolved, and some unsolvable; crowded schedules.

For all of us, re-entry usually means back to work, back to school, or back to some other routine. Such return to regular responsibilities sometimes feels confining. Not so my re-entry from Russia!

For three weeks I had lived amid the rules and regulations of Soviet society. I had been surrounded by the sameness of state-approved architecture, state-approved schools, state-approved television, newspapers, drama, travel, speeches—state-approved everything. I had felt the sullen resentment of the people who must endure it all year after year. Now I was back home and free. No matter the backlog of work, the stack of mail, the meetings lined up—I was free.

The tragedy of gifts wasted, spirits stifled, prophets suppressed, and lives sacrificed well deserves our anger. Love for our brothers and sisters in the Soviet Union demands a persistent and perceptive concern for their human rights. Our concern should be expressed through prayer and through persuasion of our government and business leaders in their dealings with the Soviet Union.

At the moment, however, I am rejoicing in our freedom here. My immigrant grandparents and parents before me delighted in their newfound freedom and opportunity in America. Their troubles in the new world they dismissed with humor. Their achievements they celebrated with thanksgiving. Their gratitude and zeal for America they passed on to their children with the full support of school and church. Together we learned to love this land—our land. I felt this love and thanksgiving renewed upon re-entry from the Soviet Union; I was glad and grateful for America.

I was puzzled too. In spite of all our freedom and all our wealth and all our power, America seems to be afraid.

Americans are afraid of the Soviet Union. Prominent government officials and commentators would have us believe that the Soviet Union is responsible for all our troubles—at least all the troubles that really matter. This rhetoric seems to have enough popular appeal to muster the votes in Congress and support among the people for multibillion-dollar increases in the arms budget. I am puzzled because I have just come from the Soviet Union and I know that they are afraid of and worried about the United States. I know that in both our societies the quality of human life is being diminished as vast resources are wasted on useless weapons. It seemed to me that the Soviets are more afraid of us than we are of them—although they would deny that. In any case, our new weapons will increase their fear and their weapons, which will in turn increase our fear and our weapons, which will in turn...

This climate of fear has stimulated the search for an enemy within as well as without. Apparently, we need a scapegoat. If our appetite for arms is to be satisfied, someone will have to starve. It appears that the poor have been chosen. A great many people seem to believe that feeding the hungry and providing work for the unemployed will drive us into bankruptcy. We are now afraid of the poor.

The poor are also afraid. They are afraid that they will no longer be able to provide food and shelter for themselves and their families. Theirs is not anxiety and anger about higher taxes and denied luxuries. It is fear that next week or next month or next year there will not be bread.

Then I begin to feel afraid. I am afraid that these two great engines of fear—fear of the enemy without and fear of the enemy within—may be out of control, that their momentum may be too great to stop. I remember that these evil, twin fears have been destroyers of civilization throughout history, and I am reminded that they are out of control in many countries of the world today. I pause then and pray for faith and for freedom from fear for us all before I go back to work.

4

Christian Citizens' Crusades

A Church Herald *column, November 27, 1981*

The religious right was on the rise through most of the 1970s. Late in the decade, they surged into presidential politics and helped Ronald Reagan defeat Jimmy Carter. One year later, they were providing support for the Reagan administration's various ideological crusades and warming up for the congressional elections. I wanted to enter a general word about Christians in politics before the public began to focus on particular candidates.

Religion and politics have been getting a lot of coverage in the news media during the last year and probably will again during the next year. Most of the attention is focused on the political action organizations of the religious right such as Christian Voice, Christian Voters' Victory Fund, Religious Roundtable, National Christian Action Coalition, and the Moral Majority.

The best known of these organizations is the Moral Majority. Its founder/leader, the Rev. Jerry Falwell, says that although most of its leaders and members are conservative Christians, the Moral Majority is not a religious organization.

The prominence of these organizations seems mostly due to media attention. Recent polls show that their actual influence is much less than they or many of their worried opponents claim. They can, of course, muster some votes, and they can raise some money. It seems, however, that generally they are being used rather than followed by the politicians of the New Right. These politicians gladly enlist the religious right when it suits their cause (the Human Life Amendment) and ignore them when it doesn't (Sandra O'Connor's 99-0 confirmation as Supreme Court Justice).

In politics, that's par for the course. The trouble is that the Moral Majority seems to approach politics as a holy war. Jerry Falwell is, of course, not the first so to meld religion and politics. In 1056 Pope Urban II preached a stirring sermon at a synod in Claermont, France. The congregation, deeply moved, boomed out *Deus vult* (God wills it). This response became the slogan of the first crusade. Popular preachers used it to stir up popular enthusiasm. Throngs marched eastward to the Holy Land to slaughter and be slaughtered—all in the name of Christ.

The fundamental error of crusaders—then and now, right or left—is the failure to distinguish between the will of God and human response to it, between the prophet and the politician. Politics needs prophecy. Now and then when a prophet cries out, "Thus saith the Lord," Christians should respond with an "amen" and with political action. We dare not forget, however, that although the word may sometimes be from the Lord, the political program is always of human origin.

Dreams, visions, and high callings are the elements of prophecy; life situations, resources, and possibilities are the stuff of politics. We need to maintain the difference. Christians may all pursue peace but differ about the defense budget or the draft. Christians may all oppose racism but differ about U.S. investment in South Africa or immigration laws. Christians may all value human life but differ on birth control, abortion, or capital punishment. Legitimate Christian citizens' movements strive to maintain such distinctions; crusaders—of either the right or the left—usually lose sight of them as they seek to increase the fervor of their followers.

Political programs parading as prophecy can be powerful. They are also dangerous. Distinctions between political advocacy and personal attack disappear as the crusade mentality takes over. Opponents become enemies, and in a holy war, enemies are often not only defeated, they are destroyed. We saw all that acted out in America during the 1950s and again during the 1960s. Some of us appear again to be in such a destructive mood.

Christian citizens' crusades are not only bad for the country, they are bad for the church. Many are deeply concerned that through these crusades all evangelicals will lose the respect they have won in recent years through Sojourners, Evangelicals for Social Action,

Bread for the World, and other similar movements concerned for the well-being of the whole world.

There does appear to be cause for concern. Jerry Falwell said in an interview published in *Christianity Today*: "What about the poor? We could never bring the issue of the poor into the Moral Majority because the argument would be, 'Who is going to decide what we teach those people? Mormons, Catholics?' No, we won't get into that."

Holding back on ministry to the poor because there is not agreement on who is going to preach to them does not exactly commend the church to the world. Readers of the *Los Angeles Times* on March 4, 1981, were probably not encouraged either to read Falwell's prediction that nuclear holocaust would likely happen in the next generation but that the Lord would take the church out of the world just in the nick of time.

Most of us must surely know firsthand the tempting lure of some form of religious escapism. We probably understand something of the mixture of fear and anger and longing for security that motivates these militant moralists. It would be hard not to in today's world. Yet, our calling is not to fear and flight, but to faith and hope and love. Christian citizens' movements can help us fulfill that calling. Crusades can't.

5
Rumors of War
and Promises of Peace

A Church Herald *column, December 25, 1981*

A column appearing precisely on Christmas day was a chance to highlight the contemporary secular significance of that long ago event, too often reduced to only "religious" significance. Expenditures for arms at the end of the '80s were of course even more insane than at the beginning—thanks in part to Christian crusades.

...world expenditures for arms and armies now exceed $500 billion per year. This is more than $100 for every man, woman, and child on the face of the earth—millions of whom have never in their lives received $100 in one year.

With the coming of Christmas, we can hardly help but ask whether the gospel of "peace on earth" is believable in such a world. The unceasing war of words, the escalating spiral of arms, and the ever more precarious balance of terror make it seem less believable. More and more people confess that they think nuclear war is likely in their lifetimes and that there is little they can do about it. Never before in history have human beings commanded so much power; never have so many felt so powerless.

During the past year I have often found myself marveling at the arrogance of modern military might. Last spring, driving through mile upon mile of Florida orange groves, I heard myself saying, "How dare we?" How dare we arrogate to ourselves the power to destroy all this?

I grope for ways to understand and remember that Emil Brunner once defined sin as "Man's God Almightiness." Yes, that's it. The power to make nuclear war is "Man's God Almightiness." And it is forbidden.

Last summer, as we were camping in the Canadian woods, slowly at first in the northern sky, and then faster and faster all the heavens were laced with the pulsating lights of the Aurora Borealis. How dare we dream of unleashing the terrrible mushroom clouds that will blot this out from human view forever? It must not be.

Our best hope that it will not be springs from another vision of the night sky.

> And suddenly there was with the angel a multitude of the heavenly host praising God and saying, "Glory to God in the highest, and on earth peace among men with whom he is pleased!" (Luke 2: 13-14).

God's promise is not merely for an external armistice; nor is it only the promise of an internal consolation. It is the fulfillment of the ancient prophetic vision of shalom. This peace of God is well-being, wholeness—life as God intended it for us all and for the earth itself: rooted in justice, offered in stewardship, and lived in love. It surrounds the whole human family, encompasses the creation, and reaches from age to age.

Yes, I know, the final fulfillment of these prophecies lies beyond history. But the mission of God in history is toward that vision. We who follow Jesus can face no other way. The Christian calling is to peace.

Christmas is a time rich with opportunities to celebrate and to practice that calling. We can open our circles of celebration to neighbors unknown, alone, far from home, or in need. We can sustain the lives of children suffering and dying from hunger today as surely as they died from Herod's sword 2,000 years ago. We can comunicate with Christian churches in other countries to share different Christmas traditions and thus begin to share our lives. We can raise the carols of Christmas and the songs of peace, believing that they shall be sung long after the "stormy clangor of wild war music" has faded away.

Justice, love, and peace shall have their way for they are God's way, and history shows that there is no other way. Walking in God's way calls us to work for arms control, for international understanding and cooperation, for peace with prosperity, for freedom of conscience, and for the personal practice and pursuit of peace at Christmas and into the New Year.

6
Freedom of Religion

A Church Herald *column, February 19, 1982*

This column is a reflection on the United Nations' Declaration on Freedom of Religion. The declaration was long delayed by the radical nature of this freedom. It makes governments anxious. I wanted to help my Reformed church readers recognize the significance of this particular freedom—too often seen as of lesser significance than the other freedoms of speech, press, and assembly guaranteed by the First Amendment to the Constitution. I hoped too that it would help them understand the religious roots of my own political commitments, which were distinctly out of step with the times and increasingly worrisome to ever larger numbers. This column provided an opportunity as well to take up that durably troublesome perception of "imbalance" in RCA and NCC criticism of the United States and the Soviet Union—and to quote one of my heroes, Thomas More.

Freedom of religion is a fairly new idea. Religious minorities were tolerated in some ancient societies, but the concept of religious liberty as a human right comes to us from the European Renaissance of the 14th, 15th, and 16th centuries. Historians call that the "modern" era.

Today, the principle of religious liberty, at least in some modified form, is affirmed in law by almost all national governments—including those socialist governments which are officially atheistic. These guarantees are, however, sometimes very limited and restrictive. Even then they are not always observed by the state, as we know from our daily news.

Oppressive governments of any kind—right or left—totalitarian or "authoritarian"—usually look askance at religious liberty, and well they might. In many such countries, religious groups are by far the largest dissenting force and frequently are among the most visible and tenacious dissenters. The Roman Catholic Church in Poland and the black churches in South Africa are outstanding current examples.

People who dissent in the name of God can be formidable opponents. Dietrich Bonhoeffer and Martin Niemoller of Germany, Beyers Naude of South Africa, and C. M. Kao of Taiwan are a few names that spring to mind. Little wonder that commentators sometimes speak of religious liberty as "the linchpin of all freedoms" and "the most crucial of all human rights." The roll is long and honorable of men, women, and children who have valued freedom of conscience more than life itself—to die, in the words of Sir Thomas More's last testimony in *A Man for All Seasons*, "The King's loyal servant, but God's first."

This radical quality of religious conviction is the chief reason why the United Nations has taken more than three decades to negotiate the declaration on religious liberty finally approved last December. Governments were loathe to give their guarantees. This declaration is an orderly, international attempt to insure and promote freedom of religion everywhere. It is a sign of hope for believers in many countries.

International support for human rights is important because it helps minimize the danger of coopting human rights into the game of international politics, public relations, and propaganda. The government of the United States, for example, criticizes human rights violations much more quickly—and loudly—in countries it opposes than similar violations in the countries of its allies—in Cuba more than in El Salvador or in Russia more than in China, both of which are Communist.

The churches, by contrast, often appear to concentrate criticism on their own nation's government and its allies. That is consistent with Christ's teaching, which requires us to apply our ethical standards first of all to our own practices—to take first the beam from our own eyes. When our governments act, we act. Our first responsibility is therefore to monitor the policies and actions of our own governments. If, in El Salvador or in other places, attacks upon the church and other violations of human rights are directly aided and abetted by the government of the United States, we must protest.

On the other hand, enlisting the help of the United States government and American public opinion in protest against violations of human rights in countries not allied with the United States, such as Cuba or the Soviet Union, can have—and often has had—the effect of hardening the attitudes of these governments and increasing the suffering of believers. A particularly harmful example of this was Senator Henry Jackson's attempt in the mid-70s to force the Soviet Union to increase the number of Jews permitted to emigrate. The Soviet Union responded by decreasing the number. Like it or not, we need to recognize that yielding to the Americans is for such governments a "loss" to an opponent. We need to act accordingly.

Always, we ought to shape our methods by their effect on our brothers and sisters under the cross. Zealous commitments to fight "Godless communism" on the left or "totalitarian oppression" on the right can easily lead to fanaticism which no longer sees the suffering people—only our self-righteous pursuit of our cause. Regular, informed prayer for suffering people can help us keep people before politics and propaganda. Names of people and information about them is available from Amnesty International, 3618 Sacramento Street, San Francisco, California, 94118.

7

A Critique of
'Christianity and Democracy'

A dialogue with the Institute on Religion and Democracy, The Interchurch Center, New York, NY, March 24, 1982

In the early 1980s, mainline Protestant leaders were worried about the religious right. The Institute on Religion and Democracy (IRD) was just getting under way, but it was already clear that the National Council of Churches would be one of the institute's select targets.

Fresh from a reorganization of its communication program, the council had just created an information committee and had named Warren Day as assistant general secretary for information. He decided to meet the challenge head-on by focusing the first meeting of the new committee on the religious right.

The highlight of the meeting was a special luncheon program with about 250 church leaders and media representatives crowded into the Interchurch Center dining room. First to speak was Norman Lear, television producer and founder of People for the American Way, described by the NCC as "an organization promoting diversity and freedom of expression thus seeking to counteract the effects of the extreme religious right." Also featured at the luncheon was a dialogue between the NCC and the IRD. The NCC was represented by its president, United Methodist Bishop James Armstrong and me; the IRD, by its chairman, the Rev. Edmond W. Robb, also United Methodist, and Lutheran pastor and author Richard John Neuhaus, who had drafted the IRD statement, "Christianity and Democracy," a sort of IRD manifesto.

Participants in the dialogue (L to R): Edmond Robb, James Armstrong, Richard Neuhaus, and Arie Brouwer. To Brouwer's right is William Howard, chairperson of the NCC information committee and moderator for the dialogue. (Credit: United Methodist Board of Global Ministries, John C. Goodwin).

Neuhaus's oral statement in the dialogue was not less pointed than the written statement, a few excerpts of which appear below in my presentation. While rereading the IRD statement earlier that morning as I traveled back to New York from Grand Rapids, I had decided that Neuhaus probably would speak in that same style and that if he were not met head-on, the IRD would carry the day. My hastily drafted statement was even more hastily edited after being run by a few trusted RCA colleagues for their comments. They had the gravest doubts about the wisdom of this statement, but I knew Dick Neuhaus from working with him on the board and in the executive committee of Bread for the World and I wanted to be ready. I was. We came off looking just fine—well reported in the media and with some ethical questions on the record for IRD and the NCC to ponder and discuss throughout the decade.

And, it would seem, around the world. Almost exactly one year later, I was in South Africa giving testimony before the Eloff Commission (chapter 10). After my extensive statement, I was asked only two questions, both unrelated to the text of my testimony. In the first, counsel for the commission wanted to know whether I was the same Arie Brouwer who had debated the IRD a few years earlier in New York. I recalled then that at the luncheon table that day in New York, I had mentioned to Dick Neuhaus that I thought I had detected in "Christianity and Democracy" traces of 19th century Dutch Reformed theologian Abraham Kuyper's notion of sphere sovereignty (which also underlies apartheid ideology). He allowed as how he had encountered the idea in conversation with South Africans.

On the way to the National Council of Churches' Governing Board meeting last November, I read the current *Christian Century* editorial which informed me that, at the meeting, I would receive a special report concerning the Institute on Religion and Democracy. As I read the report, I registered the feeling that it was probably an overreaction. Specifically, it seemed that in most places where the reporters found connections, they deduced conspiracies. I did wonder about the tactics of the Institute on Religion and Democracy (IRD) disclosed in the report but thought it best to wait and see. New political action organizations, like newborn babies, should be excused for demanding attention.

In the intervening months, I saw a few stories in the press and I heard a little gossip. In January, Warren Day asked me if I would participate in a "dialogue"—I think he called it—with the leaders of the IRD. I readily agreed—partly because Dick Neuhaus, one of the participants, is an old partner in political action (a partnership that I hope will continue after this dose of Dutch Reformed tough love).

I agreed, too, because I believed that the National Council of Churches, the World Council of Churches, and "475" in general need to engage our critics. Like other bureaucracies, ours are subject to group-think, and we are tempted to filter out the facts that do not fit our favorite theories. Outside critical perspectives can help to deliver us from those evils. I myself so much enjoy railing against these bureaucratic machinations that sometimes I think I am a victim of the group-think which opposes group-think!

Sometime later in January, or perhaps in February, the institute's statement, "Christianity and Democracy," (which is at your tables) appeared on the scene, describing itself as an explanation of "the reasons for the Institute on Religion and Democracy." Some of my friends told me it was, in their words, "well done." Again, my copy came to me courtesy of the NCC at its February Executive Committee meeting. (I do hope that the institute paid for all that xeroxing!) The statement was distributed in connection with the announcement of this event. I was grateful *that* day for Bishop Armstrong's description of *this* day in terms something like a discussion between concerned Christians with differing views and not a confrontation—a spirit which he has just exemplified and I wholeheartedly endorse.

That weekend, I read the statement. I was amazed and appalled. What, I wondered, are my friends reading, if this by comparison seems "well done"? My rereadings have not helped.

My greatest difficulty with the statement is its use of unethical means—an old and dangerous problem for political religion. For a time, I wondered if this was perhaps a case of critical candor gone awry—of overstatement and exaggeration to make a point. But that is too kind—even innocent—and after Billy Budd, we Calvinists dare not be innocent! This is not mere overstatement. This is, to use one of the document's own countless overwrought words, "mendacious posturing." It is argument by implication, innuendo, and insinuation. By document's end, the leaders of the church have been cast, if not into the outer darkness, at least into "the shadowed corners of bureaucratic power." They have been labelled as "apologists for oppression" and condemned as purveyors of "lies and half-truths." The play-acting continues apace. Philosophical and ideological cloaks part to reveal knives flashing in the dark. And if these verbal stilettoes should perhaps strike in error, then the wounds, in Jeremiah's imagery, are to be healed lightly. They say and I quote, "We are prone to err and we live by forgiveness." Ahh, what freedom! what licence! But, how, more than three decades after Dietrich Bonhoeffer, can responsible Christian leaders seek so to lave themselves in cheap grace? Don't they know that it won't wash?

"Christianity and Democracy" asserts (on page 3) that "leadership in an open church is marked by candor and never by contempt for the convictions of those with whom we differ." Well and good— even exemplary. Yet, just across the page, following an assertion that "anti-Communism is an indispensable component in discerning the signs of the times," we read that "those who do not understand this have not recognized the bloody face of our age and, however benign their hopes, can contribute little toward the establishment of a more humane world." One may, I think, be forgiven for detecting the faint odor of contempt. By page 12, there is no mistaking it. After a recitation of views which it opposes, this document claims that "this combination of lies and half-truths conceals a host of cultural and, more often than not, racial prejudices." And three paragraphs later, other opposing views—troublesome views to be sure—are actually called "contemptible." One can only conclude that the counsel given to others on page three has been, by page twelve, swept away on a sea of rhetoric.

The substance of the document is no less problematic. The root of error seems to be its preoccupation, even its obsession, with the "threat of totalitarianism." Peter Steinfels puts it succinctly in the current issue of *Christianity and Crisis:* "One thing and one thing alone, occupies the whole stretch of the political horizon; everything else is eliminated." True to form, "Christianity and Democracy" claims that "Christians must be unapologetically anti-Communist." I oppose Communism. I think Christians should oppose Communism. But that is not at all the same as saying that Christians should be anti-Communist. We Christians should not allow ourselves to be defined by our opponents in terms of what we are against. We must reserve that privilege for ourselves—in terms of what we are for. It was after all the people of God whom Moses led through the Red Sea—not the anti-Egyptians! Christians who define themselves in opposition to the evils of the day, however monstrous, freeze themselves in a particular historical moment and rob themselves of the great tradition which spans the ages—a loss this conservative cannot countenance.

There are other problems, plenty of them. I can only mention a few. Most of them are related to the theological and political imperatives that crop up now and again in this document. The history of the church knows few dangers more fearsome than theological imperatives or few legacies more terrrible than the wrack and ruin they have wrought when melded with political imperatives. In my own tradition, we remember Hugo Grotius imprisoned and Jan Van Olden Barneveldt beheaded by a government cowering before the Canons of Dort. For us all, there are the Crusades. Like those ancient theological imperatives, those of this document are ideological distortions adduced to undergird faltering politics.

And as for political imperatives, they are the hallmarks of the very totalitarianism against which this statement claims to set itself. By placing its trust in political imperatives, the Institute on Religion and Democracy demonstrates yet again that sometimes comic, sometimes tragic, fate of extreme opponents condemned to recreate one another in their respective images.

Time does not permit treatment of a cluster of other errors: sweeping generalizations and careless assumptions about America's market economy, the peculiar reference to America's Jewish citizens, the tendency to allow a favorite political ideology to take hostage the Gospel of Christ, the failure to recognize that declaring a favored political form to be *necessary* is an effective denial of the lordship of Christ over history.

These and others I pass over to return to my original point. "Christianity and Democracy" declares that the Institute on Religion and Democracy is pledged to the goal that our churches be open churches. Very well, then. Deal with us as we are. Away with the masquerade of straw men that populate this document. Perhaps there still are tucked away somewhere in the warrens of this building a few Billy Budds of the left who have not seen the true face of Stalin; or who scan the East each morning looking for the rising of Mao's new man. But where are these the prevailing views? Or is it merely that someone has failed to notice that his brand-new, neoconservative research library is made up of reprints?

I freely admit that "apologists for oppresion" is a clever piece of rhetoric. But what shall it profit in the end, if one now exchanges the truth for a neatly turned phrase?

8

The Race of Death

An address to the World Conference of Religious Workers for Saving the Sacred Gift of Life from Nuclear Catastrophe, Moscow, May 10-14, 1982

This conference was one of the most highly visible media events in which I was involved with the churches in the Soviet Union. In May, 1982, 588 delegates and observers from ninety countries descended on Moscow at the invitation of the Russian Orthodox church. They represented all major faiths in the world, and a few less familiar. Thirty-one of the delegates were North-American church leaders, each personally invited. One of the number was Billy Graham, on his first visit to the Soviet Union and invited to address the conference. Because I then chaired the NCC's Committee on U.S./USSR Church Relations, I also received an invitation to address the conference.

I was pleased, but concerned as well. It would be my first experience addressing a major interfaith conference. I would do that as a representative of the faith which more than any other in the modern world had oppressed and persecuted persons of other faiths. I would also be speaking as a citizen of the country generally believed to be primarily responsible for the world arms race—and that at a time when Ronald Reagan was giving the world

new grounds for those suspicions by beginning the
massive build-up that would mark his administration.

I decided to address the concerns pertaining to
participation in the conference at the beginning of the
speech. Some other concerns did not lend themselves to
such direct treatment. For example, at that very time the
United States was exploiting religious belief for political
advantage, making the most of "the Siberian Seven," a
group of Pentecostalists who had taken refuge in the U.S.
Embassy. Prior to leaving for the conference, we
Americans who had been invited received many letters
from private citizens expressing concern about the
Siberian Seven as well as a letter signed by twenty-seven
United States senators urging us "to raise this and other
urgent human rights cases." We did, in private meetings
apart from the conference but reported in the media, thus
neither derailing the conference nor compromising our
witness.

Further, the United States Department of State
arranged a special briefing to warn us that the conference
was a Soviet propaganda ploy—which we of course already
knew, but thought it was worth the risk.

In the RCA at that time, we were in the midst of the
most severe budget crisis I had experienced in all my
fifteen years on the denominational staff. To meet it, I
had been asked to resume my work as executive of the
denomination's General Program Council as well as
continue as general secretary. Once again, I drafted on the
run and ran it by some of my RCA colleagues and
ecumenical friends. One of my most trusted RCA
advisors told me I ought to give it up as a bad job and tell
the Russians I didn't have time! More than a little taken
aback, I stuck with it nevertheless.

On the Sunday evening before the conference, indeed
while most of us were en route to Moscow, Ronald

Reagan addressed the nation concerning the need for a strong U.S. military and warning the American people about the dangers of the American peace movement. The next day, the U.S. Embassy provided us with copies of the speech.

The first day of the conference fulfilled the State Department's worst fears with an endless round of speeches laden with pro-Soviet, anti-U.S. propaganda. The text of my speech had earlier been delivered to the conference organizers and copies distributed to the press. Already I had been heavily lobbied by my Russian friends to remove from my speech the reference to Afghanistan. I decided instead to prepare a few lines warning about the dangers of turning the conference into a propaganda war (they appear in paragraphs five and six in the speech— which were not included in the official conference report printed some months later by the Russian Orthodox church!)

When the second day of the conference followed the same propagandistic approach, I consulted a few friends and resolved to make the additions in my address when I spoke later that morning—following immediately after Billy Graham—which further increased my anxiety! About mid-morning, the conference chair was taken by David Preuss, bishop of the American Lutheran church, and a member of the conference presidium. As he took the gavel, he made a brief statement of concern about the anti-American tone of the conference. Shortly thereafter, I made my statement. The media claimed that the two of us turned the conference around. That was more credit than we deserved, but our remarks were well received and the conference did turn out to be a good experience. Because of the high visibility given to the conference in the U.S. media, my speech received a fair amount of attention and was printed in full in a number of places including *World Encounter* (fall 1982), a magazine with a mostly Lutheran readership and in the *Holland Evening Sentinel* of Holland, Michigan.

Two years later, I concluded my article "Together on the Way" (explained in chapter 1) with this paragraph:

> The conference achieved a degree of notoriety in the United States considerably beyond what we had expected. Mostly this was due to the attendance of Billy Graham and, even more, to some of his remarks about religious freedom in the Soviet Union reported (and sometimes distorted) in the U.S. press. That public media attention no doubt increased the number of requests we received from various groups to report on the conference. I confess my own surprise both at the intensity of the interest and also at the willingness, even longing, of the people to hear and believe the desire of the Soviet people for peace. There is a movement out there, and it is building wider and deeper among the people for peace. One day, it may reach high enough so that our two governments will help our two nations to bridge the gulf between us. Meanwhile, we in the churches will continue to walk together on the way.

We are an assembly of various languages and cultures. We have come from many nations. We hold different beliefs. Yet we are all members of one human family and together we treasure the same sacred gift of life.

It is this common humanity which brings us together and which opens our spirits to one another. Our witness to life, however, can be made only in terms of our own experiences as they are shaped by our respective faiths and cultures. I speak to you, therefore, as a Christian because my understanding of the gift of life is shaped by the teachings of Jesus Christ and by my experience of the Holy

Spirit whom we Christians confess to be "the Lord and Giver of Life."

I speak to you also as an American. Although these two traditions of faith and patriotism can sometimes be related, they may never be identified with one another. Loyalty to Christ, in fact, often requires churches to witness against government policy.

This is true today with respect to the arms race. Increasingly, the churches in the United States are denouncing the arms race and America's participation in it as a violation of our national honor, an intolerable immorality, a contradiction of our deepest beliefs, and a source of estrangement from the human family. Our protests include support of a nuclear freeze, participation in Ground Zero Week, and other forms to be reported to this conference.

The interest of our government in our attendance at this conference and President Reagan's speech last Sunday suggest that we are beginning to be a force to be reckoned with. Although the primary focus of the American churches is on the policies of our own government, we of course also lament the participation in the arms race by the Soviet Union and other countries. Our emphasis on U.S. government policy is directly related to our responsibility as citizens of that country. This emphasis should not, however, be interpreted to mean that we consider the United States to be unilaterally responsible for the problems of the world. The threat to peace has many causes. They are manifest in the policies of many governments. If we do not address this wide range of causes in this conference, we will run the risk of further polarizing our world, thus deepening and making more dangerous our divisions.

This point is of preeminent importance to the peace movement in the United States. The depth of vision of this conference and the breadth of its critical perspective may well make the difference in whether it helps or hinders that movement. I do not suggest that the government of the United States should not be challenged or criticized. All governments should be. I do suggest that the propaganda war is also a war without winners. I therefore want to urge us all not to allow the policies or political alignments or propaganda of our respective governments to set us against one another or to obscure our commitment to one another and to the whole of humankind. Our calling in this conference is beyond that of any nation-state. Our task transcends all the governments of the world. It can be subject to none. Our commitment in this conference can be to nothing less than the life of the world.

We are gathered here as peoples of faith, not representatives of our governments. We should make the most of our freedom and our unity.

We should not allow our protest against the arms race to be reduced to a struggle for partisan political advantage. The arms race is a race towards death for us all—instant, undiscriminating, all-consuming death.

Of such death, Hiroshima and Nagasaki stand as tragic memorials. I call up the memory of these two cities because in them we have seen actually displayed "the catastrophic consequences of the arms race and nuclear war" on which I have been asked to report for this conference. Hiroshima and Nagasaki are not think-tank scenarios to be debated by military strategists, recalculated by computers, or manipulated by propagandists. They are human life and dehumanizing death.

The first atomic bomb used in war was dropped on Hiroshima in the early morning of August 6, 1945, by order of the president of the United States. The bomb destroyed everything in a two-mile radius. At the epicenter, human beings were incinerated; metal and stone melted. Sixty thousand buildings were reduced to ruin. A fire storm sprang up two miles wide.

One hundred thousand people died almost immediately. Another 100,000 followed them into death—most of them killed by the effects of radiation. All together more than one-half of the population of the city was annihilated.

We are told that the survivors, dazed and broken, stumbled away in an eerie, deathly silence. Some 10,000 wounded made their way to Hiroshima's 600-bed Red Cross hospital. Only six doctors and ten nurses were there to help them.

We know these few. But we cannot know, we cannot feel, the almost total immersion in death experienced on that August morning. Surrounded by destruction, overwhelmed by loss, driven off by the holocaust and the smell of thousands of burning bodies, torn between the drive to save one's self and the obligation to save others—these feelings are known only to the survivors. Through nearly four decades they have struggled for ways to tell the rest of us. "I hear phantom voices crying for help," writes Ken Nakagawa. "I cannot forget." We must not forget. Remembering Hiroshima and Nagasaki is our best hope of not repeating them.

But death does not wait until the end of the race. We are dying even as we run. "The arms race," said Pope Paul VI, "kills without firing a shot."

The arms race is killing the earth. Precious natural resources formed through long eons as an inheritance for the ages to come are depleted in one generation. Fired on altars of concrete and steel, they are molded into instruments of death, while their ash is cast out to foul 10,000 lakes and rivers. Nuclear wastes pollute the atmosphere, the ocean, and the earth itself. The most terrible of these wastes, plutonium, retains its power to kill for 250,000 years— five times longer than humans have walked the earth. Our children's children are being condemned to a life endangered by a morass of nuclear waste.

The arms race is killing our economies and the people they support. In the industrialized market-economy countries, the spiralling costs of militarization spawn the plague of inflation and unemployment and destroy productivity. In countries with planned economies, militarization erodes ideals of social equality and distorts economic and social priorities. Growing arms budgets postpone and threaten efforts to meet fundamental human needs.

The arms race is killing our sense of historical continuity. The possibility of global disaster calls the future into question. Without a sense of the future, the past seems pointless and the present seems meaningless—barely worth living and hardly worth preserving.

The arms race is killing our cultures. Science is being reduced to a search for new military technologies which in turn take on lives of their own and consume ever more of our best minds and highest skills. Cultural exchange between opposing nations is held hostage to international politics and, when practiced, is harnessed to political propaganda. Public support for education and the arts is sacrificed to the gods of war.

The arms race is killing our political systems. Increasingly, governments try to solve disputes through military force rather than through political processes. Vietnam, Afghanistan, El Salvador, and Poland are only a few examples. Militarism is a scourge upon the nations. Posturing, propaganda, secrecy, and deceit are becoming the norms of governmental behavior. Even arms reduction talks are used to justify an escalating arms race.

At the root of all this destruction is an attack upon the life of the human spirit itself.

The arms race is fueled by fear. Fear is a failure of faith. When faith has failed, a part of us has died. Fear fixes its eyes on the enemy. Goals are eclipsed. Even the purpose of military forces is no longer assessed. Blind, unreasoning fear takes over and becomes the only measure—more, more, ever more guns and tanks and submarines and missiles and bombs—in a futile attempt to assuage our fear.

But our fear is not assuaged because fear cannot be cast out by force. Fear impedes human contacts. Fear reduces our common humanity to stereotypes and fixations—capitalists, communists, imperialists, terrorists, to name a few. Through these and other slogans and epithets, people are dehumanized—judged to be totally evil, deserving of death—even total death, which is possible only through total weapons. The human spirit that accepts this, that accepts the idea that world peace can be achieved through holding a whole world hostage to nuclear destruction, such a human spirit has begun to die.

The arms race is thus, in essence, a spiritual struggle—a struggle between the powers of life and death. Therefore, we cannot trust our governments to solve the problem. "It is better," says the Psalmist, "to take refuge in the Lord than to put confidence in princes" (Psalm 118:9). Princes may favor arms reduction today, deploy missiles tomorrow, and call out the troops within the week. Government officials are committed to the systems that have given them power and that keep them in power. Usually they embody and espouse the values of those systems. Frequently they are the captives of those systems. They must be judged by their deeds and by their deeds alone. Their words no longer matter.

Confronted by the powers of death in the nuclear arms race, we Christians are finding that we have no other recourse than to take refuge in the Lord and to renew our confession of faith in the one who has disarmed the powers and triumphed over death and the grave—even Jesus Christ our Lord. In Christ, we are given hope— even when there is no hope—and we are saved from despair. In Christ, we receive the gift of faith and we are able to believe that the peoples of the earth can live together in peace and justice. In Christ, we are loved without fail, and we learn that to seek to save our lives through military might or any other means is to lose them, and that to lose our lives in love and service to the world is to save them. In Christ, we protest against the race of death. We choose life and we search for peace across the barriers of different cultures, ideologies and political structures. We choose to nurture our relationship with the churches in the Soviet Union, a relationship which we consider to be an important corrective to the dangerous opposition of our two governments. We applaud the intent of this conference designed to nourish a fragile new consensus about the future of humanity. We are happy to join hands in this global circle of people from many lands and many faiths as together we draw on the resources of our deepest commitments to foster our common search for peace and life.

Meeting with the press in Moscow near the end of the conference. Bishop Karoly Toth of the Reformed Church in Hungary and president of the Christian Peace Conference (CPC); Arie Brouwer; and Andria Manjato of Mauritius, vice-president of CPC. (Credit: A.D. Photo, J. Martin Bailey).

9

America the Beautiful

A Church Herald *column, July 23, 1982*

I struggled with my country because I loved it—just as I struggled with my church because I loved it—and with the council and its member churches because I loved them. My critics sometimes failed to see that. I longed for them to know. In this column, I sought to show my love for country.

The worship experience described here happened in the Riverside Church where we worshiped occasionally in the early '80s. On this Sunday—and always on the few other times I heard her sing, I was inspired too by Clamma Dale's singing. Profoundly moved, I had a story I wanted to tell—and a brother to memorialize.

"America the Beautiful" was the offertory anthem on the Sunday before Memorial Day. Black soprano soloist, Clamma Dale, offered it, she said, as a prayer for her country.

O beautiful for spacious skies,
For amber waves of grain...

These first few words immediately stirred boyhood memories of the great plains with their endless skies open in all directions above the golden fields of grain rippling in the wind.

The rest of the stanza recalled a trip with my parents from Minnesota to California. On the second day of westward travel across the plains, we saw on the far-off horizon what we thought to be a bank of low-lying clouds. Gradually from the deep, lavender haze sharper forms emerged, exquisitely portrayed as "purple mountain majesties above the fruited plain."

O beautiful for pilgrim feet,
Whose stern, impassioned stress
A thoroughfare for freedom beat
Across the wilderness!

Those impressions of a nation molded by religious passion are part of our national heritage. They are quickened for me by associations with our own pilgrim bands led by Van Raalte and Scholte, beating another thoroughfare for freedom through the wilderness of Michigan and Iowa.

The third verse tapped other memories, deeper still.

O beautiful for heroes proved
In liberating strife,
Who more than self their country loved,
And mercy more than life!

I remembered:

The induction notice coming to my brother in the autumn of 1950.

The line of men, looking frightened and insecure to my teen-age eyes, waiting to board the bus for boot camp in the early, grey dawn on a street corner in Pipestone, Minnesota.

A few months later, the arrival of my brother's orders for service in Korea, followed by good-byes, knowing they might be our last, before my parents drove him to the troop train in Omaha.

The letters that came back from Korea full of barely concealed loneliness and anguish.

The long gap in the fall of 1951 when no letters came.

The surprise of leaving the house one Sunday evening for a youth fellowship meeting only to be met at the door by the village policeman and our pastor on the verge of tears.

The confusion of knowing without being told and the numbness when the telegram was read.

The pain—the sharp, searing pain—of a military funeral in the First Reformed Church and then in the Hillside Cemetery of Edgerton, Minnesota.

The story of a survivor who told us that my brother had put his own body between an enemy grenade and the lives of three other members of his squad.

My father's unanswered "why?" which he eventually no longer voiced, but which echoes still in the words of Job engraved on my brother's headstone:

In Memory Of

P.F.C. EDWARD JOHN BROUWER
June 9, 1927—October 12, 1951
The Lord gave, and the Lord
hath taken away;
blessed be the name of the Lord.

On that cold, February day when the sound of taps drifted across the cemetery and while the flag was folded, we took comfort in believing that the Korean War was a struggle for freedom. History has denied us most of that comfort. We know now that the Korean War was partly a result of political calculation and miscalculation between the United States and the Soviet Union, partly the fruit of a struggle in our foreign policy establishment, partly a means of resolving the rivalry between the branches of our own armed services, partly a way to quicken a faltering economy, and partly, only partly, the result of a struggle against communism. For this, my brother died.

For this, tens of hundreds of thousands of other peoples' brothers have died. There have been 29 million combat dead in this century. For this, we stand today poised on the brink of global destruction.

There is a better way.

O beautiful for patriot dream
That sees beyond the years,
Thine alabaster cities gleam,
Undimmed by human tears
America! America! God shed his grace on thee,
And crown thy good with brotherhood
From sea to shining sea!

I often think of these lines when I catch a glimpse of Manhattan by night from the windows of an airplane returning to New York— the lonely beacon of the Statue of Liberty, the countless windows of the World Trade towers, and the changing, multicolored lights flooding the Empire State Building—a thousand torches in the night, shining testimony to the glories of human creativity, skill, and power.

An hour later, on the street, I am face to face with the dirt and deterioration and I know that the words of this last stanza are truly a prayer we need to pray—for America and for the world. We need to pray that our nation and all nations may pledge themselves to patriot dreams that sees beyond the years—and beyond our national boundaries to encompass the world God loves. We need to pray that God may give us the wisdom to know that building a better society and a better world for all is the way to peace.

10
Summons to South Africa

Testimony in support of the South African Council of Churches presented before the Eloff Commission of the Government of South Africa, Pretoria, South Africa, March 18, 1983, and a report to the NCC Governing Board, San Francisco, CA, May 11, 1983.

Many of the programs of the South African Council of Churches were created to help those brutalized by the apartheid system: the homeless, the political prisoner, the hungry, the poor. Because of its opposition to apartheid, the council had been accused repeatedly by the government of being political. In addition, punitive actions had been taken against the staff of the South African Council of Churches (SACC).

On November 19, 1981, the State president appointed a commission of inquiry into the South African Council of Churches and charged it to investigate the history, purpose, and finances of the SACC as well as "any other matters pertaining to the SACC, its present and past office-bearers or officers and other persons connected with the SACC, on which the Commission is of the opinion that a report should be made in the public interest." Named to chair the commission was the Honorable C.F. Eloff, Judge of the Transvaal Province Division of the Supreme Court of Africa.

The commission began its work by collecting several volumes of background information on the SACC and the ecumenical movement. It also sent investigators to several countries including the United States, "to make some determination of the level of support for the SACC." During their visit to the United States, the investigators of the commission did not contact the National Council of Churches or any of the churches which are known to be supporters of the SACC. On the contrary, many of their appointments were with American individuals and organizations known to be critical of the churches' involvement in justice issues.

In September, 1982, the Eloff Commission began public hearings which continued until March of 1983. During the hearings, the two basic contentions of the commission staff were that the SACC had misused funds and served as a channel of funds to political organizations; and that the SACC was being manipulated by overseas churches because it received major program support from them.

The council was vulnerable to these charges in part because as a matter of long-standing policy, council funds had been used to underwrite legal defense of black political prisoners and sustain their families. In the face of such activities, financial support from within South Africa had declined so that soon the council depended for nearly all its support on overseas sources, with the European churches, especially in West Germany, as major donors.

Moreover, the council freely admitted that its financial records were in disarray, partly as a result of lax management over several administrations but also because records were deliberately not kept of the names of some individuals who were assisted or the purposes to which funds were put. It appeared that the council would have difficulty accounting for several hundred thousand dollars of the more than 10 million dollars it had received from 1977 to 1981.

To meet the second charge of manipulation by overseas churches, the SACC appealed for witnesses from its partner churches and councils in West Germany, Holland, Denmark, and the United States. All responded. Dr. J. Oscar McCloud of the United Presbyterian church and I were sent on behalf of the National Council of Churches of Christ in the U.S.A.

The first of the two following documents is our report to the Governing Board, which Oscar asked me to write. The first part also appeared as a column in the *Church Herald* (May 20, 1983) from which I have drawn the title for this chapter.

Our report we had time to prepare. Not so, our testimony. When we agreed to go—on very short notice— we were under the impression that our testimony would be a formal statement mostly prepared for us. On the eve of our departure, were handed a packet of background materials, told that the situation was highly fluid, and extended good wishes!

That need to write our own testimony was problematic but also liberating. It left me free to focus on the conflict between the gospel and the ideology of apartheid. That decision was confirmed en route as I read Bishop Tutu's own testimony before the commission, a copy of which we found in our packets. Its spirit is evident in the following excerpt:

> "Everything we do or say and everything we are must be tested by whether it is consistent with the Gospel of Jesus Christ or not, and not by whether it is merely expedient or even acceptable to the Government of the day or whether it is popular. To understand the nature of the Council, its aims,

objectives and activities requires that you appreciate the theological raison d'etre of its existence. Without this biblical and theological justification you will almost certainly misunderstand what we are about. Consequently, I want to underline that it is not the finances or any other activities of the SACC that are being investigated. It is our Christian faith, it is the Christian churches who are members of the SACC who are on trial. It is our Christianity, it is our faith and therefore our theology that are under scrutiny and that the central matters at issue are profoundly theological. As a Commission you are being asked to determine whether our understanding and practice of the Christian faith can pass muster. We are under trial for being Christian. It may be that we are being told that it is an offense to be a Christian in South Africa. That is what you are asked to determine. And that is a theological task through and through."

Happily, just before departing I had decided that my favorite ecumenical sermon might be of some use! I used it as the theological heart of my testimony. I also made the most of my special Dutch Reformed relationship to the Afrikaners who dominate South Africa and my sense of their use of biblical imagery in mythologizing their own history. When we returned to the Khotso house (Zulu for "house of peace") after giving our testimony, Bishop Tutu was dancing with joy. He had already received an angry phone call from the commission saying, "No more sermons." I had, it seems, struck a nerve. He was delighted. I was pleased. The long urgent trip had been worth the effort.

More than worth the effort. I had stood arm-in-arm with Beyers Naude, long one of my heroes, visited in the homes of my friends Desmond Tutu and Alan Boesak, and met their families and developed friendships with a number of other South Africans as well as my traveling companion, Oscar McCloud.

Greeting Bishop Desmond Tutu at "475" in the early 1980s when Bishop Tutu was general secretary of the South African Council of Churches

A Report to the Governing Board of the NCCC USA

"So you have come to visit our mad and beautiful country." An unusual greeting, but South Africa is an unusual land and our host, Beyers Naude, an unusual man in an unusual situation.

Long in the forefront of opposition to apartheid, Beyers Naude was banned by the South African government in 1977 for advocating and organizing opinion contrary to the policies of the ruling National Party. Banning is a South African punishment directed specifically against those who have been effective in communicating opposition to the prevailing ideology of white supremacy. The person banned may not write for publication, speak in public, be quoted by name in South Africa, or even speak privately to more than one person at a time. (After more than five years of banning, our host was now permitted to speak to more than one person simultaneously.)

Banning is one form of South African madness. The South African Council of Churches (SACC) is now confronted with another form of madness clothed in a recommendation from the chief of the Security Police that the council be declared "an affected organization." Such a declaration would prohibit the receipt of funds from overseas and deprive the SACC of 80-90 percent of its support. The police argue that the council is a tool of foreign conspiracy (read Communist) operated under the direction of "the world church."

All testimony is being taken by a commission of inquiry called the Eloff Commission, after the surname of the judge who chairs it. Such commissions of inquiry are used by the South African government from time to time to "investigate matters of public concern."

Bishop Desmond Tutu, general secretary of the South African Council of Churches, took us directly from the airport to the hearing room so that we could "get a feel for the situation." The feel was conspiratorial. The Rev. Case Roos, Synod president of the Netherland Reformed church, had given testimony that morning and was being cross-examined by the attorney for the commission. The questions were frequently based on second-hand sources. They were full of inferences, innuendoes, and insinuations. Under the guise of an inquiry for facts, the attorney for the commission was conducting a fishing expedition, hoping to catch a conspiracy.

That night, our hosts invited us to join other overseas witnesses at dinner. After dinner, we watched a film shown to the Eloff Commission a few weeks earlier as part of the Security Police's case for declaring the SACC an affected organization. We watched Bishop Tutu preach a gospel sermon. In an interview, he warned against the dangers of injustice. We observed Peter Storey, white Methodist minister and president of the SACC, preach to his racially mixed Johannesberg congregation. We heard Allan Boesak speak of the need for freedom. We saw the people of South Africa's churches celebrating their Christian faith and hope in worship. We watched for evidence, until as the credits flicked across the screen, we sat amazed that this film could be the case *against* the SACC. Then we sat, sobered at the paranoia that could be read into these gospel promises of peace, signs of "the total onslaught on South Africa."

Sitting among those South Africans who resist apartheid in the name of Christ, we had a powerful sense of people living daily by the strength of the gospel, nourished by the bread and wine of life offered in the Eucharist. How else, they said, can we be saved from assimilating the harshness and madness of those we oppose? How else can we keep from sinking into anger and despair? How else can we maintain our sense of humor about South Africa?

In presenting our testimony the next day, we particularly stressed our conviction that the SACC would not be the object of inquiry concerning alleged financial and management irregularities if the council were not an articulate critic of apartheid. Second, we stated that this policy and all other policies of the SACC were of its own making and not ours, and that our support was given in response to specific requests of the SACC. Thirdly, we explained that we supported the work of the SACC because its commitment to justice in society, truth in politics, and peace among the peoples were gospel commitments integral to the church's mission rather than secular political programs as Lieutenant General Coetzee, chief of the Security Police, had charged. Fourth, we declared that any action of the government would not and could not cut us off from the Christians of South Africa, but rather that the government would succeed only in further isolating itself from the world community.

Later that day, we went to visit with Beyers Naude, who opened our visit with the greeting with which we introduced this report. At the end of our visit, we stood together, a Black Presbyterian minister and a Dutch Reformed minister, both from the United States, with our arms around one another and our banned Afrikaaner host, also a minister of the gospel, praying for peace and justice and freedom for all the people of South Africa—Black and White.

But for now, the madness prevails. For anyone outside South Africa, the situation is incomprehensible. How can a cluster of some 4 million Whites think they can forever hold more than 20 million Blacks in bondage, without vote, without justice, without freedom, without shelter, even without bread? How can they turn words inside out so that "homelands" are places where the people assigned to them have never lived and where families are systematically torn asunder as fathers are forced to work and live in faraway cities visiting their families only rarely? How can they designate certain areas in which Blacks are required to live and then refer to them as "Black spots"? How can White South Africa continue to believe that it can define Black South Africa?

Even the luxuriant beauty of the land plays a part in the madness. Blacks, and other people who are not certifiably White, may view the extraordinary beauty from the public highways and sometimes even in the far distance from within the "Black spots" to which they are confined. But they may not possess the land—even for a roadside picnic. Some, in self-defense, have decided no longer to notice the beauty of the land. For others, the deprivation feeds anger or despair. The more resilient are able still to drink in the beauty with joy and thanksgiving as they wait in faith and hope for the day when South Africa will be "my land" as well as "your land."

Of special concern to the churches—all churches—is the role of the Nederduitse Gereformeerde Kerk (NGK) as the architect and ideological mainstay of the policy of apartheid. Incredible as it may seem, this church and the other Dutch Reformed churches in South Africa claim that the scattering of nations described in Genesis 11 as God's punishment on human arrogance in building the Tower of Babel is not really punishment at all, but actually the working out of God's will for the nations. The people of the earth, they say, should be kept separate—with the Whites in control.

In our testimonies, we had noted that our two churches had both been active in extensive discussions with the NGK. The United Presbyterian church had participated in consultations with the NGK in September, 1973, and in June, 1980, to no avail. In the summer of 1981, it declared apartheid a heresy. The Reformed Church in

America had engaged in a thirty-year dialogue with the NGK about apartheid until, in June of 1982, it voted to "suspend further dialogue until such time as the NGK renounces apartheid and enters into conversation on an equal basis with other Reformed churches in South Africa." In August, 1982, the World Alliance of Reformed Churches meeting in its 21st General Council in Ottawa, Canada, declared that a condition of *status confessionus* exists with respect to apartheid. The Lutheran World Federation had taken such an action already in 1977.

The NGK nevertheless persists in its heretical dehumanization of other people. This heresy prevails because of a romanticized piety which reduces spirituality to sentimentality; a legalized ethic which reduces human relations to imposed legislated arrangements; and a rationalized theology which reduces justice and freedom to abstract principles. Thus, people are cut off from other people, first in the minds and hearts of the powerful and then in their laws.

Regrettably, the Reagan administration, claiming United States self-interest, supports the government of South Africa as a bulwark against Communism and as a bastion of free enterprise in Africa. United States business supports South Africa through heavy investments which strengthen the economy and the political power of the ruling National Party. Consequently, the resistance movements are seeking support elsewhere, wherever it may be found. America is thus on the side of oppression rather than on the side of freedom.

The problems, it must be said, are totally unlike those we face in the United States—politically, numerically, and economically. At least in law, the United States government has been on the side of justice for the oppressed, whereas the South African Nationalist government is the source of oppression. When everyone shares power equally in the United States, Whites will still be in control. In South Africa, Blacks will be in control.

No one expects that kind of change to come peacefully. Blacks expect that one day tens of thousands of them will die. The South African Council of Churches works in that highly charged society *as the only remaining peoples organization in South African society where Blacks and Whites can meet one another openly and as equals.* Maintaining its ministry is, thus, urgently important for the sake of all the peoples of South Africa.

Indeed, for all our sakes. When the revolution comes, the United States will also be confronted with a choice. We are on the wrong side now. It is also the losing side. But by lending it our strength, we are prolonging the struggle and multiplying the suffering.

The government of South Africa, and our own government, must *know now* that the churches in the United States and their members do care about the suffering of our sisters and brothers in South Africa. They must *know now* that we think it completely wrongheaded and unjust to restrict the work of the South African Council of Churches. Letters of support to the South African Council of Churches, P.O. Box 31190 Braamfontein 2017, Johannesburg, South Africa, are urgently needed—NOW.

American business should *know now* that their investments do perpetuate injustice in South Africa by making it possible for the prevailing political power to persist in its policies of oppression. Our churches and our members should divest now in protest.

We who confess Christ need not, and cannot, wait for the revolution to come before we choose. The choice for us is clear. The gospel compels us to step forward and to stand with the oppressed. We must encourage all those in South Africa who are joining together to support peaceful change. We must oppose those, especially in the White churches, who support the system of apartheid. We believe that the gospel requires that we place our support behind the Black churches and the SACC, that freedom, justice, and peace may come to that land.

Statement Before the Eloff Commission, Pretoria, South Africa

Mr. Chairman, first allow me to thank you for permitting me to present testimony to this commission.

My name is Arie Brouwer. I am an ordained minister in the Reformed Church in America. Since 1977, I have served the denomination as its general secretary. I am testifying today on behalf of the Reformed Church in America and on behalf of the National Council of Churches in Christ in the United States of America, which I serve as a member of its Governing Board and Executive Committee. I am also a member of the Central Committee of the World Council of Churches. I chair the National Council of Churches committee on relationships with churches in the Soviet Union and I am active in cultivating relationships with churches in socialist societies, thus seeking to strengthen their position and witness. I also represented the Reformed Church in America at the 21st General Council of the World Alliance of Reformed Churches in Ottawa, Canada, August, 1982.

I might say in passing that the ecumenical relations of the Reformed Church in America worldwide are coordinated through its Commission on Christian Unity. That commission is meeting this week during the time of my trip to South Africa. Although it is their once annual meeting and I am its executive officer they have released me from that meeting in order that I might be directly involved in this ecumenical relationship with the South African Council of Churches and its member churches which the Reformed Church in America considers to be one of its most important relationships with any church body anywhere in the world.

The importance attached to this relationship is related to the long history of relationships between the Reformed Church in America and the Dutch Reformed churches in South Africa. The first congregation of our denomination was founded in 1628 on the southern tip of Manhattan Island in what was then Nieuw Amsterdam—about the same time as the Dutch Reformed churches were founded on the southern tip of Africa. Our churches in North America and in South Africa spring from the same ecclesiastical and ethnic roots in the Netherlands. Our piety too has traditionally taken on similar experiential forms, heavily influenced by the Old Testament and frequently finding expression in the plaintive pleas and exuberant praise of the Psalms.

I may say, Mr. Chairman, that this common heritage is personally precious to me since my immigrant mother herself taught me the treasured cadences of the Dutch psalter as she learned to sing the Lord's song in a strange land.

These common origins and ethnic bonds are treasured in our church.

They were the main impetus for beginning, more than two decades ago, an extensive, and intensive, correspondence and conversation with the NGK about the policies of apartheid. We were especially distressed that those to whom we were twice bound (both as brothers and sisters after the flesh and as brothers and sisters in the faith) should espouse as gospel a doctrine which was and is inherently in conflict with the gospel. We were, and are, puzzled and distressed that a people who had suffered so terribly at the hands of oppressors during the Boer War could themselves put on the heavy mantle of oppressors. We therefore took up the apostolic teaching to admonish and exhort one another while at the same time recognizing and confessing our own failings and shortcomings. Indeed our interest in the South African situation was motivated in part by our awareness of and participation in racial oppression in the United States and the efforts of the churches during the 1960s to shake off that oppression.

Our discussions with the NGK have continued intermittently almost up to the present time. In 1979 our General Synod sent to the NGK a lengthy response to its statement on *Human Relations in the South Africa Scene in the Light of Scripture.* The response of the NGK received in the autumn of 1981 did not seriously engage our fundamental points of criticism. Rather it dealt in large part with a lengthy explanation of the ethnic complexities of South Africa and set forth both implicit and explicit defenses of "separate development." We in the Reformed Church in America do not discount the complexities of the South African situation. We do however, insist that the gospel not be tailored to that situation. We hold rather that the gospel must be fully affirmed at all times and in all places so that in the light of its grace we can openly and freely confess our sins and thus escape the judgment of God.

To claim, as the NGK does, that God's judgment upon sin in scattering and separating the peoples of the earth from one another (Genesis 11) should rather be seen as the working out of God's purpose for the world, is to turn the Bible inside-out and to set the stage for a denial of the gospel. What judgment will befall those who then use this false gospel to uphold sinful and oppressive structures which crush the life out of God's children we do not know. We do know that we must cry out against such a false gospel and against such an evil policy. There can be no compromise on this point. Apartheid and separate development are contrary to the Word of God. That Word cannot be compromised. We must stand and confess whatever the difficulties and whatever the cost.

During more than two decades of correspondence and conversation, the NGK has again and again and again failed to engage the issues we have raised. Instead they have side-stepped, misinterpreted, and set aside those issues with pleas for continued "tolerance, patience and love."

We in the Reformed Church in America finally and reluctantly concluded that these discussions had failed and indeed that they had become counterproductive. We found that they were being used to deflect attention from the absence of dialogue here in South Africa and to put at ease what should have been an uneasy conscience in the NGK for not conducting such dialogue. Because of the failure of these talks—*and it was because of the failure of these talks, because of the refusal of the NGK to deal with these issues*—the Reformed Church in America decided in June, 1982, to "suspend further dialogue until such time as the NGK renounces apartheid and enters into conversation on an equal basis with other Reformed churches in South Africa."

We and other churches around the world have taken such action neither vindictively nor punitively, but in great sorrow and with much prayer in hope that in the growing international silence, the NGK and the other white Dutch Reformed churches in South Africa will find the grace and the will to give ear to their Black brothers' and sisters' cries for justice, peace, and freedom and to hear in those cries the renewing and saving word of the living God.

We in the Reformed Church in America have begun to hear their cry—at least in part. Slowly, too slowly, in the last few years we have built bridges to those *on the other side* of the barriers of apartheid—to those in the NGK in Africa, the Sendingkerk, the Reformed Church of Africa and to those in the Broderkring and in the Alliance of Black Reformed Christians of South Africa, and finally in the South African Council of Churches. We have moved slowly and very reluctantly to sever our ties with the NGK, yet we have been compelled to do so because those ties had dwindled to little more than ties of the flesh which are now in conflict with the ties of the Spirit which bind us to our Black sisters and brothers. In them we have found our brothers and sisters in the Spirit believing the gospel in spite of everything in the world around them. We have found them walking in faithfulness on the reformed way. Hoping against hope, they have blessed us.

During that same period we have moved with equal reluctance away from a policy of advocacy with American corporations doing business in South Africa in the hope of changing policies which would bring about justice. The failure of these efforts—*and again I emphasize that it was the failure of these efforts, and the unwillingness of the corporations and the government of South Africa to listen* that compelled us to adopt a policy of prudent divestiture—prudent in that we are still open to conversations with corporations that show genuine signs of change.

I rehearse all of this, Mr. Chairman, so that you may know that I speak today as one who is bound to the Afrikaner people of this nation by ties of blood and history and heritage. I speak as one whose initial impressions of South Africa were formed not by liberation movements or by cries for justice from the poor and oppressed. I speak as one who grew up experiencing a sense of family solidarity with those who had struggled valiantly against their English oppressors, solidarity with a people with whom we shared a treasured faith. I and many others with me in the Reformed Church in America have been compelled *against our natural sympathies* to turn away from this solidarity with the Afrikaners in order to embrace another people suffering oppression. Whatever word I have spoken on other occasions, and do speak here today against the policies and practices of this government and of the Dutch Reformed churches which have fostered and do still foster the policy of apartheid, is spoken *against* the current of those powerful natural sympathies and with a prayer that those natural ties may one day again be a source of joy.

For the present and under the prevailing conditions, this cannot be. The people of the Reformed Church in America have declared that it cannot be. The churches of the Lutheran World Federation and of the World Alliance of Reformed Churches have declared that it cannot be. Many of the member churches of the National Council of Churches have declared that it cannot be. I testify here today on their behalf because our faith demands that we join our voices with those who oppose the policies of apartheid. In order to speak the truth, we are compelled to condemn apartheid unequivocally and without qualification. So today, in the name of God, the Reformed Church in America and the National Council of Churches of Christ in the United States of America stand here in solidarity with the South African Council of Churches and its member churches.

In the name of God, I say. There are those who claim that the South African Council of Churches in its work of justice and reconciliation conducts a secular program. Nothing could be further from the truth. The church is God's agent of reconciliation *for the world*. God's purpose is not merely to bind together the church in Christ. It is to bind together the whole world and all its peoples. Ephesians 1:9-10 says that in almost exactly those words. For the church to stray from that purpose or to settle for anything less or to permit itself to be diverted from fulfilling that purpose in the world, is for the church to be unfaithful. For this government or any government to hinder the church of Christ in that purpose is for that government to obstruct God's purpose for the church. No amount of Orwellian obfuscation or doublespeak can conceal that fact from the world church or from other people of goodwill scattered among the nations.

This mission of the church to participate in God's mission to unite the world is firmly rooted in the biblical story of creation. The Bible says that the creation was called into being by the word of God. The biblical account's repeated emphasis on the creative word of God teaches that the world was intended for God's communication with the creation and especially with the human creation.

When Adam and Eve broke their connection with God and thus broke the connection between God and the creation, God's judgment was almost immediately offset by the promise of a Savior to reconcile God and his human creation and to reconcile all creation to itself, and to God.

When shortly thereafter the peoples again set themselves together against God, God scattered and separated them. And once again God showed mercy. From one of those scattered bands of people God called out Abram and Sarai to be blessed in order that they could be a blessing to all the families of the earth. They were to become a holy nation—an instrument of God's saving purpose for the world. In the unfolding history of that nation, God repeatedly renewed the covenant with the holy nation, and charged the prophets to call the people and their kings and priests to keep the covenant. The prophets revealed a God who called for justice and truth to realize the promise of peace. This God showed a special partiality for the poor, the widow, and the sojourner. The prophets who showed partiality for the rich and the powerful thereby demonstrated that they were *false* prophets and not the servants of the Lord God of Israel. Prof. David Bosch has put this point well in his testimony before this commission, in saying that the treatment of the poor, the orphan, the widow, and the sojourners "at the hands of the privileged and the authorities became the touchstone for the way in which society as a whole was judged." The pattern of God's judgment is inexorable. The wise kings of Israel heard and obeyed the word of the Lord and realized God's promise of peace. The foolish kings did not hear, did not obey, and did not survive—and the land perished with them. The judgments of the Lord are true and righteous altogether.

The words of the prophets eventually coalesced in the vision of the peaceable kingdom which the New Testament writers saw fulfilled in Jesus Christ who is our peace. Our Lord's own declaration of mission in Luke 4 is a paradigm of the prophetic call to justice and peace.

"The Spirit of the Lord is upon me,
because he has chosen me to bring good news to the poor.
He has sent me to proclaim liberty to the captives
and recovery of sight to the blind;
to set free the oppressed
and to announce that the time has come
when the Lord will save his people"
Luke 4:18-19

We have already noted that Ephesians, the most comprehensive of New Testament books, sets forth God's grand design that all things and all people be united in Christ. This is an incredible dream. Little wonder that the human heart and mind and will fight against it with unfaithful deeds and false ideology. But it is an abiding dream which has survived sword and fire and hanging and starvation for century after century. God is making the world one, however we humans may struggle to divide it for our own purposes.

In Ephesians, *alienation, separation, and division are described as the essence of God's judgment on sin.* And not only there. That is the message of the whole long history of human alienation, to which I have already alluded, beginning in the third chapter of Genesis where Adam and Eve are separated from one another by shame, from God by guilt, from the animals by fear, and from the earth by hard labor and the threat of returning to the dust in death.

Finally, in the familiar story of the Tower of Babel recorded in Genesis 11, this alienation infects even the language of the human community. People are no longer able to understand one another and they are driven to the separate corners of the globe.

All this is background for the good news proclaimed in Chapter 2, verse 13:

"BUT NOW," says the writer,
Christ has brought the Gentiles near
Made Jew and Gentile one
Broken down the wall
Abolished commandments and ordinances
Created one new humanity in place of two
Reconciled both to God in one body through the cross
Preached peace to both
Given both access in one Spirit to the Father
Made the Gentiles no longer strangers, but fellow citizens
and members of the household built upon one foundation.

That is the central insight of Paul's ministry. Hebrew of the Hebrews, Pharisee of the Pharisees, proud son of Abraham, persecutor of Christians, despiser of the lesser breeds without the Law saying, "*We are one, we are one.*" The divisions are destroyed. The barriers are broken down. See what Christ has done. If God in Christ can bridge this unbridgable gulf between Jew and Gentile, the deepest division of Paul's experience, then he can destroy all divisions including that between White and Black in South Africa. His eternal purpose to unite all things in Christ can be brought to fulfillment.

In Chapter 3, the scripture teaches that God will do this *through the church*. Not the world-wide church of the twentieth century, but a ragtag assortment of the weak, the poor, the ignorant, the despised. Their unity is the wave of the future, the sign of things to come, *the demonstration of God's purpose for the whole of creation.*

The mighty structure of imperial Rome may crumble under the weight of history but the church of Christ will endure through the ages as a sign of the age to come when all divisions shall be destroyed, all barriers broken down and we shall all be one.

With Chapter 4, the apostle launches into some specific instructions as to how this unity given in Christ is to be lived out in the church. The church is one.

There is one body and one Spirit, just as you were
called to the one hope that belongs to your call,

One Lord, one faith, one baptism,

One God and Father of us all, who is above all and through all and in all.

Eph. 4:4-6

It was such teaching that led the founding fathers of the world ecumenical movement earlier in this century to speak of the divisions among the churches as a *scandal.* Unity, they said, and the Bible says, is not merely a desirable option; it is a part of the essence of the church. We confess it each time we use the Nicene Creed when we say, "I believe in One Holy, Catholic, and Apostolic church." *Unity is an article of our faith.*

The church is compelled to unity by God's call to express and demonstrate God's eternal purpose of binding up all things in Jesus Christ. Councils of churches are signs that God in Christ can redeem even the differences that divide us and make them again the *diversities which enrich us and thus give us a fuller experience of being human.* As a White man I testify that I cannot know myself as a human being created in the image of God as long as I deny—or try to deny—that same knowledge and experience of human dignity to my sisters and brothers who are Black. When they are diminished, I am diminished.

Ecumenical organizations like the South African Council of Churches are promises—promises that fear can give way to freedom and that love can overcome estrangement. The councils of churches are foretastes of the unity which may be ours by moving closer to one another as we all are drawn together in Christ.

Of course living out these promises will bring the councils of churches into conflict with the world. It happens in South Africa; it happens in the United States; it happens in most countries around the world. It even brings the councils of churches into conflict with the churches because the councils have been asked by the churches to inhabit a land which the churches have themselves not yet reached. The councils are the servants of the churches, but they are also called to challenge the churches by being signs and foretastes of the one great universal Church which is still coming into being.

The end of God's purpose is vividly portrayed in the vision of John the Apostle in Revelation 21 and 22. Against the background of a new heaven and a new earth, the new Jerusalem comes down from heaven as a bride adorned for her husband. We may best understand this city as representing the church about to be fulfilled in union with its Lord. In that great and glorious vision we see fulfilled God's long mission of binding together the broken nations. A mission begun with Abram, signaled in the captivity in Babylon, and portrayed in the tongues of Pentecost, we see fulfilled when we read that the leaves of the tree of life set in the heart of the city of God are given for the healing of the nations.

We have seen then that the mission of the church and of the councils of churches is to be a sign, foretaste, and instrument of unity, justice, and peace, and reconciliation in the world and that *it is thoroughly biblical.* It is first of all the central burden of the prophets. It is also our Lord's own perception of his calling. It is the mystery at the heart of the church which is brought to fruition in the fulfillment of the church in the new Jerusalem. To call this work a secular program is to challenge God's purpose for the world and commission to the church. In its work for justice and peace, the South African Council of Churches has not strayed from this mission of God. It is doing the long work of God to bind us all together again in communion with one another, with all creation and with the Creator.

It is generally known, and I am sure is known to this commission, that this calling to shape society in accordance with God's law has traditionally been a special burden of the Reformed churches. I do not therefore repeat here the teachings of Calvin and other leaders of the Reformed churches to the effect that the state dares to infringe on this calling of the church only at its own peril.

In summary, that teaching proclaims that Jesus is Lord, that God will protect the church, and that God will prevail in history. Beyers Naude and others may be banned and, God forbid, Bishop Tutu or Allan Boesak be separated from their own people and from the world church. But the word of God will not pass away. New prophets will be raised up. The will of God will be done among the nations.

This call to unity which I have been expounding from the scriptures which is the only rule of faith and practice in our Reformed churches, is of course also a mainspring of the ecumenical movement. In that movement we seek to be obedient to the apostles' teaching to build up one another in love, and to bear one another's burdens.

In recent years, this bearing of burdens has included offering financial support to the South African Council of Churches. It should be noted that the Reformed Church in America and other member churches of the National Council of Churches offer support to councils of churches in many parts of the world. We have offered this support to the South African Council of Churches because the majority of the people in the member churches of the South African Council of Churches are economically deprived and therefore unable to alleviate the sufferings of their sisters, brothers, and neighbors without increasing their own suffering. Their sisters and brothers and neighbors are also our sisters and brothers and neighbors. To deny our financial assistance to those already once deprived by unjust economic structures would therefore be to do them a double injustice. It will also deny us our responsibility to fulfill our Christian vocation. General Coetzee's statement that this cutting off of the South African Council of Churches would result in its (I quote from the summary available to me) "emancipation from foreign control and enslavement of foreign funds" is an inversion of reality and therefore gravely in error.

To suggest that the South African Council of Churches is an instrument of international conspiracy is to compound injustice. The truth is that we in the United States and elsewhere overseas are uniquely indebted to the South African Council of Churches and its member churches for enabling us to render service through them. In this service we have received blessing far above what we have given. The breadth and strength of the service rendered and the courage of witness which inspires it has given us all hope and cause for rejoicing. For example, after a recent showing of the National Broadcasting Company documentary called "Land of Fear, Land of Courage" our finance office received a number of contributions simply marked "Tutu." The strength of the South African Council of Churches is our strength.

This ministry I have been describing is the ministry of the South African Council of Churches and its member churches. We overseas partners are called to hold up their hands, to support them in prayer and through our gifts. We do of course often designate those gifts, but we do so at their request and according to their sense of need. The council does inform us concerning the use of those funds. But we have and we seek no authority in the direction of its work. The mission is God's. The South African Council of Churches is God's instrument in this place, accountable to its member churches.

With the special epistemological privilege of the poor and oppressed, God's people in the council and in its member churches have dreamed dreams of service and seen visions of justice beyond our capacity to conceive, much less direct. We respond because their dreams and visions are glimpses of the kingdom of God. We are pleased to walk with these our sisters and brothers towards that kingdom of peace and justice and truth and freedom. To suggest that our doing so is an international conspiracy is to fly in the face of the facts. It is to found a case on fantasy, paranoia, and falsehood. The whole record of the modern ecumenical movement disproves such false theories. It emphasizes, rather, the calling of the world church to be in solidarity with, and at the service of, indigenous churches in every land. To seek to dominate such churches or councils would be untrue to ourselves and unfaithful to our Lord. To join General Coetzee in using these prejudicial opinions as a basis for declaring the South African Council of Churches "an affected organization" would be an act of extreme prejudice without foundation in fact, and directly opposed to the record.

I assure you, Mr. Chairman, on behalf of a great company in the member churches of the National Council of Churches in Christ in the United States of America, that although such a declaration may cut off the flow of funds to the South African Council of Churches, it will not cut us off from that council. Christ has broken down the walls, including those which may be erected through such machinations as declaring an organization "affected." We are united in one body. We do belong to the one family of God. We will not be cut off. The unity of the church is a central conviction of our faith and a central commitment of our churches. The blood of the martyrs across the centuries and throughout this century has sealed that faith. It is renewed year by year in miracles of reconciliation which transcend national boundaries no matter how firmly they are fixed or how carefully they are guarded or how highly they are raised. The Spirit of God recognizes no boundaries. God moves at will in the world.

No, Mr. Chairman. To declare the South African Council of Churches "an affected organization" will not isolate the South African Council of Churches. It will, however, further isolate this land, which already stands alone in the world. Such a deed will again testify against this nation in the councils of the nations. More tragedies will follow upon those which already weigh heavily on this land—more plagues one might say—until its peoples, all its peoples, White as well as Black, are free. For they will be free. God's people will be free. God has promised that the people will be free and the word of God will not return to God empty.

But why must so many die first? Why must Black women, Black men, and Black children suffer every day? Why must the whole nation and its peoples be held hostage to fear?

Our support for the South African Council of Churches is given for the sake of South African and *all its peoples*. In our view—more and more widely held—the South African Council of Churches is the only surviving mass movement in South Africa where Black and White can come together to speak openly to one another. It is an oasis of grace and peace in a land of injustice, anger, guilt, and fear. It is a sign, a foretaste, an instrument of a new and peaceful society for South Africa. It is the last best hope of this society. It is a light to this nation and to the world. I say with all reverence and respect, for God's sake, for your sake, for all of our sakes, do not try to extinguish that light.

Thank you, Mr. Chairman.

Being arrested for demonstrating against the South African apartheid system at the South Africa Embassy, January 24, 1985, Washington, D. C. (Credit: United Methodist News Service, Robert Lear).

Praying for peace in St. Pierre Cathedral, Geneva, Switzerland, November 17, 1985, on the occasion of the Reagan-Gorbachev summit meeting. L to R: Rev. Henry Babel, USSR; Bishop Longin of Dusseldorf (Russian Orthodox Church); Rev. Arie Brouwer, general secretary NCCCUSA; Metropolitan Filaret of Minsk & Byelorussia; Robert Neff (Church of the Brethren), vice-president, NCCCUSA; Deacon Rena Yocom (United Methodist Church), vice president NCCCUSA; Rev. Alexei Bichkov, general secretary All-Union Council of Evangelical Christian Baptists, USSR; Asochik Aristokesian, (Armenian Orthodox Church), USSR. (Credit: WCC Photo, Peter Williams).

11
Christ is Our Peace

A sermon in St. Pierre's Cathedral, Geneva, Switzerland, November 17, 1985, on the occasion of the gathering of church leaders from the United States and the Soviet Union at the time of the meeting between President Ronald Reagan and General Secretary Mikhail Gorbachev.

Given Ronald Reagan's long history of fervent anti-communism and his characterization of the Soviet Union as "an evil empire," there was quite a lot of surprise and even more anxiety about the first Reagan-Gorbachev summit. Rather than simply addressing them yet again with public statements, my colleagues and I at the council decided to invite the Soviet churches to meet with us in Geneva to pray—to witness as well, but mostly to pray. To a few of us, that seemed like the right idea at the right time. Because of the long pent-up frustration of the peace movement in the Reagan era, dozens of U.S. groups were planning to be present in Geneva to make statements. It seemed to us that the churches were in the best position to make a joint witness by praying together as Soviet and American Christians.

That decision, welcomed by some, raised the anxiety and frustration of others. Was the NCC, and its still relatively new general secretary, backing off from the NCC's historic stand of public witness? The sermon that follows was to some degree intended to alleviate those anxieties.

It was also intended to encourage the Soviets. The joint venture here launched was a new experience. The American churches enjoyed and exercised much more freedom vis a vis their government than did the Soviet churches. Some of the Soviet leaders feared that being thus publicly teamed with the American churches in such a highly visible situation could lead to embarrassment and even endanger the fragile relationships with their government. Others wanted to seize the opportunity to enlarge their freedoms. In my sermon, I wanted as discreetly as possible to give the latter a place to stand without pre-empting the freedom of the former.

Our prayers together were, we thought, fruitful, and meeting to pray between summits became yet another tradition in US-USSR church relations (except for the hastily arranged summit in Reykjavik). We later allowed ourselves to wonder occasionally if there were a connection between the difficulties encountered there and our absence!?

Through various ecumenical and denominational networks, we were also able to enlist unnumbered Christians all across the United States to join us in prayer. The same was done in the Soviet Union, and elsewhere around the world as well. Our joint prayers in Geneva thus became a connecting point and symbol of those much larger numbers. Indeed, even in Geneva, that jaded capital of international conferences, the cathedral was filled with worshipers at the special midafternoon service at which this sermon was preached.

A few paragraphs in the text that follows will seem familiar to those who have just read the preceding chapter. This sermon too is based on what was then my favorite ecumenical sermon, which I usually preached under the title, "The Gospel Centrality of Christian Unity." For this volume, I have deleted from this chapter the repetition (particularly the exposition of Ephesians 2 and Genesis 3) as much as could be done without damaging the continuity of the text.

We Christians from the Soviet Union and the United States are not here to spiritualize the divisions in our world. They are deep and terrible. They are harsh and historical. Nevertheless, we are here to witness that division is neither the first word nor the last word in history. We believe that unity is the beginning and the end of all things.

The scriptures begin with the bold statement that there is one God and that this God has created the heavens and the earth and all that dwell therein. On the eve of the meetings of President Reagan and General Secretary Gorbachev we call particular attention to our belief that all the peoples of the world are children of God. We are all one family.

We see clearly that this family is deeply divided. The scriptures reveal that alienation, separation, and division are the essence of God's judgment upon sin. The story of peace and unity and harmony is hardly begun in the first chapters of Genesis before we are plunged into the whole, long history of human alienation....

This alienation reaches its climax in the familiar story of the Tower of Babel when even the language of the human community is broken. People are not only unable to understand one another, they are driven to the ends of the earth. They are walled off from one another by cultural, economic, political, and ideological barriers behind which breed fear and hatred instead of the joy and love God intended to flourish.

We, today, experience these divisions with a global intensity never before known in human history. The geopolitical divisions of East and West exert their pressures everywhere in the world. In these days they are focused in a particular way on the meetings in this city. Intensifying them are the even more pervasive pressures of poverty, hunger, disease, world-wide violation of human dignity, and all other manner of injustice.

In the early Christian era these divisions were focused most sharply in the alienation between Jew and Gentile. No one felt this more keenly than the apostle Paul, Hebrew of the Hebrews,

Pharisee of the Pharisees, proud son of Abraham, persecutor of Christians, defender of the faith. And then by a miracle of grace— apostle to the Gentiles....

From the apostle's experience of grace was born the central insight of the Pauline tradition. Divisions are destroyed. Barriers are broken. In Christ, Jew and Gentile are united.

This is more than good news for Jew and Gentile. This is a universal gospel. If God in Christ can bridge this unbridgable gulf between Jew and Gentile, then God can heal all divisions. The eternal purpose to unite all things can be brought to fulfillment.

In the next chapter of this letter we learn that God's purpose includes using the church in a special way to bind up this broken world. The author of Ephesians is of course not speaking here of the great worldwide church of the twentieth century. There is no thought here of the tens of millions of Christians in the United States, or in the Soviet Union, or of the hundreds of millions of Christians scattered around the globe. These words are written to a ragtag assortment of the weak, the poor, the ignorant, the despised, scattered around the borders of the Mediterranean.

To them this letter says: to you God has made known the mystery of the ages. You are the wave of the future. You are the sign of things to come. You are the demonstration of God's purpose for the whole of creation. The mighty structure of imperial Rome may crumble under the weight of history but the church of Christ will endure through the ages as a sign of the age to come when all divisions shall be destroyed, all barriers broken down, and we shall all be one.

Historically, this appears to be impossible. But with God all things are possible. For the author of Ephesians, only a doxology can express this faith:

> Now to God who by the power at work within us is able to do far more abundantly than all that we ask or think, to God be glory in the church and in Christ Jesus to all generations, for ever and ever. Amen
>
> Ephesians 3:20-21

From this lofty vision the author moves quickly into a set of specific instructions as to how this unity given in Christ is to be lived out in the church, in the family, and in the world. There is here, I repeat, no spiritualization of the brokenness of the world. There is on the contrary an explicit recognition of the hard,

historical work that needs to be done in order to fulfill the purpose
of God to bind up the broken world.

This is the calling which draws the churches toward unity and to
prayer. We believe that our unity in Christ is a sign that God can
redeem the differences which divide us and make them again the
diversities which enrich us—thus giving us a fuller experience of
being human. We dare to believe and we are bold to hope that the
renewal of community within the church is a sign of renewal for
the whole human community.

It is this unity for the sake of the whole human community to
which we testify here in Geneva as we gather from the churches
within our two lands of the Soviet Union and the United States. We
bear witness that our common humanity is more important than our
different citizenships. We bear witness that the single spiritual bond
of our common faith is more powerful than all the forces of the
world which seek to divide us.

This calling to unity is an arduous calling. Knowing this full well,
the author of Ephesians concludes by urging the readers of this
letter to "be strong in the Lord and in the strength of the Lord's
might" (6:10). We need to draw on the deepest resources of our faith
to nourish our spirits—to find the inner strength to stand against the
external forces which seek to divide and to destroy. We need to
pray—without ceasing.

We who gather here from the churches in the United States and
in the Soviet Union as guests of the church of Geneva, find our
strength in Christ. Our longing for peace is for all the peoples of the
world. We share this longing with people of many faiths and with
all people of goodwill.

One of the great symbols of this longing for peace for all the
peoples of the world is the United Nations, the fortieth anniversary
of which we have just celebrated. Across from its secretariat
building stands the Isaiah Wall. On it are engraved the familiar
words of that prophet which are visually represented nearby in a
strikingly powerful human figure, beating swords into plowshares.
All the world knows that sculpture is a gift of the Soviet Union to
the United Nations. It is therefore of special meaning to us today. It
is made the more meaningful when we see this familiar image in
the context of the full vision of the prophet Isaiah. That vision is a
vivid picture of the nations flowing together in peace and unity. It is
in turn the inspiration for the vision recorded in the closing
chapters of the Bible when the apostle John sees the end of human

history culminating in a great cultural harvest of the "glory and honor of the nations."

This is the harvest for which we pray together during these days. Our prayers are made strong by the prayers of millions of believers in both our countries and around the world. With many voices in diverse tongues but with one spirit we pray that the processes of history may come to fruition, that our lives and the lives of our children's children may be fulfilled. That together we may nourish the heritage which belongs to us all in the human community. That we may pass on the gifts of God and the fruits of our human endeavors from generation to generation, enriching the lives of each succeeding generation, building a human community founded on justice in which all of God's children, young and old, male and female, may live out their days in freedom, peace, and hope in a world made new every morning.

Listen again and believe:

Now to God who by the power at work within us is able to do far more abundantly than all that we ask or think,

to God be glory in the church and in Christ Jesus to all generations, for ever and ever. Amen and Amen.

12
The Bombing of Libya

A letter to President Ronald Reagan, April 18, 1986

For both the RCA and the NCC, I sent dozens of letters to the president and other government officials, sometimes supporting, sometimes opposing proposed government policies or actions. Often those letters were more or less written by one or another church or council committee or assembly or drafted by staff closer to the action than I. Although I usually helped form these drafts in some way, I did not conceive them and they are therefore not included in this volume.

When in late March, President Reagan had provoked an armed response from Colonel Qaddafi by sending military planes into air space Libya claimed as its own, we had sent such a telegram of protest drafted by staff colleagues. A few weeks later, the president again sent American military planes against Libya, this time to bomb it in a "surgical strike" aimed at Colonel Qaddafi himself. I thought the situation demanded an immediate response, even though my key advisors for this issue were traveling overseas.

President Ronald Reagan
The White House
1600 Pennsylvania Ave., N.W.
Washington, D.C. 20500

Dear Mr. President:

Following the U.S. military action in the Gulf of Sidra in late March I sent you a telegram on March 25 urging restraint in the use of armed force, asserting that international disputes are properly addressed in international institutions in accordance with the norms of international law and warning of the dangers inherent in precipitous military action.

Since the bombing of Libya earlier this week, we have received telegrams from around the world strongly supporting this message. For example:

From the Uniting Church in Australia: "Our church respects the right to counter terrorism but not the right to effect a disproportionate terrorism in reply."

From the Federation of the Protestant Churches in Italy: "We express our deep solidarity with your dissent from USA government conduct in the Mediterranean area. We reaffirm our equally radical dissent from any terrorist as well as military action. Both fail to remove the causes of our present conflicts and on the contrary speed up the spiral of war and death..."

The Europe Resource Sharing Group representing many churches in many nations "...deplores American attack on Libya and consequent escalation of tension in Mediterranean area. We support NCCC in its efforts to influence U.S. Administration calling for restraint and sanity. We believe we cannot fight terrorism by terrorism. We uphold your witness for peace in our prayers."

A message from the General Secretary of the All Africa Conference of Churches speaks of this as another example in a consistent pattern of the "victimization of the African continent" and continues "we pray with the American churches that the vicious circle of violence will stop before it is too late."

The World Council of Churches (WCC), an international organization representing 305 churches worldwide, quotes from our March 25 message to you and then says:

> "The WCC supports the NCCC-USA and its member churches in their efforts to build public opinion and to influence their government along these lines."
> "The military action by the USA is fraught with serious consequences. It is likely to lead to a new spiral of violence and also heightens tensions in a region which is already volatile. The WCC is deeply concerned about the spread of international terrorism, but is convinced that it cannot be solved by acts of war or violent retaliation."

This immediately preceding paragraph from the WCC message expresses a deep conviction held by Christians worldwide as well as by peoples of other faiths. If the United States, on the contrary, follows what the New York *Times* editorial on April 15 called the "emotionally satisfying" course of giving Colonel Qaddafi what he deserves, matters are only made worse. We Americans have long since recognized the dangers of such actions in our domestic life. We have therefore moved to prevent such vigilantism precisely because it has often given license to vengeance even while masquerading as law.

We dare not ignore these lessons too painfully learned in our own history when we act internationally. Actions such as the bombing of Libya do not merely tarnish our image in the world, they corrode the soul of America. The more the United States takes such actions, the more we are shaped by these actions in the very image of those whom we seek to destroy. Terrorism thus met begets more terrorism and terrorists. Each act increases the spiral of violence causing more loss of life—including, as is also already being reported, more loss of American life. Your action is not then merely an attack on Libya, it is an attack on America. First by increasing the danger to Americans everywhere from more acts of terrorism and second, by attacking those traditions and values which have given the American experiment its significance for the rest of the world.

In 1981 the National Council of Churches restated this historic vision of an America in which: "government would promote the common welfare and secure the blessings of liberty for all....Justice and compassion would reign in alabaster cities that stretched from sea to shining sea and the bountiful resources of a favored land would be thankfully received and gladly shared with the whole human family, as the nurturing providence of the Creator meant them to be. This America would be known in the world for its compassion, its deep desire for peace and justice, its commitment to human rights and human decency. It would stand as a beacon and model, a city set on a hill, its power stemming from the irresistible example of a just, caring and peaceful people sharing life and treasure generously with all the people of the earth."

It is regrettable in the extreme that these visions which have nourished our nation and have been a source of hope to other peoples have been so casually set aside by your administration. I know that at the moment your actions are enjoying widespread support among the American people. Even the nation's leading newspaper, the New York *Times*, in its lead editorial on the morning after the attack, condoned the combination of America as prosecutor, judge, and executioner. It dispensed with what it itself described as the "jury" of international opinion which cautioned against precipitous action, dismissed the killing of civilians by stating that it appeared that the United States had tried to avoid "innocent casualties," ...and proclaimed that the "emotionally satisfying" feelings of revenge with which the editorial began were actually "the sober satisfaction of seeing justice done."

But as those of us who read the prophets know, justice is not achieved by the vengeful flexing of military muscles. Justice requires us to address the deep underlying issues of injustice. Your recent actions in the Gulf of Sidra and the bombing of Libya have made the exceedingly complicated issues of political, economic, and social injustice even more complicated and emotion-laden. The widespread support among the American people—even in the face of deep protest around the world—is not an atmosphere conducive to rethinking those policies.

Yet Mr. President, we pray in the name of God and for the sake of America and the world, you will turn away from these destructive policies of military confrontation to lead us in the ways of justice and peace. The United States has at times played a constructive and courageous third party role in the Middle East peace process. Only thus can we avoid the escalation of violence, deal effectively and constructively with terrorism, and make possible a peaceful world.

Very truly yours,
Arie R. Brouwer
General Secretary

13
Nonviolent Civil Disobedience

A presentencing statement of five religious leaders arrested in the rotunda of the U.S. Capitol Building, March 4, 1987

Sometime early in 1987, several churches decided to organize a lenten protest against U.S. action in Central America. The protest would open with an act of civil disobedience in the Capitol rotunda on Ash Wednesday to be repeated each Wednesday thereafter throughout Lent.

Committed as I was from my youth to the American political process, civil disobedience was for me a last resort. On Central America, I thought we had passed that point already in 1981 (see chapter 2), so I agreed to participate when invited by Avery Post, president of the United Church of Christ, which had spearheaded the campaign.

On Ash Wednesday, more than 200 Protestant and Roman Catholic church leaders gathered to pray and sing hymns on the Capitol steps. Each worshiper held a white cross inscribed with the name of a Nicaraguan killed by the Contras. The five of us scheduled to be arrested were then signed with ashes by America Sosa, leader of the COMADRES (Mothers of the Disappeared) for that group in El Salvador. As the ashes were passed among the worshipers, they also helped one another tie on sack-cloth arm bands as symbols of their commitment to work for peace. As the service concluded, Avery Post made a statement on our behalf.

The five of us, John Humbert, general minister and president of the Christian Church (Disciples of Christ); Joseph Nangle, justice and peace coordinator, Conference of Major Superiors of Men; Doris Anne Younger, general director, Church Women United, and Avery Post and I then led the group of worshipers into the rotunda. There, we five knelt in prayer while the worshipers stood around us in support. It was, in the words of Avery's statement, "a gentle trespassing in a revered area of our nation's Capitol building." Ignoring orders to cease and desist, we were arrested and led away to be booked and jailed while those who supported us asked quietly in song, "Were you there when they crucified my Lord?" According to the Washington *Post*, "They continued through several choruses of the haunting old Negro spiritual until an officer cut them off with a warning that they, too, would be arrested if the singing continued."

The crucifixion of course, was in Central America, not in the rotunda. For that, the police had been forewarned and the arresting officers courteous throughout. While waiting to be booked in the corridor below the Senate chamber, one of the officers standing guard asked me why we were demonstrating. Hearing my explanation, he said he agreed with our position. "Why," said I, "do you and I see this so clearly and up there (in the Senate) they don't?" Said he, "If you are making a hundred thousand a year, you can't understand anything!"

We spent a few hours in jail that evening, but slept in our hotel beds—wondering what it would be like if we were indeed sentenced to the year in jail which our offense could entail.

In court the next morning, I made the following statement for us all on our behalf. This too, was a more or less gentle affair. The judge told us that he took more stock in St. Peter than in Ramsey Clark—even though he had once worked for the latter. I learned later that being Greek Orthodox, he still followed the former! An hour or two later, we each paid our ten-dollar charge for court fees and we were free, although each now with a conviction on his or her record.

Your Honor, we would like to make five brief points in defense of this act of nonviolent civil disobedience.

First, nonviolent civil disobedience is not our ordinary means of political discourse. The churches with which we are associated have been consistently involved in the political processes of this country from the very earliest days up to the present moment. Indeed, many of our churches and ecumenical organizations have offices in this city for that very purpose.

Second, nonviolent civil disobedience at moments of political crisis has been a part of the Christian tradition from its very beginning. The case for nonviolent civil disobedience has never been better or more simply put than by Saint Peter in the words, "We must obey God rather than men."

Third, nonviolent civil disobedience is an important part of our American tradition and has often been the means for significant social and legal advance in our society. The ministry of Martin Luther King, Jr. is the outstanding example in our recent history. There are many more. The freedom to engage in such responsible nonviolent civil disobedience is to us an especially valued part of the liberty and heritage we treasure here in America. We recognize full well that this right is not enjoyed throughout the world and rejoice in our freedom to exercise it here.

Fourth, we have taken this action on behalf of people who have neither voice nor vote in our political processes but who are deeply affected by decisions made in the United States. Indeed, many of them, men, women, and children, are being killed every day. We have tried every possible ordinary way to bring about a change in these policies of death. We believe that the extraordinary means of nonviolent civil disobedience is required at this time.

Finally, Your Honor, many of us who stand here before you have for several decades had the privilege of traveling the world and meeting with Christian sisters and brothers in other lands. Our friends overseas have frequently faulted the United States government for destructive policies while taking care not to blame the American people. That is changing. We are all being held responsible now. We all now know enough that we are all responsible. We must change our government's policies. Nonviolent civil disobedience is one means to seek such necessary change of policy. We note, in fact, that former attorney general Ramsey Clark has said in court testimony that protest demonstrations are a legitimate and effective means of altering national policy. We respectfully state, Your Honor, that we believe that means should not be stifled.

14

Freedom for Soviet Jews

Remarks at a mass mobilization, the Mall, Washington, DC, December 6, 1987

The Reagan-Gorbachev summit in Washington, DC, again provided opportunity for the churches in the US and USSR to be symbolically present to one another in prayer. In Washington, we would also likely get more American media attention than we had in Geneva. (We did.) The Jewish community in the United States had decided to make the most of the media opportunity by staging a massive "Mobilization for Soviet Jewry" in a "Freedom Sunday" rally on the Mall in Washington, DC. The program called for representatives of various communities to make brief (two minute) statements of support. The NCC was among those invited.

That invitation sparked a heated debate within the NCC staff and its constituency fusing the feelings of tensions in relations between Christians and Jews, between peace and human rights, and between domestic politics and international affairs. Noting that he had "learned from the New York *Times* yesterday that you will be addressing the rally," and appreciating "the importance of expressions of solidarity between the Christian and Jewish communities," one informed and sympathetic but deeply concerned constituent wrote, "Nevertheless, your presence at that event cannot but express the support of

the member churches for demands that particular changes
in the internal life of the USSR must be a prerequisite to
disarmament." He concluded, "...I have always been
proud of the role of my denomination and of the NCC in
pioneering in US-Soviet relations. Your participation in
the rally Sunday will not accord with this tradition."

Having received that letter of concern immediately
prior to the event, I decided to respond after the fact.
Over 200,000 gathered on the Mall. They heard two-
minute statements from a host of American community
leaders including the majority leader of the Senate,
Robert Dole; the speaker of the House, Jim Wright; the
vice president of the United States, George Bush, and
many others. The negative effect on the disarmament
talks did not materialize. Reports in the Jewish press
were very positive.

To my friendly critic, I was able to write, after
expressing appreciation for "the opportunity to discuss
our concerns with one another" and underscoring the
NCC's continuing concern for Soviet-American
relationships, that:

"Freedom Sunday"...was organized by the major
institutions and most responsible leaders of the
American Jewish community. However media
advertising might have colored the event, the
intention from early planning stages was not to oppose
the summit, nor to convey a message that disarmament
ought not to proceed until the human rights of Soviet
Jews were assured. The mobilization aimed to affirm
the peace process (and I think did) while at the same
time clearly stating the necessity of physical and
religious freedom for Soviet Jews. With this double
emphasis I felt that my expression of NCC solidarity
was an important witness, and consistent with our

overall support of human rights and religious freedom worldwide.

This expression of concern on the part of Protestants and Orthodox, like that brought on behalf of Roman Catholics by Bishop William Keeler, was welcomed warmly by the Jewish community. The presence of the National Council of Churches and the National Conference of Catholic Bishops made it clear that the Christian community in the US shares in what all too often seems like a solely Jewish concern for the rights and freedom of Soviet religious minorities including Soviet Jewry. The shared commitment to human liberation, peace, and justice, which represents a large part of Christian-Jewish relations, was made visible in our participation on December 6 and I believe has strengthened those relationships. I enclose a copy of my remarks for your information.

Also enclosed is an excerpt from the *Jewish Week* which reports on the rally for Soviet Jewry. There is here at least the suggestion that we may, with the National Conference of Catholic Bishops, have been involved in another form of pioneering. I hope you will agree and that you will go back to being proud of the role of your church and the council.

It is a privilege to represent the National Council of Churches before this assembly today. Christians join with Jews in bearing witness to the teaching of the Hebrew prophets that peace is the fruit of justice. *We believe therefore* that basic human rights, and particularly the right to practice and to hand on from generation to generation one's faith, are essential to a just and peaceful society in any and every nation and in the whole world. We therefore today lift our voices with yours, our Jewish sisters and brothers, in testimony that concern for religious freedom is necessarily part of a true and enduring peace.

We in the churches in the United States have been joined with the churches in the Soviet Union for more than three decades.

Together we have struggled to build bridges of understanding to preserve and to protect the world from nuclear destruction. At the same time, we have tried to enlarge the boundaries of religious freedom in the interest of an enduring and lasting peace. "Glasnost" has increased our hope, but it is just beginning, and we must help to carry it forward.

While in the Soviet Union last May, I met with one group of Jewish dissidents who, encouraged by glasnost, told me that they were testing the policy by trying to establish a new synagogue in Moscow. With them, we give thanks for every sign of hope. With them, we are encouraged to call for more such signs, for more freedom to emigrate, for more freedom of religious instruction, for freedom of rabbinical education, and for more, many more reopened synagogues.

We are therefore pleased that "human rights" is formally on the agenda of this summit meeting. Both by conviction and from our reading of history, many of us hold that freedom of religion is the first freedom. History has also taught us that a government's treatment of Jews has often demonstrated its most oppressive attitude toward all peoples of faith, just as a government's treatment of Blacks has often demonstrated its most oppressive attitude toward all people of color.

I therefore believe that American Christians are duty bound to join with American Jews in support of freedom for Jews everywhere, including in the Soviet Union. With you we sing the song of the psalmist looking for that day when righteousness and peace shall kiss each other. As part of the worldwide church, we Christians have a global commitment to liberty and justice for the whole human family. We want all the peoples of the world to be free and to dwell in peace. We are with you, therefore, today in support of freedom for Soviet Jews. We are with you not only for today, but for everyday.

15
We Shall Pray

A joint message of USSR and USA church leaders to President Ronald Reagan and General Secretary Mikhail Gorbachev on the occasion of their meeting in Washington, DC, December 7, 1987

In the debate concerning Freedom Sunday, the NCC's Office of Christian-Jewish Relations saw my participation in "two quite different public events linked by an inner logic of commitment to human liberation." One question in the minds of others who opposed my participation was whether the Soviet church leaders would see that "inner logic" or would they who had come to pray for peace feel unduly pressured about human rights.

To me, that was a risk we had to take. We had habitually respected the right of the Soviet churches to make their own witness in their own place in their own way. A right respected, I thought could also be a right exercised. If participation was the right thing to do, we should do it.

My participation in the rally would, however, intrude slightly on the vigil in that I would need to arrive at the National Cathedral at least one hour later than agreed, even after having requested and received the right to be an early speaker at the rally. Such a late arrival would make it impossible for me to welcome our Soviet guests and could complicate the final negotiations on our joint statement—both of which were usually sensitive matters for the Soviets. Our friendship withstood the problem of protocol, however, and the joint statement passed muster without a hitch.

Like "Choose Life" in chapter 1, this statement too, was a joint effort. Unlike it, this document was first drafted by others. In its original form, it dealt mostly with the issues to be under discussion at the summit. Longing again for a tone like that of the "Choose Life" statement, this time to convey clearly that we were indeed to gather first of all for prayer, I recast it from start to finish—so much so as to make it a new document—even though indebted to the original, and of course to the whole history of our dialogue with the Soviets (a similar procedure of drafting and redrafting had been followed for the brief statement at the rally recorded in the previous chapter). The Soviets by this time trusted us enough that if the jointly agreed substance, on which they had been consulted, was dealt with to their satisfaction, they were content to leave the form to us. Just as we sometimes amused ourselves by meditating on the significance of our absence from Reykjavik, so also we sometimes allowed ourselves to wish that the relationships between the leaders of our two governments would be as well developed as our own.

> Grace and peace from God the Father and the Lord Jesus Christ who gave himself for our sins to deliver us from this evil age, according to the will of God to whom be the glory for ever and ever. Amen (Gal. 1:3-5).

Two years ago leaders of churches in the USSR and the USA met in Geneva as you, President Reagan and General Secretary Gorbachev, held your first summit meeting. Together we offered prayers of thanksgiving for this potential improvement in relations between our governments, and of intercession for a positive outcome. As we departed, we expressed our sincere hope that you, our nations' leaders, would meet again soon "for the signing of specific accords which (would) regularly and increasingly reduce the sphere and severity of confrontation between our nations."

The hastily arranged meeting in Reykjavik, though it produced no tangible accord, showed that agreement on significant disarmament measures was possible. Now you, the leaders of our two nations, each bearing responsibility for terrible arsenals capable of devastating the planet, meet again. Your declared intention is to sign an INF agreement: an agreement which would eliminate a whole class of nuclear weapons. According to some experts, these Intermediate Nuclear Forces are among the most destabilizing and dangerous arms in the world.

We congratulate you and our governments for the considerable efforts made by both sides to reconcile differences through negotiation, making such an agreement possible. We view this as a response to the prayers of millions of Christians in our two lands and to the longings of many millions more peace-loving people around the world. Thanks be to God.

As in Geneva, we shall engage throughout this summit meeting in a vigil of prayer and worship, symbolically linking the believers of our two countries whose hearts are joined in prayer in special services and vigils being held across the Soviet Union and the United States. We know that believers of many different confessions in neighboring countries and lands far beyond our respective borders are praying together with us for a positive outcome of this meeting. We are sustained by this worldwide community of faith, and together we thank God for this community and for the World Council of Churches through which it is continually nourished and renewed.

Our presence here together is a manifestation of our shared Christian vocation to break down all the barriers of division and enmity which stand in the way of expressing our common humanity. Never before in human history have peoples separated by great distances, languages, races, cultures, and traditions been so intimately and inescapably bound together in struggles for survival, justice, and dignity. To accept division and to acquiesce in imposed enemy images is sin whose wages in the nuclear age are indeed death and destruction.

Our own churches have been divided for centuries by differences of doctrine, language, culture, tradition, and nationality. We confess that we have yet to resolve many of these differences. We rejoice nevertheless that for more than three decades we have been in regular dialogue, exchange, and common reflection unbroken by the periodic escalations of tension between our two governments. At times our churches have provided one of the few stable points of contact between the American and Soviet people. Our presence together again in these days is an expression of our commitment to remain together. We are pledged to provide a human bond between the peoples of our two nations. We pray that our being together may also be a sign of hope to other peoples around the world whose lives are directly affected by the conflict which has characterized U.S.-Soviet relations for decades.

We dare to hope that the discussions you are about to hold will not be limited to an INF accord. We shall pray therefore that they will open the way to rapid progress in other areas as well. Specifically, we look for the following signs: the early conclusion of a Comprehensive Nuclear Test Ban, steadfast action toward the elimination of both long range ballistic missile systems and tactical nuclear weapons, and a firm agreement that outer space will be used exclusively for peaceful purposes.

We shall pray as well that the peoples not be asked to pay the terrible price of accepting more conventional weapons in exchange for nuclear weapons, but that you accelerate negotiations on mutually balanced reductions of conventional forces.

In our prayers, we shall also acknowledge that our two states are heavily involved in the international arms trade. Such arms are used in regional conflicts whose terrible price is being paid by people in many different parts of the world. Recognizing that regional conflicts have been on the agenda for discussion between our two nations since the Geneva summit, we shall pray that you, our national leaders, will hear the cries of pain and death which rise to God every moment of every day and that you will fulfill your responsibilities as world leaders by curbing the arms trade. We shall pray further that you will join together in supporting efforts to resolve regional disputes by negotiation.

We offer our prayers for peace in the light of the prophetic vision that peace will be the effect of righteousness (Is. 32:17). We pray not merely for the absence of war and the removal of weapons. We pray for justice and we pray for peace through justice.

Finally we shall pray to God that you, our brothers Ronald and Mikhail, may be given hearts strong in courage; minds enlightened by wisdom; and spirits overflowing with compassion that you may do all that lies within your power to preserve the sacred gift of life and to realize the promise of life fulfilled for all the peoples of the world.

We shall make these prayers in the name and in the spirit of Jesus the Christ who came in order that all the peoples of the world might have life and have it abundantly.

16
Faith, Hope, and Love

A reflection at the close of a prayer vigil conducted by leaders of the churches in the Soviet Union and the United States in the National Cathedral, Washington, DC, December 10, 1987, in connection with a meeting of General Secretary Mikhail Gorbachev and President Ronald Reagan.

The week of this prayer vigil was for me both a terrible week and a wonderful week. The wonder is noted in the text below and was centered in Washington. But I was hardly in Washington that week. Long before the summit had been scheduled, we at the NCC had planned a three-day staff retreat which we urgently needed. At this time, we were only a few weeks past the culmination of the first searing confrontation between me and Church World Service which was to plague us for the next eighteen months. The staff was deeply divided. The depth of those troubled feelings, combined with complicated staff travel schedules, made it unwise to attempt to reschedule the retreat. So I shuttled back and forth, missing most of both events. At vigil's end, utterly exhausted, but buoyed by the events of the week that turned back the Doomsday Clock, I offered this statement of thanksgiving.

I have the privilege of making a closing statement of thanksgiving on behalf of the American Christians who have been praying with our friends from the Soviet Union. As I reflected on what I would say, I found that throughout these last several days I have been experiencing within me a quickening sense of hope.

Hope, of course, is one of the great themes of Advent and, therefore, it is particularly important and meaningful that we should be feeling this sense of hope during these days. I say we, because I am not alone in this sense of hope. The public media have talked about a quickening sense of hope—even in this, one of the most jaded cities of the world. A city which, as one of the newspapers says, "has seen it all, and somehow seen something new this week."

Those of us who struggle for peace and justice, particularly in this decade of the 1980s, have sometimes almost resigned ourselves to defining victories as those times when we have kept something bad from happening. This week there is a sense that perhaps it is possible for something good to happen. This morning at breakfast, I learned from Harriet, my wife, that hope was the theme of the church service I missed last Sunday morning because I was in Washington with you. One of the things she carried away from that service was a statement that the person who can make the greatest contribution tomorrow is the person who feels the greatest hope today. It is not insignificant to have a quickened sense of hope, and I am deeply grateful that together as American and Soviet Christians we have been able to deepen our sense of hope.

For the first time in the cold war arms race, we have in this treaty not just a control of things to keep them from getting worse, or even another arrangement for things to go on getting worse under the guise of being controlled. No, this treaty marks, *for the first time*, an actual reduction of nuclear arms and of that particular threat to the world. People in the United States, people in the Soviet Union, people in many nations around the world are rejoicing at this one step. It is a small step, but a significant step, not only for the progress it makes by itself, but for the steps to which it leads. I cannot help but think of Neil Armstrong's statement when he took the first step on the moon—perhaps here too, this one small step this week may lead to a giant step for humankind in the future. We dare to hope for it again, as we may as well, when next year we meet together in Moscow.

I found that I could not think of hope without thinking of love. My first feeling when I learned that the visa for our brother Alexei Bichkov had been denied by our United States Department of State was one of frustration, anger, outrage, unbelief—or disbelief to be more precise. But that feeling changed. And what I have been feeling mostly in the last two days is a sense of loss because the community of love that we have established with one another is not complete without him. That led me to think about those of us who have been on this pilgrimage for much more than a decade. During that time, some of the people with whom we have shared the pilgrimage have passed on to glory, and I realized that the circle of love we have built together encompasses them still.

I also recognize and celebrate and give thanks for the fact that our circle of love has been expanded in this week. A closer bond between the clergy and staff of this cathedral and the staff and officers of the National Council of Churches has been forged. I think that has meaning for the future and I am deeply grateful for it.

This morning as I drove my car rather hurriedly into the garage at the Interchurch Center and thereby received the disturbed attention of the passengers of another car that was driving very carefully into the Interchurch Center, someone came over from that other automobile afterwards and said, "Someone in our car pointed out that the person driving that car was the general secretary of the National Council of Churches." He then lifted out of his briefcase the little booklet about our relationships called "Together On the Way," and said, "I wanted to come over to say to you that I believe that what is happening in Washington this week is in some measure a proof of what you all were talking about in the 'Choose Life' meetings in 1979." I don't know to what degree that is true. It isn't important to know to what degree that is true. But it is something to give thanks for. The circle of love we have built together includes many people who do not know most of us at all in any personal way.

And as I think of hope and love, I must also, of course, think of faith. Sometimes the love we have for one another does not meet the tests that we set for one another. We do not meet one another's expectations; sometimes we even fail to keep our commitments to one another. And, therefore, we also need faith—faith that what we are about is in keeping with God's will for the world.

I had the privilege the other night of sitting next to George Kennan, who some five to seven years ago proposed a 50 percent reduction in nuclear arms. I said to him, "Would you have believed that such a reduction could now be seriously discussed in the political world?" He said, "I would hardly have believed that, and I would hardly have believed the torturous way we have followed in order to come to the possibility of discussing it." So, I give thanks in faith, in hope, and in love, and pray that our faith may be strengthened, our love may be deepened, and the reach of our hope may know no bounds as we continue our prayer and life together.

17

Eight Essential Elements
of Ecumenical Credibility

An article in the Ecumenical Review *(Vol. 40, No. 1), January 1988*

When I came to the council as general secretary in 1985, its credibility was being sharply questioned—as was that of the WCC and the conciliar form of the ecumenical movement in general. In response, most of the council's member communions undertook reviews of their relationship with the council. The Episcopal Church's committee for such a review included my old friend George McGonigle, whom I had come to know in the 1970s when he became a member of the NCC's Governing Board. We saw the world very differently and often argued opposite points of view in the board's deliberations, but respected and enjoyed one another.

During the course of my meeting with the Episcopal Church committee sometime in the middle months of 1986, George summed up what he wanted for the council in three words: simplicity, accountability, and credibility. That felt right to me and I used those concepts as the subject of my next two reports to the Governing Board. When in May of 1987, I addressed the questions of credibility, my report was widely quoted and I was urged to submit it to the *Ecumenical Review*, which I did in a slightly edited version. Published in January, 1988, it had by that time also been reported in full in the summer 1987 issue of *World Encounter.*

The churches' quest for credibility is the major impetus for the ecumenical movement. "That the world may believe..." is the most familiar, the most enduring, and the most compelling reason to seek the unity of the church.

It is therefore of significant concern that questions of ecumenical credibility have been raised more sharply in the last decade than in any other period since the launching of the modern ecumenical movement at Edinburgh in 1910. It is true that the Federal Council of Churches was frequently attacked by fundamentalists and other reactionary forces in the 1920s, '30s and '40s, but the highly influential, old line, establishment, Protestant churches could weather the storm well enough. After regrouping in 1950 under the banner of the National Council of Churches, they maintained much the same course, albeit with increasing difficulties in the '60s and '70s.

Through most of the same period, the World Council of Churches was enjoying a well deserved recognition for solid theological work in thoroughly deliberative assemblies shaped by a congenial combination of American pragmatism and European theology. It seemed the best of both worlds, in the days when those two worlds dominated the ecumenical movement. True, a few northern eyebrows were raised and a few western rumblings provoked by the massive entrance of the Eastern European Orthodox into the WCC in 1961 and the emergence of the Third World as an undeniable ecumenical force at the Church and Society Conference in 1966, but there was no serious reaction.

Then, in 1978, came the deluge, with global media attention and right-wing attacks focused on the World Council of Churches' grant to the Patriotic Front of Zimbabwe. Nothing the councils or the churches could do could stem the tide. The image of the World Council of Churches as a radical body supporting violent revolution had become firmly fixed in the public psyche of the North and the West.

In that same psyche, all the images of all the councils, and some of the churches, tended to blend and blur in one undifferentiated mass of distortion. The controversy did eventually subside and the distortions did gradually slip into a state of dormancy, where they remained mostly undisturbed until the early 1980s. Then suddenly, they were jolted back into life by a double-barreled attack in two highly popular media, the *Reader's Digest* and CBS's "Sixty Minutes".

The churches and the council must of course meet these attacks when they come—and we have. Nor can we altogether ignore the occasional skirmishes with which our less constructive critics seek to distract us. But our credibility has much more to do with *who we are* and *what we ourselves do* than with what others say about us and our actions. *Credibility is build from the inside out.*

Compassion

The central element in our credibility is compassion. "If I have not love, I am nothing," says the apostle—and so does the world. So in fact does that familiar ecumenical text with which I began this report: "...that the world may believe." Through all this long and broken but nevertheless ecumenical twentieth century, we have somehow allowed ourselves to continue to use these words in the truncated form of a slogan of western Christian imperialism left over from a previous century.

But these treasured words are more than a slogan. In fact they are not properly a slogan at all. Listen to them in context: "I...pray...that they may all be one; even as *thou, Father, art in me and I in thee*, that they also may be in us, so that the world may believe that thou hast sent me....so that the world may *know* that thou hast sent me *and* hast *loved* them even as *thou* hast *loved me*." The heart of this message is love. It is *love within the church* by which the world is led to belief; and belief is desired for the world in order that it may know that it is *loved by God*.

How could it be otherwise? These are the closing words of the great high priestly prayer offered by Jesus just before his great sacrifice of love. They are recorded by the apostle of love at the heart of the gospel of love. Love is the heart of credibility.

We therefore all have cause to rejoice in the fortieth anniversary of Church World Service. Through all the years of this council's life and for four years before that, Church World Service has been the outreach arm of the churches' ministry of compassion. The effectiveness and efficiency of that ministry has made an immense contribution to our credibility.

The special quality of Church World Service springs from the fact that Church World Service is the churches gathered in this council working together through the churches gathered in other councils, for the life of the world. CWS is an integral part of the ecumenical movement. Bound to the life of the churches and their people, it cannot be a detached agency distributing food and material resources from afar. In the family of Christ's church, relief and justice cannot be separated.

In the beginning, it was hard to raise enough money for relief. Forty years later, money is no longer the primary issue. Our first concern is rather the nature of our partnerships and the quality of the relationships they develop among churches and peoples.

Church World Service, once among the largest of such agencies, is now small compared to agencies based in Europe, which it helped to rebuild, or compared to parachurch agencies based in the United States. The flow of vast amounts of money through these agencies challenges us in the ecumenical movement to hold fast to our sisters and brothers who live in suffering and poverty, and to continue to press the issues of justice and injustice even at risk of further diminishing the resources which are available to us. We know too well that people will release great torrents of money for relief, while those who struggle against the structures of injustice must often survive by finding a few streams in the desert. The challenge before us is to change that dynamic. We who follow Christ dare not settle for less than justice. Salvation, for both the giver and the receiver, requires solidarity.

Conviction

A second critical element in our credibility is, therefore, conviction—and the courage of our convictions. One notable example of such courage in the history of the council—strange as it may *now* seem—was the publication of the Revised Standard Version of the Bible. And another—strange as *it* may now seem—is the action of the Fifth World Order Study Conference, meeting in Cleveland, Ohio, in November, 1958, which advocated that "steps should be taken toward the inclusion of the People's Republic of China in the United Nations and for its recognition by our government."

Still another is the witness of the Rev. Eugene Carson Blake, then chair of the council's newly organized Commission of Religion & Race, whose act of civil disobedience on July 4, 1963, against the laws of segregation in Gwynn Oak Park in Baltimore, Maryland, led to his arrest. To that headline event may be added the stories of the little known but countless numbers of persons from the churches who participated in the struggle for civil rights—and do so still.

Greeted with consternation and derision by most of the public, these actions kept hope alive for others. History has vindicated the minority. What seemed to many at the time to be a loss of credibility, is today an abiding moral asset. The same process is now underway with respect to our witness for justice and peace in Central America and South Africa.

For these witnesses and their deeds we give thanks. Yet, difficult and courageous as their actions have been, and are, one major challenge to the credibility of our convictions requires of us a very different kind of courage—the courage to face our own middle-class, mostly white, liberal guilt. Guilt stalks all of our assemblies, seeking whom it may intimidate. But actions motivated by guilt lack integrity and conviction. They shrivel our spirits instead of making us strong. They foster resentment and backlash, rather than love and solidarity. And in the end they do not stand because they are built upon the sand.

We may therefore celebrate no less the action of the Governing Board, meeting in November, 1984, concerning the FLOC-Campbell dispute. Confronted with a call to boycott, the board chose instead the way of mediation. Not that mediation is always superior to advocacy. That depends on the issue and the times. My point is rather that our credibility depends on discerning the difference and on our courage to choose. That in turn depends on the openness of this fellowship of love and grace to give us the freedom to affirm and to engage one another so that we may act with the strength and wisdom of our combined convictions.

Catholicity

A third element in our credibility is our catholicity. Many who attack our credibility claim that we are no more than a declining band of liberal Protestants gathered more for politics than for prayer. There are of course many of us here, most particularly those from the nine Orthodox communions, who do not remotely fit that description. There are many more of us here who might be described as liberal Protestants who would reject that label, myself among them.

I wait with eager anticipation for the membership in the council on January 1, 1988, of the Evangelical Lutheran Church in America. The presence among us of so large a church that has named itself evangelical may finally force some of the most committed ideologues among our critics at last to be confounded by the facts. Will it not then be evident to all that we are a community with a strong evangelical, liturgical, and ecclesial commitment to the unity of the church in order that the world may believe and know that Christ was sent of God in order to demonstrate the love of God for the world!?

We are a people united in that most evangelical of principles, our common faith in Christ. We hold this unity in Christ to be more important than *whatever* may separate us. In response to that unity given by God in Christ through the Holy Spirit, we have committed ourselves *to be together* with one another in community; and, so far as our differing convictions permit, *to act together* in the world. Ronald Sider, the chairperson of Evangelicals for Social Action, had it just right when he said, "It is long past time when any Christian dare refuse to listen, share, and worship with other Christians who confess Jesus Christ as God and Savior according to the scriptures."

This we do precisely for the sake of credibility—in order that the world may believe and know that it is loved of God. In that same spirit, we invite all who share that conviction of the overarching importance of unity in Christ to walk with us on this way and to act together with us as they are able.

At the same time, we recognize the challenge of our incompleteness. Most particularly we look for greater presence among us of the Roman Catholic church and of conservative evangelical churches. But even now, they are not absent from us. A survey conducted for a meeting of the staffs of the NCC and the National Conference of Catholic Bishops on January 8, confirms the fact of extensive cooperation with the Roman Catholic church. We rejoice as well in the recent consultation sponsored by the Commission on Faith and Order, together with Fuller Seminary's David J. DuPlessis Center for Christian Spirituality, on the subject of "Confessing the Apostolic Faith from the Perspective of the Pentecostal Churches," which has notably strengthened those relationships. All these may be read as signs of an increasing catholicity, and as incentives to continue to take up the challenge.

Even while confessing our ecclesiastical incompleteness, we at the same time celebrate and accept the challenge of another kind of catholicity. This council is not only a community of communions. It is a community of communities represented particularly by the caucuses of minorities and women. The differences among these various communities within the council and its several parts are no less complex than the relationships among the communions. A source of unceasing challenge, they are also, I am persuaded, a cause for celebration. We are therefore attempting to create in this council a community in which women and minorities enjoy the full dignity of their humanity in order that we may all be human together.

This striving for inclusiveness is too often seen by its detractors as merely a matter of politics. Even its advocates sometimes see it as solely a matter of justice. But in these two years as your general secretary I have understood ever more deeply, frequently through the words and deeds of President Cousin and the leadership of both caucuses, that inclusiveness is first a matter of the well-being of us all and the wholeness of the ecumenical movement. To be sure, in Christ there is neither male nor female, bond nor free, Jew nor Gentile, but this is so, not because anyone is negated. It is so because each and all are fulfilled. Inclusiveness is faithfulness to our vision of ecumenical wholeness and therefore essential to our credibility.

And still another element of credible catholicity is our commitment to the fullness of the gospel. In Hans Kung's words, "Whoever preaches one half of the gospel is no less a heretic than the person who preaches the other half of the gospel." I remain convinced that an essential ingredient of this commitment to wholeness is a visible manifestation of worship and evangelism in our program structure and therefore press on toward a commission of that name—however long the road.

Commitment

A fourth element in our credibility is our commitment to one another in this community of Christian communions. A recent outstanding example of the power of community commitment in the life of the council was the Presidential Panel. Again and again I have heard testimony that it was able to address difficult issues over a prolonged period of time because of the quality of its life together. Its members speak of the experience still with warmth and affection for one another.

Another example worthy of mention is the experience in the elected staff retreat last October when we made a conscious effort to address together the presence among us of racism, sexism, classism, agism, and other "isms." We approached the experience with varying degrees of enthusiasm, anxiety, and confusion. We shared with one another, listened to one another, and questioned one another. We emerged with a common commitment "to the creation and development of a multicultural and inclusive community in the NCC," and a readiness, even eagerness, for next steps toward a fuller life together. We are taking some of those steps and intend to open the way for more in our staff retreat next October.

On a smaller scale, I found myself—to echo John Wesley— "strangely bonded" with Doris Anne Younger, Avery Post, Joseph Nangle, and John Humbert, as a result of our engaging together in a common act of prayer and civil disobedience on Ash Wednesday for justice and peace in Central America.

Blest be such ties that bind! They nurture the life of the movement. But even here, there is much to challenge us. If as a council of churches we do no more than *call* the churches to unity; that is, in Dietrich Bonhoeffer's terms, cheap ecumenism. No, we must *demonstrate* in our life together in this community—in staff and among the communions—the unity we envision for the churches and the world. I am persuaded that we have only begun to discover the possibilities of this way of community life together.

Coherence

Concern with community leads naturally to a fifth element of credibility—our coherence as a council. Here too, we are making progress. A report presented to the United Methodist Council of Bishops by its Special Committee on Ecumenical Activities and Relationships judged the National Council of Churches to be "...a stronger organization today than it has been in some years..." and that it is "...more responsive to its membership and at the same time unequivocal in its witness to the total gospel."

Noted as well with approval was the most visible sign of increased coherence in the council, the work of the clusters (an administrative and legislative grouping of the council's program units), both in the Governing Board and in the staff. Of particular significance, I think, is the strengthening of the core functions of the council gathered in the Unity and Relationships Cluster. Here the churches interact at the deepest level of their being through the Commission on Faith and Order; local and regional expressions of ecumenism are linked together through the Commission on Regional and Local Ecumenism (CORLE); and the council is enabled to be a more effective instrument of the ecumenical movement for racial minorities and particularly for the Black churches through Partners in Ecumenism and the Commission on Justice and Liberation.

Competence

A sixth element in our credibility is competence. We have first a kind of practical competence that comes from presence among the people. In the development of programs of child advocacy, in meeting the drought crisis in the Southeast, in working with people for freedom almost anywhere in the world, the church is "on the ground," with the people, in a way that very few if any other institutions are. In addition, we have a kind of competence that comes from the moral authority of advocating not for ourselves but for others—as a "disinterested party" seeking the common good, rather than as one more special interest group seeking its own good, often at the expense of the common good.

However much we may celebrate the "on-the-ground" credibility of the churches, we must confess that to those same "grassroots" we often seem to be in the clouds—shrouded in fog and mist. It need not be so. But if it is not to be so, then we must speak more in terms of the universal language of the church—which is the language of faith. We must also find ways to expand opportunities for ecumenical learning—to open to all the members of the body the experience of life in the *Oikumene* which has enriched and opened our spirits to the world and cast out our fears of its peoples.

We are tested not only at the grassroots. We are also challenged in the groves of academia and in the halls of government. University of Chicago ethicist James Gustafson claims that the churches have lived "too much off of indignation, and not enough on deliberation." Bishop James Malone, in a November, 1984, presidential address to the United States Catholic Conference, reminded his fellow bishops that "our impact on the public will be directly proportionate to the persuasiveness of our positions." The point is indisputable; and all-pervasive.

Our credibility is conditioned by every statement we make. Each instance of competence enhances credibility. Each instance of incompetence destroys credibility—not only on *that* issue, but of the council. A rising tide of confidence lifts all boats—at least those with sound hulls. An ebbing tide beaches all boats—no matter how sound their hulls. It follows then that the more closely we bind ourselves together in this community, the greater is our responsibility to one another and the more we need the courage to say "no" when our "yes" will lack competence.

The results of competence can be very significant and enduring. Nearly a decade after the drafting of the Middle East Policy Statement we can testify that it has weathered uncommonly well both the ebbs and flows in one of the most troubled areas of the world, as well as dramatic and erratic changes in US government policy. Indeed, there is evidence that this statement has helped to keep United States government policy from even greater vacillations. In another instance, careful study and analysis of the facts in preparation for the Policy Statement on Child Day Care led to at least fourteen states using portions of the NCC policy statement as a basis for their legislation. The issues addressed in our Policy Statement on Genetic Science for Human Benefit, approved last year, are the stuff of this year's lead stories. And the carefully crafted, much debated—and once postponed—Policy Statement on Ethical Implications of Energy Production & Use, adopted in 1979, was years ahead of its time.

Indeed, any review of the council's policy statements over the nearly four decades of its history cannot help but leave one impressed with their aggregate wisdom as well as their courage. Often they were far ahead of their time, and their wisdom was mistaken for foolishness. This is dramatically apparent in the NCC's 1983 Policy Statement on the People's Republic of China, which could begin by referring to the NCC's 1966 policy statement on the subject and say of it, "Almost all of the recommendations in that statement—calling for people-to-people and intergovernmental normalization of relations—have been realized."

Consistency

A seventh element in our credibility is our consistency. We are frequently charged with a selective indignation which is targeted mostly at the United States and its allies. A related charge is that we seem explicitly to exclude socialist societies, and especially the Soviet Union, from our indignation. These charges have of course been responded to repeatedly and at length both in defense of what we have done—as well as in amendment of what we have and have not done. The record in fact shows that we have frequently stood against the abuses of human rights and other injustices in many countries, including the Soviet Union.

Yet we recognize that no body so public as ours will ever be able to meet everyone's particular criteria in such sensitive and complex issues. It is all the more important, therefore, again to remind ourselves, and others, that we are *churches in the United States* and that we are the *Council of Churches in the United States of America*—and happy to be so. The policies of our government are therefore our first and foremost political responsibility. This is the more true because of the pre-eminent power of this nation in the world which shapes and influences the public policy of many other nations.

We of course have no such relationship or responsibility to the government of the Soviet Union. Our responsibility in this respect is two-fold: first again to our own government and to the oft-obsessive conduct of its foreign policy regarding the Soviet Union; second, to support the public witness of the churches in the Soviet Union so that their voice for justice in their own society may be heard and heeded.

We have cause to rejoice in our own path-making programs in this regard. We have helped thousands of people in our churches to get enough firsthand information to enable them to discern for themselves the wisdom or foolishness of our government's policies. And in the Soviet Union itself we have borne massive public witness to the centrality of the churches and their faith in a still officially atheist society. At the same time, we have urged the diligent use of every means to just and peaceful resolution of conflicts and sought to show by example ways this can be done.

In critiquing the relationship between the super-powers, and among all the other powers, we seek always, above all else, to insist that the nature of the action we take, public or private, confrontational or conciliatory, is determined not by our own political advantage or popularity, but rather to serve the cause of Christ, while seeking to protect the lives and serve the well-being of those whose basic human freedoms are denied, keeping particularly in mind the victims of human rights violations.

Communication

An eighth element in our credibility is the quality of our communication. Under attack by the *Reader's Digest* and CBS in the early 1980s, the council's Information Office, together with the cooperation of the communication offices of many of the member churches, struggled valiantly to win a hearing for the truth. The story, however, is very much like that of David and Goliath—without the five smooth stones!

We can not hope to equal the power of the public media, but we must make every effort to increase our information and interpretation functions. We have a story to tell. We have a witness to make.

There is much more to be said, but time would fail me to speak of CROP walks, the Revised Standard Version of the Bible, the Uniform Lesson Series through which thousands of children and adults have been nurtured in faith, the *Yearbook of American and Canadian Churches* which has been the authoritative source in its field for half a century, of countless testimonies offered and amicus briefs filed to defend the religious and civil liberties of a wide array of unpopular movements and religious groups—even those who when they are not overwhelmed by their troubles, find the time to attack us! And what more shall I say?—of lives saved, prisoners freed, families reunited, hope renewed, health restored, and the vision of the new heaven and the new earth held firmly above the horizon of history for thousands who would otherwise despair.

And that is what makes our credibility of critical importance. Most of the time we can afford to laugh along with our critics. Indeed, we would often do well to be the first to laugh. Laughter frees us to learn. The matter becomes serious—deadly serious—however, when questions about our credibility become attacks on our credibility intended to weaken or destroy our capacity to stand against injustice. In such times our greatest resource is our common commitment to one another in Christ. To prepare for *such* times, we must at *all* times so live and speak and act that we may be heard and seen in the churches first, and through them in the world, as Christians bound to one another in love, committed to the whole gospel, through the whole church, for the whole person in the whole world. Then having done all, we will be able to stand.

18

A Millennial Greeting to the Russian Orthodox Church

Presented in the Bolshoi Theater, Moscow, June 10, 1988

The 1000th anniversary of the Russian Orthodox church was eagerly anticipated around the world for at least a decade. And debated too. Since the originating event took place in Kiev, some Ukranians saw it as one more particularly nettlesome example of Russian imperialism. Many in the Soviet Union (and elsewhere) wondered if a church under persecution ought to be celebrating. The arrival of glasnost met part of the second concern but made it more possible to express the first. Nevertheless, celebrate we did, a great gala event—or rather series of events—attended by many world religious leaders and much in the news in the United States and around the world.

Planning of the event, however, left more than a little to be desired. With a thousand years to celebrate, it seemed that I might have had more than twenty-four hours' notice that I was expected to make a speech! Seated just behind and above me on the stage in the Bolshoi was Gunnar Stalsett, general secretary of the Lutheran World Federation, camera at the ready. A few weeks later I received from him a picture of my hand moving across an illegibly scrawled and heavily edited yellow pad. The picture was labeled, "Last-minute preparation!?"

The list of speakers was long, as were some of the speeches. To everyone's astonishment and great pleasure, Raisa Gorbachev sat through it from start to finish. I myself took the greatest pleasure in presenting the birthday greetings to the Russian Orthodox church from American children (see below).

I enjoyed it so much, in fact, that afterwards, a Danish Lutheran bishop whom I did not know approached me to wonder, "Could it be that you yourself are an unusually tall child?" Well, yes, of course.

Displaying a Crayola Brigade birthday card from Wesley Park United Methodist Church, Grand Rapids, Michigan, in the Bolshoi Theater, June 10, 1968. Seated on the platform are church leaders from around the world. Second from the right in the front row is Raisa Gorbachev. (Credit: Martin Bailey).

Your Holiness, Your Beatitudes, Eminences, Excellencies, sisters and brothers.

With great joy, I greet you on behalf of the forty-two million believers in the thirty-two member communions of the National Council of Churches of Christ in the U.S.A., and the heads of those churches, many of whom are present in this hall.

With you we give thanks to God for the victories of the resurrected Christ recorded in the one-thousand year history of this church, filled with triumph and with tragedy—and with triumph over tragedy. This history is a strong witness to the everlasting mercy and faithfulness of God and to the faith of the people through many times of trouble.

With you, we remember all those, known and unknown, who have lived and died in the Lord throughout those ten centuries. And especially those who have died under the cross, sealing their witness, their *martyria*, with their blood.

With you we rejoice that in the providence of God, and through the brilliant, tireless, and courageous work of Mikhail Sergeyevich Gorbachev, *glasnost* and *peristroika* should have arrived in time for this jubilee. We are hoping and watching and praying that the celebration of this thousand years of *chronos*, or calendar time, may in truth be a moment of *kairos*, or kingdom time.

Toward that end, we rejoice with you in the opening and building of churches, the return of monasteries to the church, and especially the Monastery of the Caves in Kiev. We wait with eager longing the fulfillment of these and other signs which will enable and empower the ministry of the church of Christ to the peoples of this great land.

The relationship of the National Council of the Churches of Christ in the United States of America with the Russian Orthodox Church and the other churches in the Soviet Union is but a few scattered paragraphs in the last chapter of your one-thousand year history. But in the story of the National Council of Churches in the United States, this relationship appears very near the beginning of our history, in the early 1950s at the height of the cold war—and it is writ large in our history. Now more than ever we are convinced that the destinies of our two nations are inextricably bound up with one another and indeed with the future of the whole human family and creation itself. This shared commitment we have demonstrated in our prayer vigils at the meetings of General Secretary Mikhail Gorbachev and President Ronald Reagan in Geneva, in Washington, and last week in Moscow. We are persuaded that our bond to one another in Christ cannot be broken. We have extended to one another the right hand of fellowship, clasped it, and we shall never let go.

We rejoice that, particularly in this decade, the Russian Orthodox church has taken a position of world leadership in the struggle for peace which we in the churches of the United States salute and celebrate.

With your many other brothers and sisters who have come from around the world to celebrate with you, we are indebted to you for many spiritual gifts. I myself celebrate above all else the way in which your liturgy has infused your people with the life of God and created a tradition that glows with the presence of God. We in the United States are also grateful for the missionary zeal of your forebears, particularly St. Innocent and St. Herman, through whose work we are pleased to number now in the membership of the National Council of Churches, the Orthodox Church in America as well as the Patriarchal Parishes together with seven other Orthodox communions.

In this millenial year, tens of thousands of people in our country are studying the thousand-year history of your church. They are learning about the people of the Soviet Union and they are receiving the spiritual gifts of the Orthodox churches. Our study guide is now in a record fourth printing (which is very good for our budget!). Many thousands of our people have visited your country (which is very good for your balance of trade!). But more important, they have come as pilgrims to your holy places. We believe that these programs have begun to contribute toward some "glasnost" and "peristroika" in the United States with respect to attitudes toward the Soviet Union.

There is one demonstration of this coming new age that has touched my heart more than any other and which I now in closing wish briefly to share with you. Hearing one of her rectors speak of the 1,000th anniversary of the Russian Orthodox church, Suzanne Nagel, a member of the Trinity Episcopal Church, Wall Street, New York, felt a deep urge to do something in response. She was inspired to launch what she called a "Crayon Brigade" of 1,000th anniversary "birthday cards" from Sunday school children in the United States to Russian Orthodox children in the Soviet Union. She brought her suggestion to the National Council of Churches— and the crayons began to move.

The trickle of cards that began in January turned into a deluge. We have now received tens of thousands of cards from thousands of different congregations across the United States which the people who have come to the Soviet Union from the United States have carried with them and distributed in this country. Almost all of these packets have come with moving letters of appreciation for the opportunity to share in the project and in the 1,000th anniversary observance. These letters will eventually be published in a book, we hope both in the United States and in the Soviet Union, as a means for our children to be talking with one another.

We have a formal gift to present to Your Holiness on some other occasion, but on this occasion I wish to present three of these birthday cards to the Russian Orthodox church. The first is from The St. Viator Church in Las Vegas, Nevada, where a group of pre-kindergarten children created a bouquet and each one of the children in the class imprinted a thumb-print on a petal of the flower. Another from the St. Alban's Church, St. Alban, Maine, it is an extension of the hands of American children to the hands of Soviet children. And still another, done in the Wesley Park United Methodist Church in Grand Rapids, Michigan, is the product of a class of Sunday school children who made a card with a thousand candles.

19
We Are Choosing Death
for Our Children

A statement at the American Family Festival on the grounds of the Washington Monument, Washington, DC, May 14, 1988

Here too and yet again, I was one of a long list of people representing various communities at an event of which in this case, the NCC was a sponsor. The statement as a whole was two or three times longer than these few paragraphs. I have deleted the rest in order to highlight in a few stark paragraphs a growing and terrible crisis in our land and around the world.

We are choosing death for our children by driving them into poverty. Ten thousand children die every year because of poverty. More than ten million live in poverty in this country. Thousands are homeless. If we would choose life for our children, we must work to outlaw poverty in this country.

We are choosing death for our children by mortgaging their future through an outrageous national debt. That debt grows ever more intolerable through the purchase of weapons of death that kill children all over the world. If we would choose life for our children we must stop the arms race.

We are choosing death for our children by ravaging their world. Natural resources, the environment, and other living things are being driven to death on a daily, hourly, even minute-by-minute basis. If we would choose life for our children, we must stop the killing of their mother earth.

We are choosing death for our children by dissipating their heritage. If we would choose life for our children, we must give them an opportunity for education where they can learn what is beautiful and true and just and holy.

We are choosing death for our children by destroying their hope. If we would choose life for our children, we must help them to believe in a world built on the well being of the whole human family—men, women, boys, girls—of all ages, all colors, all nations, all cultures.

20
On Signing the Williamsburg Charter

A statement at Williamsburg, VA, June 25, 1988

The 1980s were marked by worldwide intensification of politico-religious conflict. The Middle East, Northern Ireland, the Asian subcontinent, these are familiar scenes of such conflict. In many less familiar places, too, factional strife fueled by religious passions destroyed community life, ravaged whole cities, and led to the slaughter of people by the tens and hundreds of thousands.

As we have seen, such controversy also loomed large in the United States, particularly in the abortion debates and in the presidential campaigns throughout the decade. Among the persons concerned was Os Guinness, a British citizen of evangelical Christian persuasion and profoundly impressed by the American heritage of religious liberty. Alarmed by signs of its erosion, he won support for an interfaith reaffirmation of America's "first liberty" in the form of the Williamsburg Charter. Drafted by a committee representative of the widest possible spectrum of American religious belief, it is an astonishingly insightful and literate document. Credit for that high quality belongs to many people, but I wish particularly to mention my colleague Dean Kelley, director of civil and religious liberty for the NCC—whose work was customarily extraordinary!

The work of the Williamsburg Foundation culminated in a public signing and celebration of the charter in Williamsburg, Virginia, June 25, 1988. The introduction to the charter stated that "Signing this Charter implies no pretense that we believe the same things...." On the contrary, it declared that "...differences over belief are the deepest and least easily negotiated of all..." "The Charter" it says, "sets forth a renewed national compact, in the sense of a solemn mutual agreement between parties, on how we view the place of religion in American life and how we should contend with each other's deepest differences in the public sphere."

Several of those who were asked to sign the charter were also asked to say "a few words" on behalf of the various streams of American religious life. My assignment was mainline Protestantism. Richard Neuhaus, the same of chapter 7, who then edited the *Religion and Society Report*, quoted my statement in full in the November, 1988, issue under the heading "An Abduction, Of Sorts," remarking, "That gracious statement, one might suppose, is about as close as mainline/oldline/sideline Protestantism is likely to get to a formal statement of abdication." Then followed a lament that I did not name a successor to the mainline Protestant establishment! Neuhaus's report concluded, "In any case, June 25, 1988, in Williamsburg, Virginia, might be noted as an historic occasion for a number of reasons, not least because it dramatically symbolized a changing of the guard with respect to religion and public life in America."

To that, I can only say, "Perhaps...," and report, as did Neuhaus, that after raising the microphone to accommodate my six-foot seven inches, I said:

It might, I suppose, be remarked that merely by standing here today I am something of a symbol that for many decades mainline Protestantism towered over the religious landscape of America.

Speaking as a representative of the unofficial Protestant establishment, I might perhaps be forgiven for lamenting its passing. But I do not lament; I celebrate.

I celebrate the growth pains of a new post-establishment age, in the profound conviction that ultimate meaning can never be directed or dictated: either by imposed authority; or by legislative action; or by cultural dominance.

Ultimate meaning must always be recognized as a matter of mind and spirit.

Only thus can faith be true.

Only thus can the people be free.

Only thus can the nation be united.

Only thus can all its citizens be equal.

Only thus can society be just.

Only thus can the world be at peace.

Only thus can God be glorified.

Signing the Williamsburg Charter, Williamsburg, Virginia, June 25, 1988 (Credit: Christianity Today).

21
Mission in the USA

A statement at the World Conference on Mission, San Antonio, TX, May 24, 1989

This conference was heir to the great tradition of world conferences on mission begun at Edinburgh, Scotland, in 1910, usually recognized as the beginning of the modern ecumenical movement. Convened approximately every seven years, this was the first conference to be held in the United States. More than a few of the several hundred persons in attendance from around the world were friends and acquaintances and former colleagues at the World Council of Churches. Since the conference opened three days after the NCC Governing Board's public debate about my continuing as general secretary, that was a matter much discussed.

And I was highly visible. In keeping with World Council custom, the general secretary of the host council was extended the privilege of welcoming the conference at its opening session. The host council was also invited to present a program describing the mission of the churches in the host country. Ours was a multimedia presentation for which I was to make an introductory statement before it was presented on the evening of the third day of the conference. During those intervening days between my welcome and this statement, many of my friends, and many others hardly known to me, expressed their support for me and the council. I began by thanking them and then did my best to bear witness to the ecumenical movement in the United States. Having already decided but not yet disclosed my intention to resign, I knew that this would be my last such statement as general secretary of the NCC.

One of our American philosophers, Casey Stengel, used to say sometimes, "Before I start to speak, I want to say something!" I will begin my prepared remarks in just a few minutes, but first a personal word. Many of you here know something of our troubles during the last days in the National Council of Churches in the United States. Unfortunately, I need to leave tomorrow to tend to those troubles, or at least try to tend to some of those troubles. I therefore cannot speak to you all one by one, so I want to say a word now—a simple word of thanks.

I have been deeply touched, as have been many of my colleagues, my hope and spirit renewed, by being here with you. Some of you have embraced me—or reached up to embrace me—others have spoken a word of courage, others have offered to listen, others to pray—one of you even remembered a helpful word I had spoken three years ago in a church assembly—and others have just reached out to touch me.

I have felt your strength flow into me and want to say thank you, dear friends. Thank you.

And now to mission in the USA...

In the introduction to the current issue of the *International Review of Mission* "Mission in Texas," Gene Stockwell observes, "To have prepared an issue on mission in the United States would have been too vast, too daunting a task." He is right; but it is our daily task and we have tried to convey it to you by enlisting the gift of music. Even so, we can show you only a few sketches in a few places.

The American folksongs you have just heard are a few windows on the soul—the many souls—of the American people. They are forms of social protest, of prophetic irony, and of human affirmation.

They are not the hymns of our civil religion. They are the gospel songs of this culture. Our civil religion is the creation of those who hold the cards. These folksongs are the creations of those who have been dealt out of the game. They are good news for the poor. That is why we have mixed them in with our American hymnody for this presentation on "Mission in the USA."

In a few minutes, you will see a few instances of "Mission in the USA"; and you will hear snatches of our songs. You will hear echoes of the Roman Catholic missions planted on these shores more than 100 years before the founding of Protestant colonies. You will hear traces of the lingering, long notes of those sturdy psalm singers who came to build a city on a hill in the wilds of New England and of those others, dear to my own heart and heritage, who came to seek new life in the Middle Colonies. You will hear the distinctive sounds of music made in America by the free churches and indigenous movements. And, you will hear the life-sustaining, life-giving, liberation music of the African-American churches of this land.

The forms of our music are many. So, also, are the forms of our mission.

> On the rocky shores of New England with its stern covenantal Puritan theology, there arose an establishmentarianism of exclusion, and the consequent Baptist and Quaker protest against it.

> In the middle colonies of New York and New Jersey, with their pragmatic political capitalism, there arose an establishmentarianism of preference.

> In Virginia, with its worldly enlightenment rationalism, there arose an establishmentarianism of privilege.

> And in Pennsylvania, among the Quakers, no establishmentarianism at all.

And then, out of the wilderness and byways, there arose a great mighty rushing wind speaking through the tongues of Jonathan Edwards, George Whitfield, Theodore Frelinghuysen, and the Wesleys. Eventually that great wind swept away all forms of establishmentarianism. It helped to move the founders of this nation to write into our constitutional Bill of Rights the guarantee for all Americans of their first liberty—the freedom of religion—in these words:

Congress shall make no law respecting an establishment of
religion or prohibiting the free exercise thereof.

Thus, unfettered and free, the winds of the Great Awakening and
its successor awakenings carried its messengers over the
Appalachians. They pressed the frontier across the Mississippi and
beyond the Rockies to the golden hills and strands of the west.
Farther to the north and west, another wind was blowing,
eastward, across the Bering Sea, carrying hunters and adventurers,
and in 1794, the first missionary monks and priests of the Russian
Orthodox church. Settling on the island of Kodiak, they preached
the gospel, worshiped God, served the people, and built churches in
the vast whiteness of the wilderness, many decades before Alaska
became a part of these United States. Eventually one of those
priests who served in Alaska returned to Moscow as Metropolitan
Innocent. And many years later an archbishop in New York
returned to Russia to become Patriarch Tikhon, the first patriarch in
almost 200 years.
Most of the American churches, however, remained impervious
to the songs and hymns of the Orthodox, until we sang them
together in the World Council of Churches. That is a parable of
ecumenical learning and sharing demonstrating that we can speak
our own tongues and hear our neighbors tongues best in a
community of many tongues.
But that was many years later. The winds that swept across
America in the 18th and 19th centuries, carried many spirits. Some
of them were harsh, very harsh. Already in their first stirrings in
New England and in the middle colonies, those harsh winds had
devastated the native American population. Now and then there was
a gentle refreshing and renewing breeze of grace and love, but
mostly the winds were rapacious. The church, to its credit, built a
few shelters against those harsh winds, but to its discredit, not much
more. When the winds died away there was heard in the tents and
tepees and wigwams and lodges of the original peoples of this land
the mournful songs and the weeping and the wailing of whole tribes
and mighty nations which had been swept away—their lands, their
goods, their culture, and their religion—gone, gone.
We had sown the wind; they had reaped the whirlwind. We are
reaping it still. The video you will be seeing a bit later will show
some of the power of that whirlwind. It will show the effects of the
social tornadoes that even now lay waste this land we love. It will

show, too, some of the shelters against the whirlwind built and sustained by the churches.

But first, a few more words about religion in America and particularly about its free exercise. For nearly two centuries now that first liberty has been guarded by our constitutional Bill of Rights. But for most of that time—indeed all of that time—some have been more free than others. The legal establishments of the colonial period disappeared, but cultural establishment did not. Indeed, it grew stronger as an increasingly acculturated mainline Protestantism became the normative religion of the nation. Catholics, Jews, and non-mainline Protestants and all others were neglected—sometimes benignly, sometimes malignantly—as the case might be. National power and foreign mission were fitted together hand in glove, much as they are still today in an even more pernicious fashion in the foreign mission enterprises of many conservative evangelical communities.

In those days, acculturation was the American way. The winds of social change in other parts of the world swept great multitudes of immigrants to these shores and into the American melting pot. Others came as captives, plucked from their native lands by the cold winds of trade in human beings, clamped in chains, beaten, starved, and sold as slaves. The churches were there—in works of charity, providing food, housing, health care, education, and many other forms of social service—sheltering people from the whirlwinds.

But some among us have not been content merely to build shelters. They have wanted to wrestle with the whirlwind, to challenge the culture, to cast out the demons. Amid the social storms, they have cried out for justice. In the 20s and 30s, following the Great Depression, the voices of the churches were heard above the whirlwind, crying out against child labor, in support of labor unions, and for health care and public education. In substantial measure their voices prevailed, and the whirlwind lost its power.

In the 1960s and the 1970s, the whirlwind again rose and fell as people of color overcame the most blatant forms of prejudice against them; and we all won a few battles in the war on poverty—and this nation finally lost the war in Vietnam.

Now it is the 1980s. And the whirlwind is upon the land again. We do not see it, and we do not hear it, as we did in the 30s and the 60s. The whirlwind has learned how to pass silently over the land. It has even learned how to unfurl our flag in order to hide its terrible work as it sweeps away the family farm, drives tens of thousands from their homes, spreads the plague of drugs and poverty, erodes the foundations of our communities and of our culture, and divides our churches.

Our churches have long been divided over our mission. We all, or nearly all, agree that the hungry should be fed, the naked clothed, the homeless sheltered. We disagree over who should feed them and clothe them and shelter them; and we disagree over how they should be fed and clothed and sheltered. Some argue that it is a question of self-reliance; others of charity; and others of the common welfare. We, who are your hosts, hold these truths, to be self-evident, that all human beings are created in the image of God. These are therefore matters of love—and of justice.

This is the America you have come to visit. These are the churches you have come to help—at the end of this violent century when the American experiment—and indeed the human experiment—is hanging in the balance.

At the heart of the American experiment is the free exercise of religion. That is true, because, as de Tocqueville noted long ago, religion provides the energy for the American experiment, and freedom is its essence.

This land, America, is preeminently the land where one can find clearly "revealed the dangerous possibilities of human freedom." Those words are from a lecture by Reinhold Niebuhr, a distinguished American ecumenist and no stranger to the World Council of Churches. In another parable of ecumenical learning and sharing, I found those words, however, in the last, the very, very last, writings of Alan Paton, the South African novelist and social critic who recalled them in this way.

> Niebuhr felt that this rather difficult argument needed some kind of elaboration, and he proceeded to drop his script for the moment, and to dwell on the dangerous possibilities of freedom in the United States itself, the fact that the American ideal of freedom meant the liberty to choose good and to choose evil, so that high endeavor lived alongside vice and corruption and decadence. He did this with a kind of sombre gravity that certainly subdued his audience, and then inflicted on them a heavy blow by saying fiercely of American society, "It's a mess." We were all silent, feeling that the world was beyond redemption, when—after a pause—he suddenly said to us with equal emphasis, "But I

like it." It brought down the house, and we felt that there was hope for the world after all.

Yes, there is hope for the world after all. And there is more hope for us in America because you are here.

A little while ago you heard the familiar words, familiar to us at least, of Woody Guthrie's "This Land is Your Land, this Land is My Land." It is not widely known that Woodrow Wilson Guthrie wrote that song in response to Irving Berlin's "God Bless America." Berlin spoke of America as "*My* home, sweet home." In fact, Guthrie's first title for his own song was "God Bless*ed* America." One of Woody's children, Pete Seeger, speaks of Guthrie's song as "our second national anthem." It surely is a great deal more friendly than the original.

And it is the truth. This land is your land as much as it is our land. According to our laws, all of us who live here have equal right to this land and its wealth. But it is not only those of us who live here. You who have come to visit us may claim it as *your* own as well. This is true not only in the general human sense that this land, too, is a part of God's creation and therefore should be equally available to all God's children. And this is true not only in the ecumenical sense that we are all one in Christ and are therefore called to share our resources.

It is true in a political and economic sense. For many of you, much that you find here has been siphoned, stolen, even robbed from your homelands. You, therefore, have a right to claim—even to reclaim—that wealth as your own—and to do so, not only here, but over all the world until Mary's Magnificat becomes the governing principle of human community.

Indeed, in the larger global perspective, we who inhabit the powerful nations are always guests. We are often uninvited guests, living at the expense of others even in our own homelands.

All this notwithstanding, we of course make bold to welcome you nonetheless. Did you notice, I wonder, that I said "notwithstanding," "of course," and "nonetheless"? Those words, especially all together, should have triggered your hermeneutic of suspicion! Yes, we do welcome you, we welcome you with open arms and open hearts. But we are a little anxious, too.

We are eager to have you because you enrich our lives and because we need your help. We are anxious, because we are not sure how you will go about helping us! If you have been following the news about the National Council of Churches in the USA, you know that we don't need you to make trouble for us. We are doing very well by ourselves, thank you very much!

We are anxious, too, because although we criticize our government at will—we do—we sometimes get a little testy when others do. The people we represent get testier still. We feel drawn in two or more directions: loyalty to them, to you, to ourselves and to this land. Yes, America is a mess, but we do like it.

And hovering around the edges of our anxiety, darting in and out, unsettling us still more is our very non-Niebuhrian American capacity for self-flagellation. You need to know that this trait is greatly amplified when visitors like you come to town—particularly in such large numbers and with such trustworthy credentials. That is our problem; we need to get beyond it.

But meanwhile, you can help us by *seeing* beyond it—by seeing both that America is a mess and by seeing why we like it.

Please forgive me then for asking you near the outset of this conference, in the practice of your duty, yes, your brotherly, sisterly, priestly, and prophetic duty, to be critical of this nation, and of its people, and of its people—it is long past time to spare the American people while criticizing the American government—we are responsible for it; please forgive me then for urging upon you the moral and spiritual methodology of that great American, Martin Luther King, Jr., who did more to change the nature of this country, to resurrect its soul, then any other American of this century.

Martin Luther King, Jr., had a haunting way of saying, "I read somewhere," "I read somewhere..." He would go on then to quote the familiar words and the stirring cadences of our Declaration of Independence or some other text sacred to our national tradition, all the while weaving a lustrous tapestry of biblical teaching. I know of no other American in this century who has equaled him in that capacity, and that is surely a major reason why he, more than any other American in this century, changed the face of this nation by freeing people of color to hold their heads up high.

Fifty years before him, Susan B. Anthony and Elizabeth Cady Stanton, followed a similar strategy, using those same sacred texts, to set free the women of this male-dominated republic. They, too, changed the face of America by freeing women to hold their heads up high.

These gifts of Sister Susan and Brother Martin are the gifts of the Spirit. They are available to us all. We need urgently to use them.

That brings us back to our songs. Susan B. Anthony and Martin Luther King, Jr., and hosts of others have sung the songs of the church and of the people as they marched. We Christians have always sung the gospel. We Christians in America have sung the gospel in camp meetings, revival services, Sunday schools, student conferences, mission conferences, and a thousand other places. You will see a few of those places now and you will hear a few of those songs. Then we will ask you to sing the gospel with us—to sing the Lord's song in a strange land—to sing the gospel for this land, for your land, for all lands.

II

For the Unity
of the
Church

22

The Future of National
Conciliar Ecumenism

A presentation to the NCC Governing Board, New York, NY, October 13, 1974

The request to participate in a panel presentation to the NCC's Governing Board came originally to Marion "Mert" de Velder, who was then general secretary of the RCA. He had to be out town, so he suggested that I substitute for him. When invited, I agreed. First presented in the Governing Board's section on Christian Unity on Friday night, the response to the panel was enthusiastic. Docketed for presentation on Sunday to the entire Governing Board in a strictly limited time frame, I decided to write it out. It was a hit. Following the meeting, *On Location* "A joint publication of the National Association of Ecumenical Staff and the Commission on Regional and Local Ecumenism" called the panel "the most interesting item on the agenda" and published my contribution (Vol. II, No. 1).

A few background notes on the text:

Bill Thompson is William Phelps Thompson, then stated clerk of the United Presbyterian Church in the United States of America. As chair of a council planning committee, he had presented to the council's 1969 assembly a long-range plan which the assembly did not wish to hear.

Following the assembly, I was asked to chair a restructure committee of which he was a member. Against that background—and I thought with more than a little irony—he suggested that perhaps I was now the Moses to lead the council out of captivity to the promised land! That conversation provided the opening motif for my remarks.

My leadership of that restructure committee was the basis for my reference to having been "for a while...the high priest of this cult." Our restructure committee fared no better than had Bill Thompson's planning committee. After the General Board's rejection of our proposals, the council tried again, this time through a Committee on Future Ecumenical Structures. The "Ecumenical Imperatives" to which I refer below were the principles advanced by that committee as the bases for its restructure proposals.

More than a decade and a half later, it seems to me that the tides of the times are still ecumenical. It seems too, that we are still failing to take them at the flood.

My view of the future of ecumenism will be understandable only if I share with you my view of our recent history. Shortly after the Detroit assembly in December '69, I had occasion to discuss the future of the NCC with Bill Thompson. He spoke of it in terms of the Exodus. I remarked that Detroit must then have been the last of the plagues! I was wrong. Since that time we have suffered every manner of plague. There have been times when I thought we had crossed the Red Sea only to find at our next meeting that I was again gathering straw and making bricks.

At the risk of being wrong again, let me say that I believe we have now come out of Egypt. I sense a growing feeling of liberation in the last meetings of the General Board. We have spied out the land and, God knows, we have done our wilderness wanderings. We are not yet out of that wilderness, but we seem to be closer to the promised land.

We have reason to be optimistic about the future of ecumenism. Ecumenism is increasingly accepted as a given in modern culture. Societal trends which have undergirded the ecumenical movement seem to be accelerating and gathering force. The Spirit of God is moving to make us one.

It seems to me that national conciliar ecumenism must discover its future in that general ecumenical context. Our future...must be found outside of ourselves, in our vision of the new heaven and the new earth.

We members of the panel were asked to comment on the "Ecumenical Imperatives". I have studied them carefully in the last two weeks and I am uneasy about them. I do not disagree with them; I endorse their content. But I am uneasy about their tone. They seem to say, "Somehow, for God's sake, we had better hang on to each other." In Dallas in 1972 we may have needed that. We are beyond that now.

I am, therefore, uneasy about the use we make of them. They are cited as the foundation for our common life. But imperatives have to do with law, and law does not give life. (As a Dutch Reformed minister reared and trained in a mixture of classical Calvinism, Reformed scholasticism, and neo-evangelicalism, I know about that from my own pilgrimage.) Legalism grows stronger as the vision grows weaker. The imperatives may have kept us in the covenant, and they may keep us there for a while longer; but they will not give us life. New life comes from new visions, new hopes, and new dreams.

Therefore, I believe we need urgently to cultivate what I am calling a national ecumenical ethos. I am not suggesting a new slogan—and I would be suspect of anyone who did. I am talking about the things we have always talked about: faith, love, justice, human dignity, peace, hope, joy. I am pleading that we articulate our ecumenical aspiration in the symbols, myths, and realities of the Christian faith. I am not calling for more theological prologues to policy statements. They are usually abstract, argumentative, and polemical. I want something experiential, confessional, and testimonial. I am talking about an ethos that comes out of a community—an extension of the liturgy.

I do not find very much community in our Governing Board. Our group relationships apart from our personal friendships tend to be manipulative and exploitative. (How can I get them to do my thing? You sign my resolution and I'll sign yours.) We have almost totally failed to practice the liturgy of the church. This morning's service of worship was a notable and welcome exception. I applaud it. In the absence of the church's liturgy we have gone after structural idols. We intone a pagan liturgy which speaks of matrix management and interagency task forces in a bureaucratic smog which we mistake for incense. (I have, myself, bowed before the Baals and worshiped in the high places. For a while I was the high priest of this cult.)

I am not suggesting that organization is unimportant. I am saying that it should not determine our ethos. I do not want our lives to be dominated by sections, unit committees, task forces, boards, and panels. I want in my ecumenical life to know myself a member of Christ.

I say all this to you because we are responsible for our future. The development of a national ecumenical ethos is the task of the Governing Board and its executive leadership. I would hope that we accept that task and give our staff a clear mandate to make it our top priority.

In my view, ecumenical staff members are first and foremost the priests and prophets of the ecumenical movement. They are charged to seek the mind of the Christ and the mind of the church, to lead us all in

hopeful exploration of the ecumenical vision;
joyful articulation of our ecumenical aspirations;
faithful cultivation of an ecumenical ethos.

I believe the people in this room and their churches are ready for that. There are many out there beyond the NCC who are ready for that. I hope we will get at it.

23
Praying for One Another

A Church Herald *column, January 23, 1981*

Prayer doesn't often make the news so people don't usually think of the ecumenical movement in those terms—even though the community of prayer is among the most meaningful forms of ecumenical life. This column was an attempt to hold up that image, relate it to other more familiar experiences of prayer, give a human face to the Week of Prayer for Christian Unity, and extend the spirit of that week throughout the whole year.

Some of my friends keep lists of people for whom they pray regularly. They often follow up their prayers with a note or telephone call to the people for whom they have prayed. They stand ready to express their intercessions in supportive action as well as in words.

The Week of Prayer for Christian Unity, January 18-25, is an occasion to enlarge our circles of prayer to include the whole people of God. Those eight days are a reminder to pray for Christians around the world and to give thanks for our unity in Christ across many countries and cultures. Begun in 1907 by Father Paul Wattson, then of the Episcopal church, the Week of Prayer for Christian Unity is now officially sponsored by many Protestant and Orthodox churches and by the Roman Catholic church.

By sharing in a worldwide circle of prayer, we enter into the witness, struggle, anxiety, despair, suffering, and hope of all God's people. We pray for people in difficult circumstances which go essentially unchanged year after year. We pray for people whose situations grow ever more dangerous and difficult.

Confronted with such apparent failure and frustration, we experience the mystery of God's will. Yet, as last year's call to prayer for Christian unity issued by the World Council of Churches reminds us, such circumstances call for ever more fervent prayer because the growth of the kingdom "depends entirely on the church's Lord and the work of his Spirit." In prayer, God renews our faith; keeps us open to the future and free to love—against the odds.

There are, of course, dramatic breakthroughs as well. One is the new freedom granted to the church in the Peoples' Republic of China. Another recent example was the release of Mortimer Arias, a bishop of the Methodist church in Bolivia. Bishop Arias was arrested in late August by the military junta which had taken over the Bolivian government. Protests about his arrest poured in from all over the world, especially from the World Council and its member churches. Due to their unceasing prayer and public outcry, Bishop Arias was spared the torture suffered by many others arrested at the same time. Finally, in early October, the Latin American Council of the Methodist church gathered in Mexico City with Mrs. Arias to review the situation and to pray. At the close of morning prayers on the second day, word came that Bishop Arias had been released.

Such an occasion for thanksgiving renews our commitment to pray for one another. Intercession is not grounded finally in these experiences of joy, however, but in the ministry of Christ. The call to intercession is nothing less than a call to continue the ministry of Christ, whose whole life and work was to intercede for us all and who does so still at God's right hand.

People who want to join in such prayer for their brothers and sisters around the world may find useful a recent World Council of Churches' publication entitled "For all God's People: Ecumenical Prayer Cycle."* The book offers suggestions for 52 weeks of prayer. Each weekly unit contains a brief sketch of a particular part of the world, the churches in it, and several prayers used in those churches....such regular and informed intercession is one way to share the New Testament experience to which Paul repeatedly testifies—that even while he prays for the churches, he finds himself strengthened by their prayers for him.

*Reissued in 1989 as *With All God's People: The New Ecumenical Prayer Cycle*. Available from World Council of Churches, 475 Riverside Drive, New York, New York 10115 or from Anglican Book Centre, 600 Jarvis Street, Toronto, Canada M4Y 2J6. (Spanish and Dutch editions are also available.)

24
Who 'Owns' the Councils?

Occasion unknown

After leaving the council in the summer of 1989, I decided to take some time off for reflection and renewal. By the spring of 1990, I was going through my files sorting out the material for this book. This article was a mystery discovery. I recall writing it but have no recollection of its occasion. I know only that the reference to the Dresden Central Committee meeting places it sometime between the summer of 1981 and 1982.

Rereading it, I was struck by its stark anticipation of many of the issues which would be at the heart of the struggle in the NCC at the end of the decade—and by its clear vision of the councils as sign of the church toward which the movement carries us.

Who "owns the councils?" "The member churches," seems to be the most common answer. It is ordinarily assumed in reports of the councils' committees and commissions, in discussions within their governing boards, and in the councils' appeals for funds.

The assumption that the councils are church-owned also underlines the sometimes plaintive, sometimes angry, questions asked by both friends and foes of the councils: "Why don't they listen to us?" "Why don't they do as we say?"

This opinion that the councils are instruments of the churches is firmly rooted in the constituting documents of the councils. A review of the development of these documents will show, however, that although the councils were *formed* by the churches, they were *created* by the ecumenical movement and were *designed to be instruments and embodiments of that movement.* The constituting documents take great care to preserve the autonomy of the churches. But from the beginning, that concern has been in tension with the desire for the councils to be more full and complete expressions of unity than is possible for an association of autonomous churches.

This dynamic tension remains a critical issue in the life of the councils. The continuing conflict over membership in the councils' governing bodies and committees is one example. Shall they reflect the structural life of the denominations—mostly male, mostly clergy, and mostly white? Or shall they reflect the wholeness of that body—mostly female, mostly lay, and in the World Council of Churches, mostly people of color? The movement question is: How can this body be ecumenical if it institutionalizes our divisions? The institutional question, for both the churches and the councils, is: How can we relate effectively to one another without representation firmly rooted in our structures?

The National Council has struggled with an uneasy "balance" on this issue of membership ever since the tumultuous Detroit assembly in 1969 issued its call for more inclusive participation. This same issue was *the* question at last summer's meeting of the World Council's Central Committee in Dresden. It focused in the debate concerning "equal participation by women and men, as a goal toward which we should move, starting with the composition of the WCC decision-making and consultative bodies during and after the Sixth Assembly."

These uneasy compromises and unresolved differences between the churches and the ecumenical movement concerning "ownership" of the councils are further complicated by the claim to ownership coming from the institutions which embody that movement—the councils themselves. Grumbling around the edges of most ecumenical meetings usually includes complaints about "staff control"; and questions like "Who are all these 'experts'?" "Who do they represent?" "What are 'they' costing 'us'?"

Staff dominance—along with every other sort of dominance— must indeed be avoided, lest ends and means are turned around and the movement finds itself serving the institution, debate is stifled for fear of institutional damage, charismatic leaders drop out—and all such other institutional nightmares are fulfilled. There can be neither master nor slave. Nor can there be mere staff functionaries. We are all together servants of the ecumenical movement and of one another. If the councils are to be signs of unity before the world, then council staff must be recognized as full partners.

Who then "owns" the councils? The ecumenical movement, the member churches, and the conciliar institutions themselves with, one hopes, the ecumenical movement being first among equals.

This primacy of the ecumenical movement is not easily realized or maintained. Powerful institutional forces both in the member churches and in the councils themselves are arrayed against it, while the ecumenical movement itself is mostly an amorphous, on-again-off-again, up and down sort of thing, with less than a century of history—at least as we know it. The movement is easily diverted or arrested—at least temporarily. We must intentionally work to keep the movement first, if we are not to be cut off from the source of our common life and energy in the councils.

The work of the National Council's Ecumenical Panel during the last triennium was such an intentional effort. It effected a constitutional change which greatly strengthened the definition and purpose of the council by constituting it as a "community of churches," rather than the "cooperative agency" it had been. The recent Cleveland EVENT of the National Council of Churches was also such an effort. The assemblies once every seven years have served a similar purpose for the World Council of Churches.

Participants in these assemblies and other gatherings have again and again identified worship as having made the greatest contribution to the renewal of their ecumenical commitment. The ecumenical movement has no other claim to primacy in the life of the councils than its service of that oneness which we celebrate in our common worship. Little wonder that the movement weakens when our worship wanes or that it is starved by the absence of full eucharistic fellowship.

The councils' primary allegiance to the ecumenical movement cannot be sustained without such common worship. Without it, we will be prone to fall into the sin of divisive loyalties to ecclesiastical family traditions or to partisan passions. The provision of opportunities for worship is a primary and essential responsibility of the councils if they would be true to themselves as embodiments of the ecumenical movement.

Delegates to the councils' governing bodies should be the first to respond. Their freedom to do so would be enhanced by a common understanding that participation in such a body carries with it the obligation of *primary* loyalty to the whole rather than to any part, including the sending church. (We do after all regard caring for the common good as exemplary in our public servants!) Insights and traditions received from one's own group would be freely offered, but they would never be binding on the delegate.

This primary loyalty to the whole would, among other things, preclude the "unloading" of controversial programs onto the councils or—its opposite—keeping the action on popular causes within the denominations. It would free the councils and their officers and staff to act as priests and prophets of the ecumenical movement: Sometimes to press the claims of the movement—and sometimes to witness against the actions of one or more denominations.

The ecumenical movement, by definition, cannot be separated from the churches. It also fails of its definition if it is captive to the churches—or to the councils. The movement must sometimes stand against, and be always free to transcend, both the churches and the councils. The churches and the councils are always to be tested by their service to the movement. Insofar as possible, the councils are to embody the movement and be a sign of that one church which is the goal of the movement.

25
Why Work for the WCC?

A Church Herald *column, April 15, 1983*

Separation from a staff position central to the life of the Reformed Church in America was for me a very difficult decision. I had contemplated it and, as the following article states, even decided it, but when the call came to the WCC and the decision had to be implemented, it was painful in the extreme. I have often referred to it as an experience of mortality. That earlier decision, and at least some of those feelings of joyful attachments to the RCA and painful separation from it, I wanted the whole church to know.

I also wanted the church to know the nature of my journey and how it sprang from my deep roots in the RCA. I wanted them to accompany me on my journey, as they had over the years. That theme of continuing the journey together, I followed right through to my last *Church Herald* column published two months later in July 1983. I called it "A Sort of Farewell," explaining that "...although I leave my post as general secretary, I do not leave the RCA or its ministry or even its denominational service—thanks to my and Harriet's appointment as World Mission Associates," the nature of which relationship I had already explained in this column.

It started in our family devotions. Day after day, year after year, my father picked up the family Bible, read a lesson, and offered a prayer. He did this at every meal—a Psalm in the morning, a New Testament lesson at noon, and an Old Testament reading in the evening. Poets, philosophers, patriarchs, kings, prophets, apostles, and martyrs marched around the table as he read. Already then on that farm near Edgerton, Minnesota, I was fascinated by this long journey of the church toward the unfolding of the end time with its gathering of peoples from every tongue, tribe, and nation around the throne of God.

The next long stride in this pilgrimage was an exegetical course in Ephesians at Western Theological Seminary. There could be no denying it. This most comprehensive of all New Testament letters stated categorically and at length that God's purpose was to unite all things in Christ (Eph. 1:9-10). That learning, together with some studies in Old Testament theology, started me on a course of theological reflection concerning the nature and mission of the church.

Pastoral Experience

As a parish minister, the mission of the church in history usually influenced, and often dominated, my sermons. There were many readings from Ephesians, Isaiah, Genesis, and Revelation—and an occasional series of sermons. The most rewarding of those series to me was a paragraph-by-paragraph exposition of Revelation, which lasted for months and committed me for life to the study of the unfolding plan of God in history.

While serving as a pastor (in Passaic, New Jersey), I was asked to become a member of the Board of World Missions. A few years later, I was appointed to chair a study on mission rationale. That study opened to me a new body of theological work on the kingdom of God. From that time to this, that kingdom has been the preeminent theme of my own theological thought, as may be seen in the policies and programs I have proposed to the General Program Council and to the denomination.

Denominational Service

My first trip overseas came while I was still pastor at Passaic and doing some volunteer work on that statement of mission rationale. The purpose of the trip was to consult with leaders of our partner churches with whom we were engaged in mission. That trip, together with another half dozen shorter trips during my decade of work with the General Program Council, opened my eyes to the growing distance between the peoples and churches of the United States and the other peoples and churches in the world. Through firsthand observation and through long hours of listening to the people in our partner churches in Taiwan, Japan, India, the Middle East, Africa, Mexico, and other places, a conviction crystallized. Somehow, some way, more Reformed Church members must have opportunities to learn what I was learning.

During that decade, I encouraged the General Program Council to increase the communication between the peoples of the Reformed Church in America and the peoples of our partner churches. We used Mission Festival '71, visits of Reformed Church pastors to India and elsewhere, visits of church leaders from abroad to the General Program Council and to the General Synod, and many other means. I and the GPC wanted our people to see and hear firsthand the challenges presented by our sisters and brothers from other lands. Many did, and in their responses contributed significantly to the renewal of both church and world.

Ecumenical Involvement

In 1977, the church elected me its general secretary. With that election came the position of my predecessor, Marion deVelder, on the Central Committee of the World Council of Churches. There, as in the earlier mission relationships and in other ecumenical relationships, nothing impressed me so much as the urgency of strong ecumenical relationships, the urgency of our common bond in Christ across the boundaries and walls of language, color, creed, custom, governments, and political interests. These relationships often helped to ensure the freedom and well-being of our brothers and sisters—some of whom were now and then absent from our meetings because they were imprisoned for their obedience to Christ. Not infrequently, our relationships in Christ made the critical difference in preserving a life.

More than anything, this need for a visible unity in Christ, stronger than all that divides the human community, inspired and sustained my interest in the ecumenical movement and its agencies. This same need constrained me to do all I could to inform the people of the Reformed Church in America about this movement and to invite their participation in it.

Ecumenical Vocation

My involvement in the ecumenical movement and my efforts to support and interpret it have led some of my friends to inquire when I would go to work for one of its agencies. I've always said I didn't intend to. My commitment was to reach the people in the churches—in particular the Reformed Church in America. That has proven difficult enough from within a denominational bureaucracy; I knew it would be harder still from within an ecumenical bureaucracy. So, I have said, "Thank you, but, no thank you."

Last summer that began to change. It's been my custom to examine thoroughly my continuing commitment to my position on the staff once in every five years. This time I concluded that it was time to leave the staff sometime within the next five-year period.

It will soon be 15 years that I have occupied a key leadership position in the denominational staff. That's a long time, and it seemed to me that someone with a different package of gifts should now take up the task to complement what I have done and to compensate for what I have not done. It seemed, too, that a different type of work for me might give me an opportunity to use my own gifts in ways that the demands of this position made difficult and often impossible. I informed the moderator of my supervising committee, Carl Ver Beek, of my decision to leave the staff sometime within the next five years.

In making this decision, I had carefully weighed the possibility of working in an international ecumenical agency and decided against it for a host of reasons. That decision, against that possibility, has greatly complicated my decision on the invitation recently issued by the World Council of Churches to become one of its deputy general secretaries. If not then—why now?

I can only say that both Harriet and I have not been able to consider this invitation as other than a call. From the first conversations last December, we have not felt free to say no. The freedom to say yes, however, has come only after a three-month struggle. Years ago we resolved to go where, and to do what, it seemed the Lord was calling us to go and to do—even if that were not particularly in accord with our wishes at the time. When we have done that, the Lord has without fail opened new doors of service and opportunity for personal growth far beyond what we had imagined. We haven't always seen that on a day-to-day or even year-to-year basis, but from the perspective of nearly five decades, we would join in confessing that it is the only way to live. So we try to be faithful, and we cannot escape the conviction that this invitation is a calling and, if that be so, the rest will fall into place.

A *Place to Stand*

The invitation is, of course, full of threat and promise. The promises are as always of service and growth. The threats are legion even if not uncommon: the stretching, and in some cases severing, of ties to family, friends, and colleagues; the barriers of language; and the challenge of working in the center of the vortex of churches, cultures, and conflicts which is the World Council of Churches.

Nothing has helped me so much in dealing with these challenges of complexity in the World Council of Churches as my sense of roots firmly implanted in the Reformed Church in America. While struggling with the decision in January, I fulfilled a commitment to pay a four-day visit to Northwestern College in Orange City, Iowa. Surrounded by the familiar Great Plains of my boyhood and in touch with family, I felt a growing sense of roots sturdy and stable enough to provide the strength to cope. That feeling has been warmly reinforced by the generosity of the General Synod Executive Committee in allowing me time to talk through with them the pain of this separation and the equal generosity of the General Program Council in appointing Harriet and me as World Mission associates, an unsalaried relationship intended to provide Reformed Church members in church-related vocations overseas with a formal and living connection with the denomination. Its chief continuing benefits are air-mail copies of *Hotline* and the *Church Herald*! But much more, it is for both of us a deeply meaningful connection with a church whose life and work we will cherish no less in Geneva, Switzerland, than we have in New York City; Passaic, New Jersey; Corinth and Holland, Michigan; Orange City, Iowa; and Edgerton, Minnesota.

26
The Councils of Churches
as Centers of Conflict

A Church Herald *column, June, 1983*

I had known a lot of conflict during my thirty or so years of active engagement in the denomination-wide institutions of the Reformed Church in America. As editor of the Northwestern College "Beacon," college student, seminarian, pastor, vice-president of the Board of World Missions, chair of the Board of Theological Education, contributing editor of the *Church Herald*, general program council executive, general secretary—I engaged the issues. In all but a few cases, we had done so without personal alienation. That had been possible in part because people with conflicting opinions could deal with one another face-to-face, person-to-person. Departing for the World Council of Churches—and likely heard from only when there was controversy—I was concerned that at the greater distance of Geneva, alienation might occur. I wanted in this penultimate installment of my *Church Herald* column to say, "Brothers and sisters, expect it!—and hold on to the family ties."

Many members of the Reformed Church in America have often expressed confusion and concern that the councils of churches are the centers of so much controversy and conflict. It may be worth noting that the councils of churches were in fact organized to be centers of conflict. They were intended to be places where the churches could come to work out their differences openly and constructively.

Much of the controversy around the councils today springs from the sharp truth that our churchly divisions are more closely linked to the world's divisions than had been seen at first. We have together discovered that the churches themselves are fragmented by the divisions in the world. We Christians do not escape being cut off from one another by income and privilege, race and sex, language and nationality, politics and ideology. We have together discovered that we cannot deal with the brokenness of the church without dealing with the brokenness of the world around and within the church. The struggle against apartheid in South Africa is the most striking example of this worldly division in the church, but it is not the only one. Many of our denominational divisions in the United States are more economic and cultural (worldly) than theological and liturgical (churchly).

These worldly divisions of the church make the struggle for unity much more difficult and controversial. Discussion of differences in doctrine and liturgy may arouse some anxiety about loss of treasured heritages or changes in familiar ways. But dealing with differences in property and privilege may well seem to threaten our whole way of life and to demand unacceptable sacrifices. Anxiety may give way to alarm.

The call to God's all-encompassing unity is, nevertheless, unmistakable. According to Ephesians 1:9-10, God's purpose "set forth in Christ [is] to unite all things in him, things in heaven and things on earth." God's plan for the ages is, in a word, unity—the unity of the church, the unity of humankind, the unity of all creation.

Unity is central to God's purpose because the crux of the world's dilemma is disunity. The core of our human problem is brokenness, alienation, separation. Division is the essence of God's judgment on sin. Through sin came guilt, which alienated Adam and Eve from God. Through sin came shame, which put distance between Adam and Eve. Through sin came fear, which estranged Adam and Eve from the rest of creation. Through sin came hard labor, which deprived Eve and Adam of the earth's abundance. The climax of God's judgment on sin is played out at the Tower of Babel. Human communication disintegrates. No longer able to understand one another, people are scattered abroad "over the face of all the earth."

Faithfulness to God's one purpose requires Christians to seek both the unity of the church and the unity of the world. To seek the unity of the church without working for justice in the world is to cry "'peace, peace' when there is no peace". To seek justice in the world without working for the unity of the church is to cut ourselves off from Christ, who is our peace.

In God's one mission, our concern for the brokenness of the world is not secular politics; it is faithfulness to the fullness of God's purpose without which our church assemblies are charades. In God's one mission, our concern for the brokenness of the church is not irrelevant doctrinal disputation; it is a search for the unifying power of the gospel without which our social vision is a mirage. God's work in church and world is one work—"to unite all things."

It is this unified call to unity that puts Christians on a collision course with all those who seek to carve up the world for their own purposes. Our calling to unity does not permit us to participate in economic structures that snatch bread from the tables of the poor. Our calling to unity does not permit us to credit the dehumanization of political or military opponents, to submit to the dictates of ideological systems, to be captive to national boundaries. Called to unity, we are compelled to oppose all devices of division in both the church and the world—whatever the controversy, conflict, or cost. The way of the cross is the only way to unity.

27

Jesus Christ—the Life of the World
(The Vancouver Vision)

A sermon at the Riverside Church, August 21, 1983

The sermon speaks for itself. All our children were present. Following the service, we had a celebrative lunch together, brought Milt to the airport for return to his home in Ohio, while Steve and Pat headed off to college in Michigan and Charla to her newly leased New Jersey apartment. Harriet and I went home to finish packing. The next afternoon, we left for ten days at our cottage in Cape Breton, Nova Scotia, en route to Geneva.

> Scripture: Deuteronomy 30:11-14,19
> I John 1:1-3
> John 6:47-51

I begin the sermon this morning with a word of appreciation for the gifts I have received from this congregation and its ministers over the years from Harry Emerson Fosdick to William Sloane Coffin. I want to say, too, that it is a very good feeling on this last whole day that Mrs. Brouwer and I are spending in the United States of America to be in one of the great congregations, which is so firmly committed to the ministry of the World Council of Churches, and to share this morning this common ministry that we have with churches around the world.

The theme of the sermon this morning is the theme of the Sixth Assembly of the World Council of Churches, which concluded just a few days ago in Vancouver, British Columbia. Some of you who were there may be concerned that you are now about to get a twenty-minute rerun of a three-week experience. I want to assure you that even my Calvinistic sense of duty does not require that!

I chose the theme of the assembly for the theme of the sermon because I want to *evoke something* of what that theme meant at the assembly and what it may mean in the life of the member churches of the World Council of Churches for the next seven years until the next assembly. A theme of the World Council of Churches is not like themes that are chosen for most of our North American church events, where they serve as little more than platform decorations and may get passing reference from the keynote speaker. A theme of the World Council of Churches is chosen carefully and well in advance—this one three years in advance—and thoroughly developed as the theme for the work of the assembly. "Jesus Christ, the Life of the World," has been the subject of biblical studies and theological reflections in Orthodox, Protestant, and Roman Catholic churches for some years. It has been the central point of books, and articles in magazines and journals. It has been explored in all kinds of events in the multiplex of cultures represented in the 304-member churches of the World Council scattered throughout more than a hundred countries over all six continents. And the richness of their life has enriched the theme of the assembly—"Jesus Christ, the Life of the World."

At the assembly itself, that theme was the focus for personal witness, community experience, and most of all, for worship. More, we are told, than was true in the worship settings of the previous five assemblies at Amsterdam, Evanston, New Delhi, Uppsala, and Nairobi. If all goes well, this theme will influence the work of the World Council and the work of its member churches until the next assembly and well beyond. I want, therefore, to say something of what that theme may mean during the next seven years.

From the very beginning, this theme was seen as a confession of faith. Three years ago in the Central Committee, I had the privilege of chairing the subcommittee which developed and presented this theme. When the subcommittee's work was presented to the committee as a whole and, indeed already in the subcommittee, some said: "How can you think of a theme like that? A theme that focuses on life when the world is groaning in death. Global death, human extinction is never more than a few hours away. Many of our people are dying from hunger and sickness and from the guns and bullets of those who are supposed to protect them. How can you think of a theme of life?" But others who lived under exactly the same condition of exploitation and suffering said again and again, and again, "It is just because we live in the midst of a world that is dying every day that we must confess our faith in 'Jesus Christ, the Life of the World.'"

There were others who said: "How can you think of a theme like that? During these last eight years since the Nairobi assembly, we have moved through decades of pain and misunderstanding in relationships with people of other faiths. 'Jesus Christ, the Life of the World', smacks again of the old triumphalism—of our Christian efforts to conquer rather than to witness. Let's take out the definite article. Let's not claim too much. Let's simply say: Jesus Christ— Life of the World." But again, others who had a right to testify because they were living surrounded by people of other faiths and in daily dialogue with them, said, "No, we do not experience Jesus Christ as one life among many. Our experience of faith in Jesus Christ is that he is the life of the world. Our faith is, to be sure, in dialogue with many other faiths. We make no judgment on other faiths. We simply say that this is our faith and it is our faith we celebrate, and it is the life we have received from Jesus Christ that we know and which we gather in Vancouver in 1983 to offer to the world."

The discussion explored many other concerns—important issues having to do with Christian worship, and particularly, the celebration of the Eucharist, with human management of the source and shape of biological life. In the end, we decided to confess our faith together at Vancouver around the theme, "Jesus Christ—The Life of the World."

Now, I underline that we decided to confess our faith—in confrontation with the powers of death, in dialogue and encounter with other faiths, in tension with one another theologically, but in unity at the point of our common affirmation that Jesus Christ is, indeed, the life of the world.

That was the Central Committee discussion three years ago. Vancouver was, of course, a much more comprehensive gathering than the Central Committee, a mere 150 people, could ever be. More than 800 delegates, hundreds even thousands of guests, with some gatherings reaching a total of 15,000 people. People from all walks of life were in attendance. Eighty percent of the more than 800 delegates were having their very first assembly experience with the World Council of Churches. Let us be clear that by no means all of us there had been face to face with death in our witness to Jesus

Christ or in our daily struggle. But some of the people at Vancouver have looked death in the face—not once, not twice, but again and again and yet again. And, in the face of death, confessed Jesus Christ as the life of the world. We wept with them. We laughed with them. We prayed and sang with them. One of the most moving testimonies, I think, came to us from a person not even in attendance, Severina, a poor Brazilian woman who could neither read nor write, whose cry of the heart was brought to us by Dorothee Sölle.

> But who really knows what it means for a woman to carry a child for nine months, weeping for the first three of them because she knows she will never see her baby grow up—and that perhaps ten times or more? Is she to love the child only to see it die of starvation within four months? Can that really be what they mean when they speak of human dignity?

From the Marshall Islands came Darlene Keju-Johnson, a young married woman who is afraid to have children because of the three tumors she carries in her body which signal the ravages of radiation sickness. From her and others from the South Pacific, we were reminded of whole islands blasted off the face of the earth—not in war but in peace through testing of nuclear weapons by the United States of America. She reported that the representatives of our government claimed they had come to protect the Marshall Islanders from their enemies. The Marshall Islanders said: "Enemies? We do not have enemies. What are 'enemies'? We have no word for 'enemy' in our language." Through her, we heard the cry of people who have lived on the Marshall Islands for generations and who are now barred from their ancestral home because our government has taken over their islands and relegated the native peoples to live on other islands surrounded by water and filled with land polluted with radiation.

These twin pressures, these pressures of poverty and war and their opposites, the calls to justice and peace, placed the most severe strain on the assembly and promise to be a point of stress and strain for the seven years to come in the World Council of Churches and in its member churches. Some Christians, particularly North American and European, tend to put first the threats to peace—other Christians, particularly those from the Third World, consider poverty the priority. They say: "Why should we worry about death at some distant future point when we are dying every day?"

This interrelationship and interconnectedness (to use two words overused at the assembly) of the concerns for justice and peace is surely one of the major issues before the church in this decade. We dare not allow the principalities and powers of this world—whether in the world or in the church—to separate these two issues and set us over against one another—some for peace and others for justice. We must remember, *always remember, that there can be no peace without justice and no justice without peace.* We must hold them together, work at them together, repeating to ourselves the words of Isaiah, who teaches us that peace is the fruit of justice (Is. 32:16-18).

I think there can be little question that the greatest *immediate* threat of global destruction comes from the nuclear arms race and the now almost hair-trigger, split-second technology that stands between us and the incinerating power of a million blinding suns. But poised as we are on the precipice of nuclear destruction every day, every hour, every minute, nevertheless, we must keep the conviction in our minds that we will make no genuine progress toward walking away from that threat unless we deal with the economic issues underlying it. Among the most powerful of the engines of war which propel the arms race is the struggle for economic domination of the world. As the superpowers and the transnational corporations wrestle and struggle with one another, the poor everywhere are ground underfoot. War devastates the Third World. There is no peace. The superpowers move ever nearer the ultimate catastrophe.

You see, once again we are back to confessing our faith. We have nothing else to live by. And even though we stand on this precipice of nuclear destruction, by faith we look for the pathway away from the precipice along the lines of economic justice. Without our faith, we would be tempted to despair—tempted to join those who say, "Yes, of course, there is no question that we are all traveling on the Titanic, but since that is true I want to go first class." Without faith, we would be tempted to join those who say: "No future" and stop planting trees or having children. By faith we believe that the birth, and the death, and the resurrection of Jesus Christ has overcome death and that Jesus Christ is indeed the life of the world.

These are two parts of the Vancouver vision. First, a confession of faith and a recommitment to the theological task of exploring the mysteries of our faith, the witness of the church in the life of the world. Second, a growing commitment to strive together for justice and peace in the world. There is a third part to that vision—a vision of the whole people of God enlisted in the mission of the church.

It is a truism to say that the whole people of God are not yet committed as one body. It was a painful experience at Vancouver, not one but many painful experiences, to deal with those moments when our divisions were more visible than our unity. There were the age-old issues of separate Protestant and Orthodox tables for the one sacrament of the Eucharist—to say nothing of the pain that the Roman Catholic and conservative evangelical tables were not even set up in that fellowship. There were the struggles for participation by the Orthodox churches, and by women, youth, and lay people in what was largely a Protestant, male, middle-aged, and ordained group, even though youth, women, and disabled did participate in the largest numbers ever. And then, and this is the point I wish particularly to underline, *there were the general calls for more participation by the churches and by the members of the churches in the life and work of the World Council of Churches.*

My sisters and brothers, the World Council of Churches needs us all to understand, as does the National Council of Churches, the terrible dilemma in these cries for participation which find voice in the councils of churches. The more those who are voiceless and powerless in the world and in their own churches, the more they find voice and power in the World or National Councils of Churches, the greater grows the gap between the councils and the churches. But the more the voiceless and the powerless do not find freedom and voice in the World Council of Churches or in the National Council of Churches, the greater grows the gap between the councils and the world of the poor and oppressed for whom Christ died.

There is no choice. We must be for the world for whom Christ died. There is only one way through this crisis which makes the councils of churches so vulnerable in a world that would seek to destroy bridges that are being built in order that enmity and hostility may be employed for political purposes and economic self-interest.

There is only one way through this crisis, so that the church of Jesus Christ scattered around the face of the earth may be a bridge across which all humankind may meet one another. And that one way is the increased interaction between the poor and oppressed on the one hand and the rich and the powerful on the other in the context of the church of Jesus Christ—like which there is no other institution on the face of the earth—in the context of that church of Jesus Christ, who is the life of the world.

Three weeks we spent in Vancouver surrounded by hundreds and sometimes thousands of people from all over the world. Again and again I thought, and as often I heard others say, "There isn't anything else like the World Council of Churches on the face of the earth." With all the tensions and pressures that drive us apart in what to begin with is a very fragile body, there is always at the center, no matter how deep the conflict or how strong the feeling, there is always at the center the overwhelming awareness of the deep and abiding shared faith in Jesus Christ, which is our central commitment and which binds us to one another even when it runs against our own self interest, because we are bound to Christ.

Assemblies of the World Council of Churches and the multitude of people who exchanged experiences with one another in the interchurch visits prior to the assembly, these are a foretaste of the opportunities for sharing life and binding us to one another which the world so desperately needs today. Deepening these experiences of sharing will be one of the major challenges between now and the next assembly and beyond.

Sharing the life of the church in other lands is a particular challenge to the churches in North America. We live here for all practical purposes on a continental island. We are given the task of witnessing to Jesus Christ in the midst of the most powerful nation in all the history of the world. We are called to witness at a time in history when that nation is grudgingly, fearfully, spasmodically, coming to terms with its loss of power while it is squared off with another colossal superpower driven by many of the same anxieties. That is our calling. But however difficult our task, the key to justice and peace is, nevertheless, my brothers and sisters, more in our hands than in the hands of any other people on the face of the earth. We can still touch that key. We can still reach out and touch that key. I believe that we can turn it and open the door to justice and peace for the world. But we need the whole people of God for that mission.

We need a church so profoundly committed to unity, *so profoundly committed to unity*, that we who live in the land of the rich and the powerful (and are ourselves rich and powerful) will be able to hear and identify with the poor so that the tie that binds us as a people of God becomes stronger than all that separates us, so that neither race, nor sex, nor age, nor nationality, nor social nor economic class nor political persuasion nor history, nor doctrinal formulation, nor any other thing in all creation can separate us from the love of God in Christ Jesus which we have for one another.

We need a church so profoundly committed to unity that when the *Reader's Digest* mounts its once-in-a-decade attack on the councils of churches, most of us will simply say, "There they go again." Or when *Sixty Minutes* sells out to the Institute on Religion and Democracy or when *Time* magazine again indulges in innuendo, we need a church so profoundly committed to unity, so profoundly committed to preserving the bridge for all the peoples of the world that the church of Jesus Christ represents, that there will be an outpouring of outrage at these attempts, not only to derogate the councils of churches, but to break the body of Christ.

We need a church so profoundly committed to unity that denominational offices will no longer need to expend energies and resources defending their commitment to Christians around the world but rather will be called to account when they do not act as part of the worldwide body of Christ dedicated to the healing of the nations.

We need a church so profoundly committed to unity that we are able within the church, East and West, North and South, to confront one another openly and honestly exhorting and admonishing one another to strengthen the body without fear of breaking it and also to set aside the posturing of our governments, to ignore the rhetoric of our politicians, to concentrate only on speaking the truth in order that we *all*, East *and West*, South *and North*, in order that we *all* may be free.

We need a church so profoundly committed to unity, my brothers and sisters, that the pain and suffering of our sisters and brothers in the Marshall Islands, or in South Africa, or in El Salvador, or in the countless other places where we are implicated becomes our pain and suffering so that we all with one voice, rich and poor, black and white, east and west, north and south, with one voice, may say: "In the name of God, *NO*. No more death, only life—life in the name of Jesus Christ—abundant, free, and full for the whole world. Amen.

28
Some Stories About Sharing

An introduction to a Resource Sharing Consultation, the Ecumenical Institute, Bossey, Switzerland, June 17, 1984

Shortly after joining the WCC staff, I was asked (read assigned!) by General Secretary Philip Potter to moderate the staff task force on resource sharing. Money, structure, turf, power—all these dynamics and more converged in that project. Nowhere were the issues raised more sharply than between the WCC and the Christian Conference of Asia. When these two groups came together for a consultation in June 1984, I was asked to open the meeting with a brief Bible study. I chose to lift up a few of the dynamics common to these New Testaments stories and our own.

(Acts 2:43-47; 4:32-5:11; 6:1-7; 11:27-30)

These stories about sharing have fascinated Christians in every age. Commentators and preachers often point to them, particularly the first story (in Acts 2), as exhibits of the exemplary spirituality of the early church—sometimes to scold us, sometimes to inspire us. Since the rise of modern capitalism and particularly since the advent of Karl Marx, these stories have had a special interest for Christians. What is the meaning of this "communism" of the early church!? Is it normative for the church in all periods? Or was this a case of excessive eschatological enthusiasm? That is, did this early Jerusalem community of apostles and disciples think that earthly possessions no longer mattered because in a few days, weeks, or at the most months, the Lord would return and they would all be savoring the milk and honey of the messianic kingdom?

Ananias and Sapphira stand out in dramatic contrast to the spirit of the community as a whole. We do not know why they agreed to pretend that they were putting their "all on the altar," but we will probably not be far wrong if we imagine their having a touch of skepticism about this riotous community enthusiasm for sharing. They may have observed other messianic communities in Judea and seen their enthusiasm destroy them. Or perhaps they sensed the administrative and structural problems which were shortly to emerge in a dispute between the Hellenists and the Hebrews because of unfair treatment of their widows and they could see that the apostles wouldn't be able to cope. Or they may have felt that the theology underlying this community of goods needed clearer articulation before they took the plunge. And then, of course, there were their own institutional, that is family, needs which might well extend beyond the life of this experiment or even beyond the life of this early Christian community.

It takes even less imagination for us to understand why they didn't express their reservation. The whole community was "on a roll." Everybody thought well of them—even the priests were showing a personal interest in joining up. Everybody was getting into the act. According to Luke, "No one said that anything he possessed was his own," and a ritual had already developed in which the money was laid at the apostles' feet, no doubt accompanied by the rejoicing and well-wishing of the community. Heady stuff.

Furthermore, all of this was likely reinforced by an emphasis on koinonia and sharing in the apostles' teaching. And probably complicated by guilt in Ananias and Sapphira that they hadn't yet gone along. Surrounded by all that enthusiasm which was already turning the apostles' teaching into a community ideology (of resource sharing perhaps), they certainly weren't going to talk about reservations. Even without saying a word, they had probably already begun to feel the isolation and to sense the distancing and to pick up the innuendos. So...they decided to go along—at least part of the way. They couldn't quite muster the courage of their skepticism. They played the game or at least acted so that they appeared to play the game.

Now what guidance can we find in these familiar stories (about these very familiar ecumenical dilemmas) for our work (and life) here together during these few days? I offer eight observations.

Sharing is a spontaneous expression of faith However much one may wish to discount the life of this early community on the index of exaggerated eschatology, the fact remains that their faith led them to share. I need not argue the point; we all know it. That is why we immediately recognize the lack of faith (as well as lack of love, of course) in the priest and the levite who passed by on the other side. And of course our contemporary world is a theater of the opposite of faith as increasingly fearful peoples and nations hold on ever tighter to what they have—and want to keep.

Sharing is deeply rooted in community life The sense of community life in these early stories is almost palpable. You can feel it as you read. The daily worship and fellowship, the joy and wonder, illumine everything and show themselves most vividly in the common ownership of property.

Pretending to share is a serious offense Peter makes it clear that Ananias and Sapphira were not under moral obligation to sell their land or to turn in all the proceeds (and there is no evidence that this is a later capitalist qualifier inserted into the text!). They might have said, "We sold the land for so and so much. We are presenting this part of it to the community." Their problem was that they pretended to go along and thereby violated a taboo.

Pooling resources does not solve all the problems Even in this early Christian community filled with eschatological enthusiasm and deeply impressed by the fate of Ananias and Sapphira, some "murmured" against others because of inequalities of distribution— one might almost say because of favoritisms shown within certain "confessional" and cultural families. We don't know whether that favoritism was due to neglect or manipulation or whatever. But we do know that pooling of resources did not solve all the problems.

Visions may falter because of administrative problems As the community grew, the apostles were overwhelmed. They recognized their limitations and created the "office" of deacon which we now think of as a separate order of ministry. This is not an incidental matter. It is quite clear that the vision itself was endangered by administrative problems.

Sharing is closely related to the growth of the Christian community In each of these three stories about sharing in Jerusalem, Luke points out that the community grew (2:47; 5:14; 6:7). Sharing is closely related to the growth of the Christian community.

Visions do not come with guarantees We know that this community of sharing in Jerusalem had a relatively short life and appears not to have been replicated in other early Christian communities. Acts 11:27-30 even seems to suggests that the Christian community in Judea was particularly vulnerable to the coming famine. The collapse of this community may of course be attributed to many reasons—persecution not least among them. But we may at least wonder if the community faltered partly because it failed to deal with the problems of the inaugurated but not yet realized rule of Christ. And we may also wonder if the community would have been better able to deal with these problems if Ananias and Sapphira had found the courage to share their skepticism. Imagination aside, the story makes it clear that visions do not come with guarantees. Even the fear aroused by the death of Ananias and Sapphira could not accomplish that—and of course our present efforts at resource sharing do not have that kind of reinforcement!

Sharing is a sober obligation of faith These stories in Acts virtually bubble with the spontaneous enthusiasm of sharing. We may, for whatever reason, even some theological reasons having to do with eschatology, be tempted do dismiss all this as visionary. But it is clear that sharing is not merely a matter of early Christian effervescence. Paul's letter to the Corinthians reveals that sharing is an important continuing expression of Christian faith—he himself considering it of sufficient importance that he gave the better part of several years to collecting an offering in Macedonia. So we may dare to think that the search for a community of sharing is worthy of our time and energy in this consultation and in the ones that have gone before and in those that will no doubt come after.

29

Towards an Ecumenical Community of Sharing—Resources and Relationships

An address to the Seventh North American Conference on Christian Philanthropy, Orlando, FL, April 15, 1986

This invitation was extended by my old RCA colleague and friend, Lois Joice, who was then chair of the NCC Commission on Stewardship. I accepted for her sake and used it as an opportunity to sum up my WCC work on resource sharing mentioned in the previous chapter.

The distinctive contribution of the ecumenical movement to the principles and practice of stewardship is its concern for the quality of the relationships in which sharing takes place. This quality of relationships has been a subject of much general concern and discussion in the ecumenical movement for many years. Since 1976 it has been a direct object of study and planning by the World Council of Churches' Office of Resource Sharing, which I had the privilege of supervising while working in Geneva during 1983 and 1984.

In June of the latter year we brought together a document called "Towards an Ecumenical Commitment for Resource Sharing." The purpose of that document was to identify some principles, problems, and practices to be considered in developing an ecumenical community of resource sharing. Each of the document's nine sections is concerned with relationships—to God, among the churches, to one another, to creation, and to the world as a whole.

In that concern for relationships, the document addresses questions of decision-making, reporting, and accountability along with the diverse and complex structures and systems through which those processes take place and which either facilitate or impede relationships.

The document is the product of a broad consensus, shaped by both those who "give" and those who "receive" as well as by those who serve as intermediaries. We may therefore take its preoccupation with relationships as solid evidence that this is an overriding issue in ecumenical thinking about resource sharing. More than the amount of money and more than the nature of the projects, the relationships in which sharing takes place are the focus of the ecumenical discussion of resource sharing.

Sharing in Community

Ecumenical sharing is sharing in community. The primary pattern for this emphasis on community is, of course, the familiar stories about sharing in the book of Acts. They are preeminently stories about community. "And all who believed were together and had all things in common" (Acts 2:44), writes Luke, adding that daily they attended the temple together and took common meals in their homes. The sense of community life in those stories is almost palpable. The daily worship and fellowship, joy and wonder, illumine everything showing themselves most dramatically in the common ownership of property. That sharing of property is clearly a sign and seal of the strong sense of community from which it springs.

We know that this particular experiment with sharing in community had a relatively short life and appears not to have been attempted in other Christian communities. But the records of the early church show that the practice of sharing remained closely related to the experience of community.

Sharing in the Eucharist

This relationship between community and sharing is most powerfully demonstrated in connection with the eucharist. From the beginning, the celebration of this sacrament has been the central act of the Christian community, both expressing and enabling its unity in Christ. From the earliest times, the eucharist has been clearly associated with acts of sharing, in the form of love feasts for the whole community as well as the collection of offerings of money and material for distribution to the poor. Many of our churches today continue that tradition with special communion offerings for the poor and needy. The most notable example of this is the observance of "One Great Hour of Sharing" on Worldwide Communion Sunday. That act of worldwide sharing strengthens the sense of worldwide community experienced in the sacrament; while the sense of community experienced in the sacrament in turn enriches the act of sharing.

Mutuality in Sharing

Sharing in community has the quality of mutuality. By mutuality, I mean that the acts of giving and receiving are inseparably interrelated because the persons who are giving and receiving are linked together in a prior personal relationship which provides the context for sharing. In the absence of such community ties, the act of giving and receiving readily deteriorates from personal relationships to subject-object relationships in which the giver acts upon the receiver as the object of the gift. No amount of giving can possibly compensate for the destructiveness of that subject-object relationship. Indeed the more giving and receiving which transpires through such a broken relationship, the more destructive it becomes. Rather than increasing the flow of giving—or unilaterally cutting it off—an effort must be made to put the act of resource sharing in the context of shared community life. This, I again underscore, is the pattern in the stories of the early church recorded in the book of Acts. The act of sharing was an *expression* of community life; it was not the *foundation* of community life.

The Problem of Dependency

Most of the relationships in which resources are shared among the churches today have started the other way around. Churches from North America and Western Europe have sent missionaries and material aid to churches in other parts of the world. Many of the churches in the other parts of the world were in fact begun by the work of missionaries from North America and Western Europe. Dependency (on both sides) was therefore built into the relationships from the beginning. As long as such dependency relationships continue, mutuality in mission is impossible, yes, impossible! Such dependency relationships can however be resolved within the larger patterns of shared community life.

The ecumenical movement has therefore, particularly in the last decade, placed great emphasis on the sharing of spiritual and cultural resources as well as physical and material resources. This broadening of the concept of resource sharing has fostered an increased mutuality in mission enabling all of the world's churches to give as well as to receive.

The result is, however, far from satisfactory. The increasing amounts of money flowing through church channels for relief and development in our ever more broken world have all too often overwhelmed the sharing of spiritual and cultural resources. Moreover, most of the traditional ties through which resources flow have been created and shaped to serve the purposes of the wealthy churches' programs of giving and sending to churches in the poorer parts of the world. Dependency is thus built into the relationships. In a word, dependency is systemic, i.e. not subject to change by goodwill without developing new patterns of sharing in the context of new relationships.

Ecumenical studies of resource sharing have repeatedly demonstrated that when one partner is always giving and the other always receiving, dependency is virtually inescapable. They have also shown that no matter how many attempts are made to "balance" the relationship by reversing the flow of resources (for example by sending people from the money-receiving church back to the money-giving church) the fact remains that the relationship is rooted, grounded, shaped, and maintained in the flow of financial resources from one to the other. The reverse flow of spiritual, cultural, and human resources is therefore frequently seen as little more than a compensating factor in an essentially financial relationship. As such, it does little more than offset some of the worst aspects of that relationship.

Equality in Community

Systemic dependency can be healed only by systemic change. *New* relationships are required which are rooted, grounded, shaped, and maintained not in dependency but in equality. Equality is the fundamental and essential element in such new relationships.

Our long-term goal is equality in the ability to provide resources. We seek to establish, in the church and in the world, communities of justice in which everyone will have enough and we will all be interdependent in communities of mutual sharing in which everyone gives and everyone receives. We are of course far from that goal. We need therefore to rely on the grace of those who receive to do so without being incapacitated by anger and resentment that another has the power to give or to withhold resources and, therefore, to give or to withhold life and well-being.

The Needs of the Giver

A first step along that road to equality is the recognition that we all come to the process of sharing with needs—with "empty hands," as one ecumenical study on resource sharing puts it. Most of us are readily aware of financial or material needs when we speak of resource sharing. We may be less aware of our spiritual needs— particularly of the spiritual needs of those who give. Yet it is true that our giving is often mixed with deep needs for self-expression or the exercise of power. It is essential that these needs be clearly identified, recognized, and confessed as a powerful dynamic in resource sharing. To meet them we need that special measure of grace which our Lord so often reminded us was necessary if the rich were to enter the kingdom of heaven.

Awareness of these needs helps to open the way to equality in decision-making. Equality means that power itself becomes an offering to the community to be exercised together within the community. Such sharing of power exercised through equality in decision-making is absolutely essential to equality in relationships and is therefore the crux of the whole matter. It is also therefore extremely elusive.

Through Self-Dependence to Interdependence

We have already recalled our Lord's teaching that the connection between resources and human sin is extremely powerful. We need not then be surprised that the problems of dominance and dependency accompanied by self-destruction on both sides have sometimes been so severe that it has been necessary for financially poor churches to withdraw from the process altogether in order to free themselves from external control and one-sided dependency. They have needed first to rediscover and reassert themselves before returning to the process free to enter into an equal partnership.

This was, of course, the point of the moratoriums, much publicized in the 1970s. They were attempts of the churches oppressed by dependency relationships to find space in which they could discover their own identity. Admittedly, this self-discovery in separation from other churches could only be partial, since each church can truly know itself only in fellowship with all other churches. But however partial, it was often a necessary step of self-dependence on the road from other-dependence to interdependence.

In thus speaking of dependence, we should not make the mistake of thinking that dependency is a problem unique to the poor churches. On the contrary. Those who remember the opening of the moratorium debate in the early 1970s will recall the cries of pain, and even rage, from the rich churches suddenly deprived of their longtime partners whom they very much needed as objects of their giving. They sounded for all the world like possessive parents suddenly confronted with their self-assertive offspring. It was thus utterly transparent that the giving churches were themselves in need—even for their own well-being, to be confronted by *equal* partners who could require them to examine their needs to give in order that they might meet these needs in a way which would be less institutionally and personally damaging among the churches to which they had been giving.

Common Tables for Resource Sharing

One ecumenical attempt to build such new relationships has been the setting up of common tables for resource sharing which bring together a number of "giving" and "receiving" churches. We have already seen that when only two parties sit at a table across which one is mostly giving and the other mostly receiving, dependency is unavoidable. Sitting together around a common table, however, makes it possible for a wealthy giving church to *receive* from a poor church to which it is *giving nothing*, thus making it more possible for them to meet as equals and for both to grow in grace.

Even these common tables of resource sharing, however, are not without danger. Precisely because they are set up as tables to share resources, they may become nothing more than more complicated patterns of giving and receiving rather than means toward mutual sharing, i.e. of life together in the community.

Sharing Through the Council of Churches

Sharing is an expression of community life. It is therefore best nurtured in the context of a wider fellowship previously established.

The sharing that takes place in such a context is thus subject to scrutiny by parties outside of that particular process. Even more important, the act of sharing is thus but one expression of a wider fellowship formed for commonly established purposes in which all share for the sake of all—and beyond the community itself for the salvation of the world and the glory of God.

It is such communities of sharing that the councils of churches are intended to provide. They are instruments of all the member churches, both rich and poor, in which all may come together on an equal footing to share in common purposes. Relationships among them are therefore not fixed by preestablished patterns of resource sharing. Rather, resource sharing takes place in the context of a community of shared life and work which all have entered as equals.

I do not, of course, suggest that all these problems are solved within the councils of churches. Far from it. I claim only that the councils provide a community setting—and in most cases, the only community setting—in which it is possible to address these questions in an atmosphere of equality.

Community as the Goal of Sharing

The importance of such communities of sharing therefore can hardly can be overemphasized. Jacques Rossel, former president of the Basel Mission which has been a pioneer in creating new relationships and structures for resource sharing, puts the point with stunning force.

The ultimate aim of sharing is not the alleviation of need, nor even a more just distribution of wealth, but the development of Christian fellowship locally and worldwide, as a sign of hope for humanity. In church cooperation in development, the partner churches have to ask themselves how far they are strengthening fellowship and how far, on the other hand, they are destroying it.... This ultimate goal—the strengthening of fellowship—must be kept steadily in view when we are dealing with the question of the appropriate use of resources. (*International Review of Mission*—April, 1984, p. 194)

To reiterate: the quality of the relationships which enables the church to be a community of justice and peace and a sign of hope for humanity is more important than the particular project of the moment or than all the projects combined.

This concern for community, says Dr. Rossel, should be the primary purpose of the reports we in the rich churches require concerning our contributions. Our first concern, he argues, should be the effect of our contributions on the quality of relationships. Our reporting should be designed first of all to hold ourselves accountable for building up the church as a community of hope for the world. This we should do

> ...by showing the disproportion that exists between what the churches spend on themselves and the amounts donated for development aid; by listing the steps taken in the process of giving that show respect for the recipients; by reporting the efforts to prevent humiliating forms of dependence from being created; by accounting for the way the church's donations have been received by their recipients.... Only after these things have been done would it be opportune to refer to reports of projects and financial statements (ibid. p.197).

Community as a Sign of Justice

This concern for community grounded in equality is closely related to a commitment to justice. If the church is to be a sign of hope for humanity, it must of course demonstrate justice in its own life. The nature of a sign, in the biblical sense of that word, is to participate in and to demonstrate in some small measure that to which it points. The church as sign, can therefore never be satisfied with internal sharing, no matter how just and equitable that may be. Since it points to God's concern for the whole world, the church will also be deeply committed to justice beyond its own borders.

Nor can the church be content with serving the *victims* of injustice. As a sign of hope, the church is, by its very nature, in conflict with the *agents* of injustice. Yet, as is well known, our actual practice is a direct contradiction of this primary commitment to justice. Service ministries, such as relief to the starving or homeless, are being supported as never before, while justice ministries, which address the root causes of this suffering, are being steadily curtailed. There is even a strong sentiment to idealize our service ministries by, for example, exempting them from necessary administrative charges.

Faithfulness to our primary commitment to justice requires us rather to see these service ministries as nothing more than necessary interim measures undertaken only until justice can be done. Instead of exempting them from routine charges, we should allocate a part of what is given to alleviate the symptoms of injustice to programs of education and advocacy which address the causes of the injustice that breaks and divides our human community. This is in fact increasingly the practice in the ecumenical movement.

Participation in the Sharing Community

If Dr. Rossel is correct, and I believe he is, that the most important aim of sharing is the development of Christian community as a sign of hope for humanity, then it follows as well that we should seek to expand the community to encompass as many people as can be included and that we should seek to root it as deeply in their lives as their spirits permit. Our purpose is to share among the people. Every effort must be made to ensure that programs of sharing do not result in resources passing from one elite to another elite; that they do not overwhelm the capacity of local communities to receive them; that they do not result in the displacement of indigenous leadership; but rather that they build up the community as a sign of hope for the world.

Participation must be cultivated among the people who give as well as among those who receive. Programs of education concerning causes of injustice are essential. But there can be no substitute for participation in the ministries themselves. A current example of such consciousness-raising through participation is the Witness for Peace program in Nicaragua. There are now thousands of Americans who have not just given money to programs in Nicaragua, and not just studied about those programs and about Nicaragua and its people. They have participated in the struggle for justice. They can tell what they themselves have seen and heard.

Stewards of an Ecumenical Community of Sharing

All of this, as the example of Nicaragua illustrates, is extremely complicated and conflictual. Quite naturally, donors (and fund-raisers!) are tempted to avoid such relationships—as are receivers who have been able to establish their own private connections! Direct bilateral relationships, free of common concern about equality and justice and participation and community, is much simpler. It is, therefore, not surprising that there is a growing trend for churches and agencies to "go it alone" apart from, and sometimes in conflict with, their ecumenical commitments.

But this is more than a practical matter. Jacques Rossel puts the issue in theological terms. He suggests that the problem stems from the rich churches thinking of themselves as *autonomous*—a self-perception which a glance at the constitutions of either the World Council of Churches or the National Council of Churches will quickly confirm. Dr. Rossel argues that the churches should rather think of themselves as *theonomous*—that is, responsible to God—as opposed to responsible to themselves. A moment's reflection will likely lead to the conclusion that the idea of an autonomous church is in fact a dangerously secular idea. No church can be a law unto itself, choosing to act in isolation from the body of Christ. The church is one. All the various churches belong to it because each belongs to God in Christ and is, therefore, equal before God.

In the deepest sense, therefore, an ecumenical community of sharing is not something we must establish. It is already given by God. We are required only to be its faithful stewards.

30

Molded for Ministry

A Homily at the Ecumenical Service of Worship for the Inauguration of Robert W. Neff as president of Juniata College, Huntingdon, PA, April 3, 1987

I first came to know Robert Neff when he became general secretary of the Church of the Brethren at about the same time I became general secretary of the Reformed Church in America. We were drawn together by our relative youth among those who held similar positions in other churches, by our shared and strong ecumenical commitment, and by our discovery of similar difficulties in being responsible for the work of the NCC's two member communions that participated in a wide range of NCC activities while being much smaller than the "big seven" who shaped those activities to fit the patterns of their own much larger staffs. More important, however, far more important, was our common commitment to justice as the rock-bottom foundation for community life in both church and world. There is more about that in the sermon that follows.

Simultaneously with my election as general secretary of the council in November 1984, Bob became its second vice-president, where he was an inspiring source of strength until he resigned in 1986, when he left his post as general secretary of the Church of the Brethren to become president of that denomination's premier institution of higher education, Juniata College at Huntingdon, Pennsylvania. Acknowledging his letter of resignation, I wrote to him then:

> You will be greatly missed. I am sure there will be a strange silence from time to time on critical issues to which your voice would have been raised. We shall do our best to listen for what your spirit is telling us.

To me, Bob extended the honor of an invitation to deliver the homily at the ecumenical service of worship preceding his inauguration. The homily presented was a variation on what was then becoming my prime sermon on behalf of the ecumenical movement, often replacing the sermon mentioned in chapters 10 and 11 above and again in chapter 33 below. This sermon was based on the central theme of John's Gospel, "I am come that they may have life, and have it abundantly" (John 10:10). My favorite gospel since childhood days, I was introduced to its profoundly symbolic depth by Dr. Richard C. Oudersluys, professor of New Testament at Western Theological Seminary, an understanding further enhanced in my relationships with the Orthodox churches. This sermon I usually preached under the title, "A Movement for Life," and drew my material more heavily from the ecumenical movement, in a fashion similar to that in the sermon "Jesus Christ—the Life of the World." On this occasion, I drew from college life. The title was Juniata's chosen theme for the ecumenical service of worship, in the course of which art professor Jack Troy molded a bowl from a blend of various types of clay thus symbolizing the various faith traditions represented in the Juniata College community.

Delivering the homily at the inauguration of Robert Neff, April 3, 1987 (Credit: Juniata College).

In the year of our Lord's grace 1831, the yearly conference of the Church of the Brethren considered the question whether it was advisable to have the sons—the daughters were not in question— educated in a college. After due deliberation the conference concluded that it was considered "not advisable in as much as experience had taught that such sons very seldom will come back afterwards to the humble ways of the Lord."

But, I have not come here tonight primarily to celebrate the progress of the Church of the Brethren from 1831 to the present time. My task is to preach the gospel; and my wish is to celebrate the ministry of Robert W. Neff who is to be inaugurated as the president of this college in these days. I have known Robert Neff for more than a decade and we have often worked together in the National Council of Churches. I have learned that here is a man who has not only read the prophets and the apostles—he has been formed by them. Time and again when issues arose in the deliberations of that ecumenical assembly and in others, I discovered that the fundamental criterion by which Robert Neff made his decisions was not whether it was advantageous or disadvantageous to various groups he served—even, I must say, to the Church of the Brethren—or by some other political standard, but rather whether it was in keeping with the gospel and whether it served justice. For that I learned to love him, and love him still. (We do miss him in the National Council of Churches. We hope to correct that situation again one day, but we're leaving him with you fulltime for the time being!)

How does a person get to be like that? How does a person not only read the Bible but be formed by it? I rediscovered in the few minutes we've had to visit together this evening how precious the word "formation" is to him. "That's very interesting," said I, "That's what I'm preaching about tonight." Said he, "I thought you might!" Formation is the subject we are considering together tonight— ecumenical formation particularly in the context of an educational institution, a church-related educational institution.

By formation I mean more than learning. By formation I mean more than experiencing. By formation I mean that process by which the spirit and the soul and the body, the whole person, is shaped, influenced—molded as a potter molds the clay—by the Spirit of God. In my title this evening, "Molded for Ministry," I am not talking about the small number of people whom we speak of as ordained ministers. I refer to the whole body of the people of God— even to the whole family of humankind ministering to one another in process of formation. Of that process I wish to say four things.

First, to be molded for ministry is to have an experience of life. Formation is not some abstraction that happens apart from life. It happens in the center of life. You whose college experiences are 10,

20, 30, or 40 years in the past now would likely share with me the recognition that even though we remember many things from those days, the most important memory is the life we experienced during those days in college. Professors played a part. Students played a part. Extracurricular, and curricular—and some noncurricular activities!—played a part. Many of us remember those 2, 3, 4, or 5 years, however many it was, as among the richest periods of our lives. That is as it should be. College is not a preparation for life, it *is* life—life in which influences to which we have not previously been exposed begin to mold and shape our spirits, our persons. We have become new persons, renewed by discovering within ourselves resources we didn't know existed; by encountering experiences that we hadn't dreamed or imagined were possible; by coming into contact with the wealth of the history and the cultures of the world that we would not have known without our college experience.

One of my own favorite memories of my resistance to that encounter with life is that of coming to college thinking it was most of all a place to acquire knowledge. I wanted, therefore, to be an English major without bothering with what seemed to be that somewhat ephemeral form of literature known as "novel." I petitioned the chairperson of the English Department, chairman in those days, if I could somehow be excused from courses in novel. "Well, Mr. Brouwer," he said to me, "you'll have to see the dean." With all the self-assurance of someone who fancied that education was simply a matter of acquiring knowledge—and that as factual and ordered as possible—I marched into the dean's office and said, "Doctor Hollenbach, I am an English major but I would like to be excused from taking courses in novel." He peered at me over his glasses and said, "Mr. Brouwer, an English major at Hope College takes novel." It was one of the shortest interviews I've ever had!

In these days as I remember my college experiences, right at the top of the list is professor James Prins of Hope College who opened the doors of life to me in American, and English, and European novel in a way I hadn't dreamed possible. I was not surprised, and immensely pleased, when he later became the first to receive the HOPE award, recognizing him as "Hope's Outstanding Professor Educator."

A couple of years ago when I made my first visit to Vietnam, I asked one of my Asian colleagues on the staff of the World Council of Churches to give me everything he could to read about Southeast Asia so that I would understand what I was about to experience. He came to me a few days later with a novel. Without that experience at Hope College I probably would have dismissed that as a way of dismissing me, but I was open to it, and found it an unparalleled way to enter into the life of the people of Vietnam.

I remember another time going out with our family of small children on one of those evenings when one simply has to get out of the house. We drove to a nearby drive-in theater where a new movie was playing about which we knew nothing. (That was still relatively safe in those days!) We drove into the theater, parked the car, and began to watch the movie. It was 2001. Some of you have seen it. I saw in the newspapers last week that it was rated as one of the ten great movies of all time. Seeing it was an experience of life unlike any other I've had. An experience of life endlessly opening as a person is drawn down the corridors of space and time through exploding dimensions of the richness and the texture and the beauty of life and on into the third and fourth dimension of the spirit. That is formation.

Formation also happens through sharing the experience of other lives. Last summer I thought I would spend some odd moments over a few days reading a biography of Sir Thomas More, written by Richard Marius. I discovered, however, that the biographer was not simply recounting the experiences or analyzing the life of Thomas More. He was exploring dozens of different avenues of all the rich life of that period. I found myself engrossed in it, being formed by it, just as I had been by watching the dramatization of Sir Thomas More's life in *A Man For All Seasons*. That's formation—shaping the whole person in an experience of life.

Formation is first of all an experience of life. It is also an experience of life with God. We Christians believe that God is best known to us in the person of Jesus Christ. Christians, Jews, and persons of many other faiths believe that man and woman are created in the image of God, and that the human being is both being and human because we carry within us the image of God. We Christians believe that image of God to be most clearly visible in the person of Jesus Christ, God who became flesh and dwelt among us. Therefore, if we want to know what God is like, we look to Jesus whom we confess to be the Son of God. We then know that God is a person of love, and of justice, and of kindness, one who when reviled, reviled not again, one who took time for quietness and peace in the midst of the multitudes, and one who could offer his life freely for the life of the world. We have some understanding of what God is like, because we have seen God revealed in Jesus Christ.

A few weeks ago Mrs. Brouwer and I went to see what many people say is the best movie on the Vietnam experience, *Platoon*. If you have seen it you will know that in it there are some people who know the experience of the image of God within them and are able in the midst of all sorts of terrible circumstances around them to maintain their sense of being human. You will also have seen that there are some people who have lost their grip on the image of God within them and are kept in their human shell only by the social pressures around them. When the social pressures around them disappear, then that creatureliness which is less than human begins to express itself by taking other human beings apart. Being formed in life with God means that the spirit of God molds our spirits so that we are human from the inside out. And when we fail to radiate the image of God, even then we know that by the grace of God we can be renewed and reformed in the image of God and once again know ourselves to be the children of God. Being molded for ministry is an experience of life with God.

One of the enriching experiences of life with God in the ecumenical movement is the experience of growth through the interaction of our different understandings of God. Someone observed sometime ago that the word "Christian" is a noun, but the words Reformed and Lutheran and Methodist and Episcopalian and all the other traditions are adjectives. So I am never a Lutheran, I am always a Lutheran Christian. I am never an Episcopalian, I am an Episcopalian Christian, and so on. This is a way of saying that what we discover in the interaction of the various traditions, which are various ways of looking at God and understanding God, is that the peculiarities begin to slip out to the edges—where they belong.

By contrast, groups which exclude and separate themselves from other groups tend to concentrate on those peculiarities and to make the peculiarities more important than the centralities. When we come together we discover that what we all have in common are precisely those fundamental centralities. Therefore, in the ecumenical fellowship, more, not less, than in unecumenical fellowship, we are able to get in touch in a deeper way with the roots of our common life. That makes for refreshment, and renewal, and re-formation. Little wonder that the birth of the ecumenical movement was marked by a rebirth in biblical studies. Christians discovered what they had in common and they found that as they discovered the centralities of their various traditions it led them back to the Bible.

And not just Christians. Some people are afraid of dialogue with people of other faiths, but the most fundamental premise for such dialogue is that a person who knows only one tradition knows no tradition. It is only as we see ourselves in fellowship with people of other faith traditions that we truly come to understand the meaning and significance of our own faith tradition. And again, one begins to discover common emphases and interests—this time in the great centralities of the human condition and the human being—and we discover that the process of formation is once again enriched.

Being molded for ministry is an experience of life with God. It is also an experience of life with God in community. One of the wonderful features of a college like Juniata (I discovered from your president that you are almost entirely an on-campus community) is the possibility of an experience of community that again is probably unparalleled in experiences most people have at other times in their lives. Into this college community come the different traditions of different communities, different church backgrounds, different family traditions, various ethnic traditions, various community traditions—traditions of all sorts. Each person comes here not just as an individual but as a person who has been shaped within a whole host of communities in which that person has participated. All these flow together into the college community.

The process of freshmen orientation is understood to be for the benefit of the freshmen, and it is. But it is no less for the benefit of the college to help it reintegrate the community into which all those different traditions flow in those first few days. The richness of all those traditions of faculty and staff and students, and the whole host of those who have gone before—who have formed the tradition of Juniata College, who have given it a particular ethos—all of that comes together. By the time that class leaves there is a new and recultivated sense of community that has been developed because theirs has been an experience unique in the history of this college— and in the whole history of the world. Everyone who participates in that experience is formed by it.

Being molded for ministry is an experience of life with God in community. It is not an accident, my sisters and brothers, that many of the people who, throughout the history of the church, and today in the life of the church, are making the most difference, are people who believe in and practice community. Whether it is the strange kind of community with God that we moderns do not very well understand of hermits living in caves in the desert, or whether it is a community such as the Essene community, or some other of the many communities throughout the history of the Christian church, there is something about the experience of cultivated community that makes people strong. It forms them. It makes them able to stand against the principalities and the powers. It gives them a sense of belonging not only to God but of belonging to God in the company of their sisters and brothers. Today we may see this in a community like the Sojourners, for example, an evangelical community representing many different traditions in the city of Washington which persists and grows stronger in its witness against the principalities and the powers because its members know that nothing can separate them from the love of God in Christ Jesus, and if they cannot be separated from the love of God in Christ Jesus, then they cannot be separated from one another.

That's the vision at the heart of the ecumenical movement. Because we all belong together in Jesus Christ we are formed and molded in community with Jesus Christ. If I am Christ's brother and you are Christ's sisters and brothers, then we are sister and brother one to another and nothing can separate us from one another, because we belong to Christ and Christ belongs to God. We are formed by an experience of life with God in community.

One more thing. To be formed in this way is to live a life with God in community and in service to the world. During the 1960s when there was a great deal of emphasis on small groups, people analyzed such groups who discovered what any Christian who had lived in community across the centuries could have told them. Groups that concentrated just on things to do, fell apart because they degenerated into collections of activists, which is not the same as community. Groups that concentrated just on meditation and prayer fell apart because they no longer had any common task to bind them together. If a group was to continue as a group and become a community then it was necessary for it to have *both* a common task *and* a means of nurturing itself. It is through life in community with God, offered in service to the world, that Christian formation occurs.

Illustrations of such formation can be found all over the world. Such as the men and women in Roman Catholic orders in Nicaragua giving the gift of their own lives in the struggle for freedom there. Last week I was in Haiti where for the first time in forty or more years, people were voting in an election. The election was greatly complicated by the fact that most of the people in Haiti are illiterate and that the Constitution itself had been published only days before the referendum. The one institution that was present all over the country and could possibly interpret for the people the meaning of the Constitution was the church. The people trusted it to do so and took a significant step toward freedom.

Such service to the world is an essential element of formation. Christians in South Africa, Christians in the United States, Christians everywhere, having known the fullness of life with God in community can find the strength and grace to give themselves to the life of the world. People who have known what it means to be loved by God and by their sisters and brothers in community are able to give themselves with abandon for the life of the world.

One can hope to experience some small part of that in a church-related college. As we live in such communities we are all writing some very important chapters in the stories of our lives. Someone has said that such stories have three purposes. They are first a way in which we recall the past, try to understand the past, or even try to recreate the past as we wish it had been. They are also a means by which we try to understand the present. And finally, they are a vehicle for projecting what we want to be.

In these extraordinarily important years for the formation of one's whole life, these college years, it is possible to write the main lines of the story of one's life in a way that will help make it possible for the story to be rich and full all the way to the end. An experience of such formation in a college setting such as this can make one a life-long member of a resistance movement that stands against anything that attempts to shrivel the human spirit. Being formed as a child of God cna mean no less. God bless you as you experience together in community that process of formation. Amen.

31

The Roman Catholic Church and Conciliar Ecumenism

A presentation at the Consultation on Roman Catholic Participation in State Ecumenical Agencies, Indianapolis, IN, September 9, 1987.

In 1984, at the request of the Commission on Regional and Local Ecumenism (CORLE) of the National Council of Churches (NCC), Joseph Witmer of the Bishops' Committee on Ecumenical and Interreligious Affairs (BCEIA) of the National Conference of Catholic Bishops (NCCB) had conducted a survey of Roman Catholic participation in regional and local councils. That survey uncovered a rapid and significant increase in Roman Catholic membership in such councils. Both CORLE and BCEIA wanted to know the reasons for that increase; what was helping it and what was hindering it. Three years later, in the fall of 1987, a group of forty-two people from seven states gathered at the Alverna Retreat House (Roman Catholic) in Indianapolis for a consultation on Roman Catholic participation in state ecumenical agencies.

Mostly, the consultants generated their own agenda. To put the issues in broader perspective, Roman Catholic ecumenist Basil Meeking, from the staff of the Secretariat for Promoting Christian Unity (SPCU), had been invited to present a Roman Catholic perspective on "The Roman

Catholic Church and Conciliar Ecumenism." After accepting, he returned to New Zealand as a bishop. Former SPCU staff member Thomas Stransky had been asked to substitute. I had been invited to present an NCC perspective. Both presentations, together with other consultation papers, were published under the title "Living Together: A Consultation on Roman Catholic Participation in State Ecumenical Agencies," John Bush, Ed. (available for five dollars from CORLE, 475 Riverside Drive, NY, NY 10115).

Well after the date for this consultation had been established, the Vatican announced overlapping dates for the visit of John Paul II to the United States. Because of duties related to that scheduling, I arrived late, stopping at the consultation en route to the ecumenical meeting with John Paul II at Columbia, SC, to which I referred in the opening paragraph of my presentation.

A few other background notes:

The union of the Lutheran churches' mentioned in this chapter is discussed in the next.

The NCCB is also incorporated as the United States Catholic Conference (USCC) and uses that identity in its relationship with governments, etc.

In the third section of this presentation, I noted the membership of the Roman Catholic churches in the Caribbean and Pacific Conferences of Churches. In 1990, the Roman Catholic churches in the Middle East became members of the Middle East Council of Churches. They are not members of the other regional conferences of churches in Africa, Asia, Europe, and Latin America.

A final note about the title: Since the word "ecumenism" was assigned to me, I accepted it even though I have used it less and less over the years and now try to avoid it altogether if possible since I have become increasingly wary of the ideological overtones of all "ism" words. I prefer rather to speak of the phenomenon of ecumenicity, and of plurality rather than pluralism.

First, a couple of personal notes: As I boarded the plane this morning, I recalled that I was last at this retreat center for a meeting of the National Council of Churches panel, which eventually led to the council identifying itself as a "community of communions." During that meeting, as is my custom, I went out for an early morning walk. I came back into the dining room to see my good friend Jorge Lara-Braud, who was then working for the National Council, simply stricken. He had just heard on the radio that Pope John Paul I had died. We went spontaneously and prayed with the community here. I think it interesting that on my second visit to this center, we are gathered to talk about Roman Catholic participation in state ecumenical agencies—and that I should be doing that on my way to a meeting with Pope John Paul II!

Next, a personal note about Tom Stransky. I asked for a change in program, because I wanted my presentation to follow his—for content reasons, as I will indicate—but also for personal reasons. I have known Tom for almost twenty years. My first meeting with him was on my very first trip overseas in 1968. I had been traveling for eight weeks in about twelve different countries. It was a wonderful trip—in spite of how that schedule sounds! At the end I came to Rome where Tom was my host—he was then a staff member of the Secretariat for Christian Unity. All my life I will treasure the memory of that visit. The experience that always springs first to mind is sitting behind Tom on his motor bike while he was taking us through Rome traffic—with my long legs sticking out on either side of him! All I could do was wrap my arms around him and hang on—which is a kind of parable of the ecumenical movement. Since that time, I have worked with Tom in World Council affairs and in other ways. I feel that I have had my arms around him ever since. I have respected and loved him for a long, long time and am delighted with his new assignment as director of the Ecumenical Institute at Tantur (just outside Jerusalem).

Now to my subject: I will talk first about the importance, from the perspective of national ecumenism, of looking at the Roman Catholic church as a world body; then about working relationships with that church in the ecumenical movement in this country; third, about some differences between local, regional, and national ecumenicity vis-a-vis the Roman Catholic church; and finally, about some of the promises, problems and challenges in relationships with the Roman Catholic church.

Roman Catholicism as a World Body

First, the importance of seeing Roman Catholicism as a world church, even when working in national ecumenism. One element is the sheer size of the Roman Catholic church. The numbers I have read vary from 400 million to 750 million. Even the lower number is larger than the entire fellowship of churches within the World Council of Churches.

Size is only one aspect. There is also the ecclesiological dimension. Ecclesiological issues involving the Roman Catholic church cannot be settled in any national conference. This is of course also true in a somewhat different way for the Orthodox churches. But it is different from most of the other churches in the National Council of Churches. For example, when the United Methodist church decided it wanted to ordain a woman as a bishop, it ordained a woman. The Episcopalians are going through a much more complicated process with conversations in the Anglican Consultive Council and the Lambeth Conference, but in most cases this is happening in the United States. I leave it to your imagination what would be required in the Roman Catholic church.

Then, of course, there is the papacy, of which we are keenly aware in these days just prior to the visit of the Pope. Planning for that visit has been done in consultation with the National Conference of Catholic Bishops, but it has been very much under the direction of the Vatican. That again is different from our work with any other group. Because Tom spoke about that at some length, I will not belabor the point, but I do want to underscore its importance from my perspective as well.

Working Relationships with the Roman Catholic church in the United States

The second matter I want to discuss is working relationships with the Roman Catholic church in this country. My first observation is closely related to the self-identity of the Roman Catholic church as a worldwide church. The idea of national churches is much more of a Protestant, and in some ways an Orthodox, idea than it is a Roman Catholic idea. Episcopal conferences in the Roman Catholic church, such as the National Conference of Catholic Bishops, have been around for only about two decades—a very short period of time. Their identity and nature is still very much subject to debate within the Roman Catholic church.

Second, I want to note the centuries-long and virulent anti-Catholicism in the history of this century. Sydney Ahlstrom, in his huge work on the religious history of the American people, says that such anti-Catholicism ceased to be a major feature in the 1960s. But it is still strong. We have seen lingering evidence of it around the visit of John Paul II. I think particularly of the hesitancy on the part of some people in the conservative evangelical communities, to say nothing of the religious right, at having their people see them in the presence of this Pope or any Pope. That anxiety is very, very strong. More than once I have been shocked to see how very strong.

A third factor is the size of the Roman Catholic church. We in the National Council of Churches now, with the union of the Lutheran churches, number about 44 million. The last count I saw of the Roman Catholic church in the United States was somewhere between 53 and 54 million. The third force in American church life represented by the conservative evangelical churches is uncountable, but is probably about the same size or a little smaller, depending on where the boundary is drawn. In spite of this numerical superiority, there is, in the hearts of many evangelicals and Roman Catholics, a rapidly declining but still pronounced residual feeling of being a minority because of having been such for so long. That feeling is still a factor in the Roman Catholic church's relationship with other churches—even though it has changed drastically in the last few years. Indeed, the tables are turning now so that the churches which dominated the culture, the "mainline Protestant" churches, are beginning to develop a minority mentality—which further complicates and confuses the relationship.

A fourth point has to do with some of the relationships between the NCC and the Roman Catholic church. One continuing vehicle for this relationship is a group called the Inter-Religious Secretaries, a meeting of the general secretaries of the National Council of Churches, the National Conference of Catholic Bishops, and the Synagogue Council of America. We meet on a regular basis to cultivate personal relationships and to deal with common agenda. Such regular established working relationships are of course very helpful in working through the intricacies of a papal visit—to say nothing of when a crisis arises. At one point in the early '70s, controversy around the issue of public and parochial schools became so severe that the general secretary of the National Conference of Catholic Bishops withdrew feeling that testimony which the National Council of Churches had entered in the Congressional Record was unfair and prejudicial toward the Roman Catholic church. The general secretary of the National Council of Churches then withdrew that particular part of the statement, although not the whole testimony. The tensions continued for a while, but the general secretaries got back together again and have stayed together.

A fifth point is the wide variety of relationships that we cultivate with one another. Those who are interested can get from my office a report on a January 8, 1987, meeting with the National Conference of Catholic Bishops staff in which we looked at a whole host of things we do together. Most of the program units of the National Council of Churches have Roman Catholic participation. In some instances, there are working groups where Roman Catholics are the chief actors. The Roman Catholic church is, however, an official member only of the Commission on Faith and Order.

Sixth, in that meeting on January 8, we did in a more formal way what we do informally all the time, namely identify points of disagreement. We simply say: on this we are not ready to work together; on this, we tried to work together, but haven't figured out how. And of course, we identified new areas in which to cooperate.

Finally a word concerning relationships with Roman Catholic orders. They have not been tabulated. One conclusion of the January 8 meeting between the staffs of the National Council of Churches and the National Conference of Catholic Bishops is that we ought to tabulate and analyze those relationships. I think it would be even more extensive than the participation of the NCCB/USCC. The orders are everywhere, God love them. At lunch Tom asked me about pressure on the NCC from the left and the right within the Roman Catholic church. We get very little of which I am aware from reactionary forces within the Roman Catholic church, but we are constantly being nudged by the people in the religious orders to take more radical stands than we do. They are a very, very good stimulus to us because they help us with the critical point that Tom mentioned of being able to take a radical stance on an issue while not developing the supercilious, self-righteous attitude that others who are not prepared to take that same radical stand do not belong in the community. These relationships are very important to our life together in the National Council of Churches.

Some Differences Between Local, Regional, and National Ecumenism.

Recently I read somewhere that being subtle is the art of saying what you have to say and then getting out of the way before it is understood! I'll take that risk here today hoping that I will not be heard as saying that one form of ecumenism in one missional zone (I prefer zone to level) is superior to another. They are different. I believe it is very important for us to recognize those differences.

Why is there so much more participation of Roman Catholics in local and regional ecumenism than there is in national ecumenical structures? I want to identify five different reasons which I do not claim to be exhaustive but each of which I believe to be a factor.

First is the obvious fact of numbers: There are more local and regional forms of ecumenism than there are national forms. Tom identified twenty-one NCCs—I have a little higher count than that, around 30—in which the Roman Catholic churches participate in their respective countries. Of course, participation in local and regional structures in this country is vast. You already have those figures.

A second factor is the relative freedom of action that officials of the Roman Catholic church have at different levels. A priest can ordinarily cooperate with a local ecumenical structure more easily than can a bishop with a regional structure, and a bishop more easily with a regional structure than can an episcopal conference with a national structure, and an episcopal conference more easily with a national structure than can the Pope with the World Council of Churches. In a hierarchial church, each step up the hierarchy further complicates the ecclesiological, logistical, and political issues.

Third, we need to reckon with the nature of the council involved. The World Council of Churches is unique—not only in the sense that it is worldwide, but also in the sense that it is the flagship of the ecumenical fleet and the symbol of the church's unity in a way that no national council or any group of national councils of churches together ever can be. The ecclesial issue therefore is raised much more sharply in relationship with the WCC than it is with a NCC. It is still less significant for state and local councils. In some ways, participation of the Roman Catholic church in the program *units* of the National Council may be compared to membership in certain forms of regional councils.

A fourth issue is the strength of the Roman Catholic church. The general pattern is that where the Roman Catholic church is equal in size or a minority, there it is more likely to participate in councils of churches. That is true in this country and it is true around the world in global regions—for example, in the Caribbean and the Pacific. Exceptions to the pattern are usually due to someone's personal leadership. (I am reminded, in this regard, of Malcolm Muggeridge's unfair but partly true characterization of the ecumenical movement. He once described the leaders of the ecumenical movement as being very like the town drunks in the village where he grew up! If they didn't lean on one another, none of them would be able to stand!)

A fifth element is the issue of history. How much anti-Catholicism there has been, in a particular region, for example. The more prejudice, the harder it is to be together.

Promises, Problems and Challenges

Now, a fourth category of promises and challenges. Let me preface this section by saying that we in the NCC are not pressing for membership of the Roman Catholic church. That was discussed at length in the early '70s. It is not being discussed now. Neither side is ready.

First, participation of the Roman Catholic church constitutes, by definition, a more full expression of Christian unity. The point can of course be made about the participation of any Christian church, but it is most assuredly true of this largest and most comprehensive community.

A second promise is a more powerfully expressed Christian witness. I mean three or four different things by that. I have alluded to the role that the religious orders can play and do play and the spiritual depth that they have given to some of our work together. Second, the Roman Catholic church takes its ecumenical commitments very seriously. When three years ago in the NCC, we put together an ecumenical agenda trying to say in short form "where we are headed," the group that responded most seriously was the National Conference of Catholic Bishops—of course, they were also six weeks beyond the deadline!

On another plane, the NCCB can bring to bear a kind of coherence and institutional connectedness that a council of churches cannot begin to approach. On the other hand, a council of churches can bring to bear the richness of the diversity and the urgency of issues raised within an ecumenical context which an episcopal conference cannot do. We need both witnesses. I would like to see more interaction between them. That interaction is not beyond the realm of possibility, but it will require movement on both sides—and it will require us to deal seriously with the ministry of the laity—on both sides. We in the NCC, for example, need to recapture some of the thoroughness (including secular competence) which we have sometimes used in the past to address some of the issues we have spoken about and practice that thoroughness much more regularly. I believe that if we take that step, there will be a response.

A third promise is the Roman Catholic church's emphasis on spiritual ecumenism. When someone from the Free Church tradition speaks of spiritual unity, I am frequently skeptical. Not so when Roman Catholics speak of spiritual ecumenism, because they do so in the context of a profound ecclesiology. Vatican II speaks of spiritual ecumenism as the soul of the whole ecumenical movement. Spirituality is the root of ecumenism. We need urgently to cultivate that in the National Council of Churches and its member churches.

A fourth contribution is the papacy itself. The problems surrounding the papacy are well known, but it is also a contribution, which the Roman Catholic church makes to the ecumenical movement. The Pope, as the Bishop of Rome, is a unique symbol of the unity of the Christian church. The challenge is to integrate a reformed or renewed papacy in the life of the church.

Now some problems. First, the challenge to the ecclesial integrity of the communions when the Roman Catholic church participates with them—which is counterpoint to the ecclesiological challenge to the Roman Catholic church in deciding to participate on a more or less equal basis with other Christian communities. The fact that most Protestant churches have, to some degree, defined themselves over against the Roman Catholic church means that they have to come to terms with what they have done with that "over-againstness." It is sometimes acted out by a kind of unfortunate deference to the Pope—which I think is just as bad as anti-papism. If the Roman Catholic church is to be truly present with us, then we must come to terms with its meaning for us in our own internal lives—our own identities. For that we need freedom from stereotypes—which is greatly aided by access to the living tradition and the people who embody it.

A second issue is the ecclesial nature of the councils. At a WCC-convened consultation in Geneva last October of all the National Council of Churches around the world, a paper was read about Roman Catholic participation in councils of churches. That paper was one of the clearest, and therefore among the most problematic expressions of the Roman Catholic stance on this issue. On the one hand, the Roman Catholic church is saying to councils of churches that they need to deal more seriously with ecclesial issues. On the other hand, it is saying that councils must not be too ecclesial! We need, I think, to do the former, and risk the latter.

Third, are the social and theological issues. They have been mentioned in this consultation repeatedly. It is interesting to note that when the NCC and the Roman Catholic church were talking together 20 years ago, they already then identified abortion as one of the most complicated issues they would need to address.

Finally, there are the organizational issues such as finance, levels of participation, etc., and, most of all, the issues of organizational culture. We in the National Council of Churches are struggling these days to deal with the organizational cultural issues in terms of the participation of the Orthodox churches, the Black churches, and some other churches even less recognized within our fellowship. That problem in relation to the Roman Catholic church would be immense.

In that milieu, the ongoing quiet work that is renewed in consultations such as this one is fundamentally important. God bless you as you try to keep trying.

32
An Ecumenical Greeting

Presented to the Constituting Convention of the Evangelical Lutheran Church in America, Chicago, IL, May 1, 1987.

The Constituting Convention of the Evangelical Lutheran Church in America (ELCA) was an event of special significance to the NCC, since it united one member church, the Lutheran Church in America (LCA), and two non-member churches, The American Lutheran Church (ALC) and the Association of Evangelical Lutheran Churches (AELC), with the understanding that the new church would be a member of the NCC as well as of the WCC. Continuing membership in both councils was to be subject to specific decision at the first church-wide assembly of the ELCA in 1989. Since the ALC was already a member of the WCC, ELCA concern about the councils focused particularly on the NCC, of which it was not a member.

In order to build confidence in the NCC as soon as possible, I was invited, as general secretary of the NCC, to bring greetings to the constituting convention. Also present at the convention were representatives of other churches, who were assembled on the platform and introduced to the convention just before I presented these greetings. Among the church representatives to whom I refer in the opening paragraph were some of the council's "heads of communions," an NCC rubric for an informal grouping of the senior officers of its member churches. These churches in turn were (and are) referred to more frequently as "communions" than as churches— an unfortunate and confusing usage, I think, with no apparent supporting rationale but with a durable history nonetheless—even though in WCC parlance, to speak of, for example, the Orthodox Church in America as a "communion" would be offensive to it and the other Orthodox churches with which it is in communion! But then, as my NCC colleague Peggy Shriver (assistant general secretary for research and evaluation) used occasionally to remind us, some things have a history even though they do not have a reason!

With delight, I concluded these greetings at the convention with the first public announcement of Dr. Dorothy Marple's nomination as assistant general secretary of the council. I announced it there because her coming would help build ELCA confidence in the council, since she had given outstanding service first to the LCA and then to all three uniting churches as executive of the Commission on the New Lutheran Church. Far beyond such confidence building, however, her coming to the council was a gift of grace to me. My expectations for her work were very high. She far exceeded them, being one of the most committed and competent professionals I have known.

At the time of these greetings, the convention was counting the votes in their umpteenth ballot as part of a laborious process they called an ecclesiastical ballot, in which various persons were nominated and then removed from consideration as, ballot by ballot, the assembly ground its way toward the election of a bishop for the church. My closing allusion is to that process, from which I thought the delegates needed a touch of comic relief! They seemed to agree.

This greeting represents that part of my work as NCC general secretary I most enjoyed—visiting the member churches on their home turf. Already in my May 1986 Report to the Governing Board I had said:

> My greatest joy during these past nearly eighteen months as your general secretary has been the opportunity to be present in the councils, synods, conferences, and other gatherings of the varied communions which constitute this community. I have rejoiced in the rich and distinctive ethos of each of these family gatherings and repeatedly found that ethos expressed with a strength and attraction that I have found both inspiring and invigorating.

The privilege and pleasure of being present in person at the "family gatherings" of the various traditions were considerably enhanced by my responsibility to address them, sometimes with a full-length sermon and sometimes with a shorter greeting and often both. Usually I went to any such meeting with the facts about that tradition in hand and a few fairly clear ideas of what to say—just in case nothing better occurred to me at the assembly or I ran out of time to prepare something on site. I then watched and listened and absorbed and drafted—usually right up to the last minute—before I spoke from notes decipherable only to me. I enjoyed it immensely.

Often at these meetings one or more people would thank me for "taking time out of your busy schedule to be present with us." At the time, I didn't take that too seriously. Now that I am no longer traveling around to such meetings, I have a much clearer idea of how much energy those activities did demand in terms of preparation, time away, and catching up. Happily, at the time, I realized that only in part and was, therefore, free to enjoy them.

Mr. Chairperson, delegates, sisters, and brothers. For one fleeting moment I thought that I would be able to bring you the greetings of the National Council of Churches from this platform, flanked by the heads of communions and ecumenical officers of many of its member communions. That would have been a more faithful representation than my standing here alone. But I trust the image lingers in your mind, even if not before your eyes.

First, I want to say how very much at home I have felt among you. I arrived yesterday in time to be a part of the program last night in which you celebrated the mission of your church and the strength your various ethnic heritages contribute to that mission. The presentation stirred memories in me of my own Dutch-American background and the strength that I continue to draw from that heritage for my life and ministry. I know that many of you do the same from your heritages.

I must also say that I felt at home physically. With so many tall Scandinavians around I was hardly more than a head taller than some of you, rather than the usual head and shoulders!

But there are more substantive reasons for feeling at home. In the mid-1980s, I spent a brief time on the staff of the World Council of Churches in Geneva. Mrs. Brouwer and I found that the congregation in which we could worship most meaningfully was the Lutheran congregation in that city. Having grown up in Minnesota you will not be surprised that I am no stranger to Lutherans! But worshiping in the church in Geneva provided me an opportunity to come to know Lutheran liturgy and community more deeply than before.

I take personal joy in this constituting convention as well. One of my brothers is a very active member of an American Lutheran congregation, indeed has been president of that congregation, in Tyler, Minnesota. I am delighted that the church of which he and his family are members is now a member of the National Council of Churches.

But there is a deeper reason still for a relationship between the tradition which I represent (being a minister in the Reformed Church in America) and the Lutheran tradition. As you know the European Reformed churches were nurtured on the Heidelberg Catechism. The catechism, as you also know, was very heavily influenced by the Lutheran community as well as by the Reformed community. Indeed, one way of describing people who have been formed by reading the Heidelberg Catechism is to say that on good days they read Calvin, and on bad days they read Luther! I may say to you that since I have joined the staff of the National Council of Churches, I have been reading a lot of Martin Luther!

Nor am I a stranger to what you are doing here in these days in your constituting convention. I have followed your work very closely over the last few years. To one who comes out of the rather more fractious Reformed and Presbyterian tradition, I stand amazed at how much you have been able to accomplish in such a short period of time. I congratulate you on it.

We have been watching you not merely out of curiosity, but because what you are doing here is of immense significance to the National Council of Churches. Our witness as a council would not be complete, not even remotely near complete, without the active participation of the Evangelical Lutheran Church in America. Your coming together holds promise of making our witness more complete and strong.

We are not strangers in the National Council of Churches to watching Lutherans merge. At the beginning of the National Council of Churches in 1950 there were three Lutheran churches present: the Augustana Evangelical Lutheran Church, the Danish Evangelical Lutheran Church of America, and the United Lutheran Church of America, all of which became charter members. They later united to become the Lutheran Church in America and, thus united, have been making a strong contribution to the National Council of Churches ever since.

I have said that we have been watching you. I understand that the Evangelical Lutheran Church in America will in the next few years be watching us. We are accustomed to that. I sometimes say to my colleagues that if we have thirty-two member communions, how does it happen that there are thirty-three of them watching us all the time? But we have been pleased to see that each member communion which has taken up a careful study of the National Council of Churches has decided to strengthen its connection with the National Council of Churches. At its most recent meeting, the United Methodist church's Council of Bishops heard a special committee report that, in its judgment, the National Council of Churches was a stronger organization than it had been in some years.

One of the points at which we are trying to grow stronger is in our relationships both to the Roman Catholic church and to

conservative evangelical churches. Of course, neither the Roman
Catholic church nor conservative evangelicals are strangers to us
now. The Southern Baptist churches, the Assemblies of God, and
the Lutheran Church, Missouri Synod, are official members of the
Faith and Order Commission of the National Council of Churches
as is the Roman Catholic church. You can help strengthen those
ties.

Nor is the American Lutheran church a stranger to the National
Council of Churches. I asked my colleagues a few weeks ago if they
would each give me a few notes about the participation of the
American Lutheran church in the various units of the National
Council of Churches, thinking that I would have a few tidbits of
information to share with you. The result runs to several pages and
we do not have that much time. Let me simply say that the
American Lutheran church participates formally or informally in
all the major units of the National Council of Churches and last
year supported its programs with nearly $100,000 in contributions.

The Association of Evangelical Lutheran Churches brings a
different kind of gift which is also very much treasured by us in the
National Council of Churches—the passionate gift of holding to
unity even in the midst of separation.

What of the future? I want to identify three major contributions—
by no means an exhaustive list—but three major potential
contributions you can make to the National Council of Churches.
First, your reclaiming Evangelical in your name. Surely that will
cause some of our critics to clarify their thinking about who we are.
Even more important, your reclaiming that essential word will, I
hope, lead to a deeper understanding of that word among all
American Christians—that it is not a *narrow* word but a *deep* word.
I like to say of the National Council of Churches that we are
organized around the most evangelical of principles: being bound
together in Jesus Christ we are persuaded that if we are so bound
together then there is nothing sufficiently important to separate us.
You can help us make that witness clear to the world.

Second: your very rich tradition of worship and the theological
content and depth of your liturgy. On Easter Monday I stood in our
staff worship service next to one of the people whose voice leads us
most often in singing in our staff groups, and heard his voice fall
silent. Later, remarking that we were singing one of the great
Lutheran resurrection hymns which was unfamiliar to him, he said,
"I was so moved by the depth of the language that I had to stop

singing just to soak up the words." We need that in the council. We need that very much.

Finally, your strong ecclesiology. We in the National Council of Churches are on a pilgrimage toward becoming a community of communions. You can help us with that. Your strong ecclesiology is essential to it.

I hope therefore that we can get to know one another very well. As soon as you are through with your elections, and your new leadership has an opportunity to settle in, we will be asking for an opportunity to pay a visit to the new offices of the Evangelical Lutheran Church in America.

Finally I want to say that you have already given us a gift. I think a very great gift. A few weeks ago, through the good offices of Bishop Crumley, I was led into conversation with Dr. Dorothy Marple, who has served as the assistant to the president/bishop during the tenures of Robert Marshall and James Crumley, and who has done so much to bring the Evangelical Lutheran Church in America to this moment of fulfillment. Through conversation with her, I have gained her acceptance to come sometime later this year to the staff of the National Council of Churches, where she will be the assistant general secretary in my office.

It is true of course that her election is not official until two weeks from now, but I am happy to report that her election is not by means of an ecclesiastical ballot!

33
No Longer Strangers

A sermon at "A Gathering of Christians: Pentecost '88," Arlington, TX, May 21, 1988

"No Longer Strangers" was the theme of an experimental "gathering of Christians." The event was suggested by the council's Presidential Panel on Future Mission and Resources, which had presented an extensive report in November 1984. The "gathering" was a suggested strategy for reaching out to conservative Evangelicals and Roman Catholics. We tried it at Arlington, Texas, in May 1988 with only modest success.

I was asked to give the opening sermon. I have included it here because it is my most "perfected" version of a sermon I have used dozens of times and places and in almost as many forms when asked to speak or preach on an ecumenical theme. (See chapters 10 and 11 for two examples.)

Most of the ideas were already present in the 1980 document, "An Affirmation of Christian Unity" (chapter 39). Here, however, the order of thought is eschatological: gift, promise, task. Earlier, the order had been historical: gift, task, promise. The significance of this seemingly small change I hope will be clear in the sermon.

I have been asked to preach this evening on the theme of this gathering, "No Longer Strangers." That theme springs from the passage of scripture read in your hearing this evening, the second chapter of Ephesians, one of the classic New Testament treatments of unity in Christ. It is therefore a rich and enduring source for the ecumenical vision. It is that ecumenical vision of the unity of the Christian church, the renewal of human community, and the healing of the nations that brings us together this evening. It is that ecumenical vision I want to explore with you in this sermon.

First, we are here to *celebrate the gift of Christian unity*. It is striking that this phrase "no longer strangers" occurs in the same passage in which appears one of the starkest pictures of the brokenness of the human condition to be found anywhere in the scriptures. Speaking to the letter's Gentile readers, the author says that they were *separated* from Christ, "*alienated* from Israel, *strangers* to the covenants, *without* God, *far off*." In all of these phrases, there is the common theme of alienation, of separation, of division—as the *essence* of God's judgment upon sin. Sin is brokenness. Sin separates us from God, from one another, from the earth, from all living things, and even from our own true selves.

That is the bad news. Then comes the good news as we read the words of the apostle, "But now." Listen to the contrast. "*BUT NOW*," says the author,

Christ has brought the Gentiles *near*

Made Jew and Gentile *one*

Broken down the wall

Abolished commandments and ordinances

Created *one new humanity* in place of two

Reconciled both to God in one body through the cross

Preached *peace* to both

Given both *access in one spirit* to God

Made the Gentiles, *no longer strangers, fellow citizens and members of the household of God built upon the one foundation.*

This passage always calls to mind the wonderful picture in early Christian literature of the resurrected Christ, again bearing the cross but using it now to batter down the gates of hell. In the words of the Orthodox liturgy he is seen "trampling down death by death." Alongside that triumphant scene, there is this infinitely tender portrayal of the crucified and resurrected Christ reaching out to both Jew and Gentile, as the apostle saw it, reaching out to all humanity as we see it, embracing them and joining them together as brothers and sisters into one human family. That is Christ's great gift to the church which we are here to celebrate. We are no longer strangers, we *are* fellow citizens, members of the household of God built upon the one foundation.

We are also here to *claim the promise of Christian unity*. The gift of Christian unity, which we celebrate, is what Christ has already done for us. The promise of Christian unity, which we claim, is what Christ will do for us.

Among the greatest privileges of being general secretary of the National Council of Churches is the experience of being received in many different congregations in many different traditions—not as a stranger, but as a brother in Christ.

Last Sunday I had the privilege of worshiping at the St. Nicholas Cathedral of the Orthodox Church in America in Washington, D.C. The occasion was a special service commemorating the 1000th anniversary of the Baptism of Rus', the beginning of the Christian church in what is now the Soviet Union. I felt my spirit moved again and indeed, "my heart strangely warmed" as many times before, by the beauty of the liturgy and perhaps even more by the wonderful family feeling of the congregation. Moving freely among the congregation with the deacons, priests, bishops, archbishops, and metropolitans in all their vested splendor were several little girls in spring bonnets and dresses, each carrying baskets filled with petals of flowers for distribution to other worshipers. That afternoon we were together again at the National Cathedral of the Episcopal church in an ecumenical celebration of the Millennial Jubilee.

All through those services, and afterwards, and still now, I kept saying to myself: How much we need one another! How much we have to give to one another! How much promise there is for reform and renewal in our being together!

How much more full of life is the gospel to me because of the Orthodox theology, liturgy, and iconography of the resurrected Christ.

How much more vital are my roots in the gospel because of the evangelical preaching and teaching of the Word of God and singing of hymns and spiritual songs in which I was nurtured.

How much more concrete is the gospel promise of a new community because of the Catholic doctrine of the church.

How much larger is my understanding of the gospel promise of a new heaven and a new earth because of the ecumenical vision.

These are a few of the promises of Christian unity. We of the National Council of Churches, therefore, *do not* in these days say to those of you from non-member communions: "Come and be like us." How could we? We are not like one another! We do not wish to be like one another! We seek to be like Christ. That is the invitation of Christ to each of us in these days and always. That is the promise of Christian unity: as we are bound together as Christ's sisters and brothers, so shall we be no longer strangers.

The promise of Christian unity is, of course, a promise of a united church. But more than that, it is a promise of a renewed community. Christ broke down walls and abolished commandments and ordinances in order to create *one new humanity*. The promise toward which we live is the promise of a renewed human community in which there is neither Jew nor Greek, neither male nor female, neither black nor white. At the same time, the promise is that everyone will be fully what they are: fully Jew and fully Greek, fully male and fully female, fully black and fully white. That is the promise of the gospel, that each of us will be born again, renewed in the image of God, so that we may be who we were intended to be and thus enrich the human community and show forth the glory of God.

It is the glorious calling and privilege of the Christian church to be the foretaste, the sign, the instrument of this renewed human community. Our Lord's familiar high priestly prayer for unity found in the 17th chapter of John's Gospel is a prayer for the fulfillment of this promise. It is a far more radical and all encompassing prayer than we usually hear. Jesus did not pray only for the church to be one in order that the world might believe that he was sent from

God. Listen: Hear Jesus say, "...that they may be one in order that the world may believe that you *love* them even as you *love* me." Jesus' prayer and God's promise is for a community of love and justice and peace through which the whole human family and all the incredible variety of creation join together in a joyous quest for one another's well being for the glory of God.

That is the long vision of Christian unity, the promise of the gospel, which draws the ecumenical movement onward. It is a search for a church united in Christ, renewed by the Holy Spirit, and witnessing to the love of God made concrete in social justice as the foundation for world peace which fosters the well being of the whole creation as the theater of the iridescent many-colored glory of God.

We are here to celebrate the gift of Christian unity. *We are also here to take up the task of Christian unity.*

It is true that the dividing walls have been broken down. That is the gift of Christian unity.

It is true that someday the stones of which those dividing walls were built will all be beautifully fitted together in the new Jerusalem. That is the promise of Christian unity.

But today, those stones are impediments on the way to Christian unity. They are rubble on the road to Christian unity. We need to pick our way around them, we need to climb over them, we need to sprint ahead in those places where the road is clear. That is the task of Christian unity, in this time between the giving of the gift and the fulfillment of the promise.

What is this rubble along the road? It has many names—too many to call, but they are not unfamiliar. Most of them are "isms"— traditionalism, racism, sexism, nationalism, classism, triumphalism, sectarianism, ecumenism. The problem is in the "ism." When the dead faith of the living is substituted for the living faith of the dead. When love of nation becomes an America-first movement giving second place to love, justice, peace, and truth. When concern for personal renewal becomes privatism. When zeal for the public order leads to the sacrifice of personal well-being. When unity is sought at any price. These are a few of the things that divide the human community and the Christian community. They are the rubble we must remove, the demons we must cast out, if we are to celebrate the gift and claim the promise of Christian unity.

That in brief is the nature of the task of Christian unity: to stand firmly on the gift of unity given in Christ; to reach out longingly for the promise of unity given in Christ.

It is frequently said these days that the ecumenical movement is in the doldrums—that the winds of the Spirit are no longer blowing upon the good ship "Oikumene." Sometimes that is true. The Spirit blows where it wills. But it is also true that we are sometimes making slower progress today partly because we are sailing into stronger head winds. We are today sailing over troubled seas which two decades ago would have forced us to remain safely within the harbors of our separations. In two short decades, we have moved from livingroom dialogues in which Protestants and Catholics were just discovering one another to be Christian to widespread recognition of one another's baptism. We are engaging directly the hard issues of intercommunion and those most complicated issues of ministry and order. And we are here together.

Yet the questions persist: Is the ecumenical movement worth it all? Do we not heal some divisions only at the cost of creating new ones? Yes sometimes that is true. But even then, it is worth it.

I like to think of the ecumenical movement as a kind of super glue which binds together what has been broken more firmly then it was bound together originally. If anything so glued is broken again, it will be along some other line, not where it was broken before. Our strength is in our weakness, even in our wounds. We must of course always beware of new divisions, but we may be confident that having dealt with our brokenness along this or that line, we have put some of the brokenness of sin behind us and, *by the grace of God we are stronger at that point than if we had never been broken.* We are free then, we are free. We are free to celebrate the gift, to claim the promise, and to take up the task of Christian unity for the sake of the whole human family and all of God's creation.

The promise of Christian unity is a glorious promise—a promise full of hope and joy and love and peace and justice. We see it by faith.

By faith we can see a promise of the churches bound together not only in one baptism and one faith and one Lord, but also, may God hasten the day, also in one eucharist and one mission and ministry.

By faith, we can see a promise of the churches offering the gifts of their various traditions and cultures at *one* altar before the throne of the *one* God.

By faith, we can see a promise of each of us who are less oppressed, standing arm-in-arm with someone more oppressed, with the arms of all outstretched in love to those who oppose the coming of the kingdom.

By faith, we can see a promise of all the peoples of the earth embracing one another around the globe rejoicing in one another's gifts and reveling in one another's strengths as they dance together before the Lord.

By faith, we can see a promise of all God's children living with enough, on a planet no longer burdened with industrial pollution and no longer dwelling in the darkness of the nuclear umbrella, but shining bright and clear to the glory of God.

By faith, we can see a world in which the promise of Isaiah is fulfilled and the desert is indeed blossoming like a rose, pointing the way to the new heaven and the new earth where we shall all with one voice say "Worthy is the lamb who was slain, to receive power and glory and blessing and honor for ever and ever. Amen."

34

Surely the Lord is in This Place;
and I did not Know It

A homily at the Presbyterian "Rite of Passage" in the Interchurch Center Chapel, New York, NY June 22, 1988

Early in my tenure at the council, a number of people urged me, some with considerable feeling, to "speak out" on several issues internal to the Presbyterian struggle toward reunion, notably the matter of office location. My more informed friends assured me that to do so would be the kiss of death for a New York location, a pattern that repeated itself again a few years later with reference to the United Church of Christ.

When the time came for the Presbyterians to leave New York, I was invited to deliver the homily at the Presbyterian "Rite of Passage" in the Interchurch Chapel. I gladly accepted and did what I could to encourage the wounded, reinforce the faithful, and keep the committed connected. I also urged my colleagues at the council to urge their colleagues to be present in the chapel—not to hear me preach!—but to let the Presbyterians know that they would be missed. We had a full house.

The full title of this homily is taken literally from the 28th chapter of Genesis, the 16th verse: "Surely the Lord is in this place;

and I did not know it!" It is, of course, a text that can be applied equally to New York, Louisville, or Atlanta.

Today we are concerned primarily with Louisville and secondarily with New York; but Louisville and New York cannot be understood without Atlanta, and perhaps we can best understand them all if first we pay a visit to Bethel.

When asked to deliver this homily, I immediately began thinking of familiar stories in the Bible that had to do with the significance of place. This pericope (Gen. 28:10-22) was easily the winner, partly because of its familiarity and partly because of the various imaginative possible applications of those words of Jacob which constitute the title of this meditation! A few of those we will entertain shortly, but first linger with me for a moment at Bethel.

The matter of place, the issue of geographic location, is of very great importance in the Bible. It is not an accidental matter for Abram to leave Ur of the Chaldeans, or for Jacob to go down to Egypt, or for Moses to come up from Egypt. This story of Jacob at Bethel has to do particularly with the struggle in the development of the faith of Israel over the question of the special presence of God at certain holy places or shrines. We Christians know that as a place of worship, a particular mountain or a particular city is not of prime importance. Spirit and truth are what matter. Nevertheless, Jerusalem is still Jerusalem and Rome is Rome and New York is New York and Louisville is Louisville and Atlanta is Atlanta. Place is important.

But if Francis Thompson, in his poem, "The Kingdom of God," could see Jacob's ladder "Pitched betwixt Heaven and Charing Cross," then is it not impossible that we can see it as well pitched between Heaven and Riverside Drive!—or Witherspoon Street, or Ponce de Leon Avenue! There are, of course, many people for whom it is quite impossible to think of angels passing between any of those places and the gates of Heaven! But we are today concerned with *our* visions—and we know that God is present with us. We also know that God need not be any less present in one place than in any other.

Another attractive feature of this story is its description of the feelings of the traveler. Jacob was not a pilgrim seeking the presence of God in a special holy place. He was a wanderer carrying out a journey he had not willingly undertaken. He was burdened with the pain of separation, uncertainty and loss—with no small cost to his family as well.

Moreover, this journey was precipitated by many bitter feelings about birthrights being stolen or sold or traded—depending on one's point of view. One can hardly, at least I could not, think of these stories without being painfully reminded of the feelings of separation, uncertainty, loss, and dislocation which many of you are experiencing. Nor could I help but think of those Presbyterian birthright matters of commitment to your own history, the ecumenical movement, the city, the world, racial/ethnic minorities, and other barely less weighty matters that have been so much discussed among you and reflected upon by us all in these last months.

Yet, against the background of all those feelings of hurt and pain and confusion and bitterness, this story has been a source of comfort, consolation, and courage—even joy—to unwilling wanderers for many centuries. It is worth noting that for us this is due not so much directly to this Bible story, but indirectly to the visions of Jacob's ladder seen by Black men, women, and children in the chains of slavery—that same institution of slavery which in such large part caused the brokenness of this church.

That takes us to the heart of the story, which is the unexpected discovery of the presence of God in an unlikely place—which I say again may be applied no less equally to New York and to Atlanta as to Louisville. Indeed, we know that it was vigorously applied both to New York and to Atlanta at the time of relocation to those sites—as well as while the offices were present at those sites, and again in the most recent process of selecting a new site.

But today we are concerned with the discovery of the presence of God in Louisville. Let me urge you to look for new and unexpected visions of the presence of God in the confluence of these two separated streams of one church. It is of course true that you are a united and reunited church and not really a new church at all—on the one hand that is true. On the other hand, it is no less true you *are* a new church, and by no stretch of the imagination merely a coming together again of that which was broken apart in 1864. This confluence of histories, theologies, communities, and ethos is quite capable of finding new visions of the unexpected presence of God. I hope you will experience it often.

For it is that renewing experience of the presence of God that will keep us bound together. It is not coincidental that Jacob's dream at Bethel included a vision of the Lord standing above the ladder and proclaiming again the covenant of which Jacob was now the custodian. I do hope, I do hope profoundly, that this time of reunion for the Presbyterian Church in the United States of America may be a time of rich renewal of that covenant by which you are bound not only to one another, but to all those who name the name of Christ. That renewed promise of the covenant which Jacob saw in his dream did after all eventuate not only in an experience of awe. It led as well to an offering of Jacob's life to God.

It has been very pleasant to be here together in the Interchurch Center. Daily interaction with one another has helped make it possible for this New York part of the Presbyterian church to make outstanding contributions to the life of the National Council of Churches not only through the services of people on the staff of the council, but also through active leadership in the constituency committees of the council. It is an illustrious roll, too long for me to name.

Our proximity to one another has made it possible for you to be easily *ecumenical by association*. Now that will be somewhat harder and you shall need to rely more heavily on being *ecumenical by conviction*. That, of course, will not be a new experience for you Presbyterians since it is the very essence of Reformed theology to be always reforming and, therefore, always seeking the unity of the church. That conviction has long been the basis of your ecumenical associations. You shall now, however, need to be more consciously aware of those convictions and act more deliberately upon them.

While we were here together in this one place, our easy association with one another strengthened our convictions both consciously and unconsciously. Now it will need to be our convictions that bring us, consciously, into association with one another. That is, I think, another point at which New York and Louisville cannot be thought of apart from Atlanta, where they have had all along to be ecumenical by conviction.

This "Rite of Passage" is then by no means complete today. It is a step along the way. When the staff cabinet of the National Council of Churches travels to Louisville in September to meet with the staff of the Presbyterian church, we will take another step. Each time we journey back and forth, the rite of passage will go on. My colleagues and I in the National Council of Churches treasure the many experiences we have had here together in this place. We pledge ourselves to continue together on the way. May God go with us all—and we with God.

35

Can the 'Mainline' Find New Life on the Ecumenical Way?

An article in the Christian Century, *February 28, 1990*

After reading the *Christian Century* issue of November 8, 1989, featuring the mainline churches, I expressed to several people my disappointment that the ecumenical movement was hardly mentioned. Bill Fore, sometime NCC colleague (assistant general secretary for communication), and *Christian Century* contributing editor, mentioned that disappointment to *Christian Century* editor, James Wall, who solicited an article. In it, I sketched in outline form a process of renewal I believed to be possible through the ecumenical movement. The article appeared in the *Christian Century* (February 23, 1990) in an edited version that I felt missed some of the nuances of the original, which I have here restored.

"Where is the 'Mainline' Headed?" That bold-faced question headlined the *Christian Century* cover for November 8, 1989. The titles of the articles and the names of the authors promised substance and discernment—and perhaps enjoyment, too. An imaginative cover map of the "State of the Mainline" projected problems, but playfully. It appeared to be a journey worth taking. It was.

But something was missing. I suppose I should have detected that already on the cover map. Criss-crossed with "Establishment," "Liberal," and "Postliberal" trunk highways and marked with an "Evangelical Interchange," there is not so much as a blue highway, bicycle path, or hiking trail for the ecumenical movement.

The authors themselves seem to assume the ecumenical movement as part of the lay of the land. They give hardly a hint, however, that those churches which have been switched off the mainline might find new life on the ecumenical way. It is an omission for ecumenists to reckon with, the more so since all four authors and the churches of which they write are, ecumenically speaking, fully accredited.

Moreover, the authors have company. the *Christian Century* identifies itself as "an ecumenical weekly." We may assume, therefore, that its readership is ecumenically oriented. My small informal survey suggests nevertheless that not many noticed the absence of the ecumenical movement as an agent for renewal.

Indeed, more than a few would have been surprised to see it delineated as a way out of the wilderness for the churches of the "mainline." Some argue that the ecumenical movement itself is at least partly to blame for the mainline's estrangement from the culture and thus partly responsible for their decline. Others argue that the ecumenical movement drains life from the churches, drawing off resources which are now badly needed within the churches themselves. Or that the ecumenical movement is having so much difficulty sustaining its own life, it can hardly have any to give away. Most add that these churches have a continuing ecumenical obligation even if it does make their lives difficult.

These are weighty arguments not to be dismissed, but to be met. To take the last first. True, the ecumenical movement is not a vast reservoir of resources for renewal. It never has been. It is not meant to be. It is more like an intricate system of conduits connecting the reservoirs (the churches), providing a means for their resources to flow among them, lowering the level in none while raising it in all—sharing in the manner of the five loaves and two fishes; sharing in love; sharing like the worshiping community which we shall shortly observe together.

Sometimes an active flow of resources among the churches does generate enough energy to create new resources which may be called "ecumenical," in an original sense. One example is the Lima

Liturgy, developed by Max Thurian of the Taize community as part of the work on Baptism, Eucharist and Ministry and used first by the World Council of Churches' Commission on Faith and Order at its 1982 meeting in Lima, Peru. Such "ecumenical" resources are relatively few in number and even they belong not to the movement, but to the church for which the movement is preparing the way. In the interim, what the ecumenical movement has to offer the churches is already largely within them. Released and received, their resources bring renewal.

The development and use of the Lima Liturgy suggests that one way these resources can be released and received is through worship. The churches are uniquely and distinctively themselves at worship. There one feels the heartbeat of tradition. Most members of the "mainline" long for a stronger pulse.

To meet that need for *renewal of worship*, the churches have mined their respective traditions; and have borrowed from other traditions and from the culture at large. Books of worship, hymnals, resource packets have rolled off the press, but renewal mostly eludes us.

The ecumenical search for renewal of worship follows a different way. It affirms much of what is in each of the traditions and critiques them as well while transcending them all. It creates new wine in new liturgies *and* new wine skins in new communities. It goes beyond borrowing rites; it shares spirituality.

It often happens something like this: A group of people from various traditions will come together to ask themselves: What does each of us wish this emerging community which we are, or which we represent, to offer to God? What forms will our offerings take? The substance of these worship offerings in many cases, but not in all, will be similar; the forms will usually be different.

As the sharing begins, so will the discoveries. In some cases, the *forms* of another tradition will be recognized as a richer way of sharing the *substance* of one's offering to God and will be accepted as a gift, such as the widely used *kyrie eleison* of the Russian Orthodox liturgy. At other points, the forms will complement one another as in the Lima Liturgy, when the Word of God is lifted up, first in the "Liturgy of Entrance," inspired by the Orthodox tradition, and then in the "Liturgy of the Word," inspired by the Reformation tradition.

Eventually, the sharing will take a form different from all the traditions yet embodying and transcending them all, of which, once again, the Lima Liturgy taken as a whole is an outstanding example and the worship in the tent at the Vancouver Assembly of the World Council of Churches an outstanding experience.

Often not only the forms of worship will be new, so will the substance. By means of other traditions, worshipers will find within themselves gifts from God they did not know and make those gifts part of their own offering in worship and in service.

It will be obvious that such renewal of worship is in an inseparable and reciprocal relationship with *renewal of community*—also much longed for in the mainline churches. The fundamental problem, I think, with the communities we know in our congregations is that they do not correlate with the communities we know in the world. In our daily meetings with people, most of us continually cross barriers of culture, race, and class. In many of our congregations, those barriers are barely visible, not because we have eradicated them but because they are outside the walls. For escapist religion, that would not be a problem. But ours is a faith to be lived in the world. Our alienation is compounded, therefore, by awareness that such closed communities contradict our Christian hope. No amount of cultivation within those confines can produce the desired experience of community. To anticipate the heavenly community we seek, the gates of our congregations, too, need to be open to the east, the west, the north, and the south.

All of us who have tried to create such open communities know how hard that is. It is difficult for congregations to cross cultural barriers. Yet, in almost every community in this country, there are congregations that would discover new life by uniting with congregations different from themselves. Perhaps the new Christian community, with the hearts of its members newly opened to one another, would also be far more open to the whole human community in that place and in the world.

Thus, the ecumenical movement could also help meet the mainline's need for *renewal of cultural engagement*. For example, ecumenical renewal of worship will sharpen the questioners' understanding of the cultural forms in which worship is expressed. Uniting two communities *across* cultural barriers will do the same— as opposed to uniting two communities of similar cultures or traditions, which may extend their lives but usually only further isolates them from the culture around them.

In a previous time of cultural establishment, skills of cultural analysis and engagement were not so necessary. The culture within the churches and that of larger community were connected. Their disconnection is in large part the occasion for the current crisis of the mainline. Skills, long disused and largely atrophied, need to be renewed. The dialogue of cultures within the churches is an excellent learning space for the dialogue of cultures between the churches and the world.

What shall we make then of the argument that the ecumenical movement is at least in part responsible for the decline of the mainline churches by contributing to their estrangement from the culture around them? First, to acknowledge the truth in that assertion. The ecumenical movement, by definition, transcends any particular culture, including our own, its globe-encircling power notwithstanding. Precisely because American culture is the most influential in the world, we who live within it urgently need the experience of cultural transcendence. We need it; we do not always like it. Some have disliked it enough to feel alienated from the churches that know their need. A few have left those churches for others more content in their acculturation.

That is the tip of the iceberg. There is far more substance to the argument that ecumenical dialogue with other cultures has helped those churches to know their own cultural captivity and to begin to open themselves to persons of other cultures, races, gender, and class. The fruit of that openness is evident everywhere, still mostly in small signs, but evident nonetheless. Leaders of the churches are aware that those small signs are the first steps of a journey which if now accelerated rapidly will free them from remaining forever frozen in the cultures of the past and enable them to become agents of cultural renewal.

Such openness is also important in the quest for *renewal of identity*, for which these denominations seem to be searching, mostly in the limited space of the few rooms in their own tradition, rather than in the whole household of God. "What does it mean to be (*insert your own denomination or tradition*)?" can never be a main question; it is always subsidiary to: "What does it mean to be Christian?"

The primary place to seek this essential Christian identity is, once again, in ecumenical worship. As we have seen, in ecumenical worship the various traditions are not negated; they are reintegrated into the Great Tradition, in which light, each of the traditions is made more rich, more beautiful. It is seen as one band, or a part of one band, in the full spectrum of the gospel and the church. Such an experience one cannot have without knowing oneself a member of the Church, One, Holy, Catholic and Apostolic, and that in a way not possible within the confines of any one tradition.

Such a new identity is an urgent need for our present situation. The old identities faded fast in post-World War II America. Mostly transplanted from a Europe that is no more, they will not suffice for an America that is no more.

The discovery of such an ecumenical identity can open the way to identification with the *Oikumene*, the whole inhabited earth, and thus to *renewal of mission*. Is there today any leader of these churches who would argue in terms of mission *to*? We are all in mission *with*—joined together, receiving as well as reaching. At least in theory. In practice, at least nationally and internationally, most mission is still conducted in denominational channels within which it is nearly impossible to find freedom from the destructive dependencies and counter-dependencies of traditional relationships—and this in spite of the pleas without ceasing from the "recipients" of such mission for a more ecumenical approach.

Why do the churches deny themselves these new life-giving identities related to the whole church and the whole world? Mostly because of the power of the old institutions in which the old identities are vested. Declining institutions they may be, but they are still strong enough to deflect the Spirit. Yet, since their strength is ebbing, they are anxious about giving it away—at least to those ecumenical institutions which seem to challenge them, as well as to promise them fulfillment in their common Christian identity.

The challenge is near at hand and easily seen. The promise of fulfillment requires a longer vision. Unhappily, the churches are mostly taking the shorter view. Some emphasize their ecclesial identities, thus retreating into their respective traditions and their accompanying cultures. Sometimes this is done in comparison with one another; more often in contrast with ecumenical institutions. (I do not refer here to the very different situations of the Orthodox and Roman Catholic churches, which lie outside the purview of this article.)

Even where that is not done explicitly, the spell of ecclesial enchantment is cast over the bureaucracies of the churches. They and their programs are presented as somehow more "churchly" (and therefore more authentic) than those of ecumenical bodies. It will not avail. The dwindling away of national denominational program bureaucracies is irreversible, a conclusion I reached not as an ecumenical executive, but long before as a denominational executive. I was not happy with that conclusion—not for the church I served nor for the nation and the world within which the national witness of the ecumenical community is of great importance. I took hope then in the promise of a meaningful future for national mission if it were done ecumenically. That hope I nourish still, but time is short. A generation of denominational survivalism has done little to stem the tide and has left stranded more than a few ecumenical programs.

To move beyond survival, the churches will need to arrest their growing tendency to see ecumenical program as a "duplication" of denominational program (and therefore dispensable). The churches can no longer afford the luxury, as they could in the 1950s, of doing ecumenical mission over and above their "own" program, as something outside of themselves. The future lies in reasserting the vision of ecumenical program as sign (however faint) and instrument (however feeble) of their common witness—which only they can make clear and strong.

Nor is this merely an obligation. The ecumenical movement is not first a duty to be discharged; it is a way of being. More than a new way of acting, the churches need a new way of thinking—a new way of seeing themselves, not only in relation to the world, but also in relation to the church. Only thus can they be set free from cultural captivity, ecclesial enchantment, institutional survivalism, confessional traditionalism and the other isms that bind them.

This new way to freedom may be unfamiliar; it is not foreign. It lies within the churches and may be glimpsed in that experience of worship described above in which the Spirit bears witness with the spirits of the worshipers, that they are members of the Church, One Holy Catholic and Apostolic. To ask the meaning of that witness is to seek the truth that will set us free. Surely we can find that truth in larger measure together than each apart.

We Christians confess that the renewal we seek is finally the gift of the Spirit, "the Lord and Giver of Life." This does not mean that renewal is out of our hands. It means rather that we need to open our hands, our hearts, our minds, and our church assemblies to the Spirit; that we need to discern the Spirit, to discover what the Spirit is saying to the churches.

To make such discernment of the Spirit the primary focus of our inquiry, would, I believe, fulfill still one more promise of the ecumenical movement, the *renewal of theology*. Searching always for the breakthroughs of God's future into the present, we would test them against past signs of the Spirit of God's future preserved within the traditions, finding our way forward in dialogue with our forebears, integrating the signs of God's future they have discerned with those given directly to us.

Such a methodology is already evident in the Council at Jerusalem reported in Acts 15. There we can see the limitations of custom and tradition giving way before the discernment of the Spirit's signs and wonders tested against the tradition until the council could, "with the whole church," declare "...it has seemed good to the Holy Spirit and to us...." Waiting in the wings at Jerusalem, were more than a few of the powers with which we wrestle still today, some of whose names have been called above. Even so, the Council at Jersualem followed the Spirit in a way that renewed and reunited the church in the first century. Following that way can do so again in the twenty-first.

III

For the Renewal
of the
Tradition

36

A Life-Embracing Liturgy

An article in the Reformed Journal, *April 1976*

By the mid-70s, the tidal wave of church growth ideology threatened to overtake the regional structures of the Reformed Church in America, and thus the denominations' church development program—and thus perhaps its future. In an effort to outrun the flood, my colleagues and I at the General Program Council launched a Reformed Church Growth Fund. The first order of business was to engage the ideologies spreading eastward from various institutes in California. Those studies and reflections deepened my already strong conviction about the centrality of the liturgy in the life of the church and gave new insights about the relationship of the church to the larger culture. Some of those convictions and insights found their way into the Reformed Church Growth Fund literature, but I wanted them to stand on their own as well. I decided to publish an article.

The *Reformed Journal* was my publisher of choice. While a pastor at the Reformed Church of Corinth, near Grand Rapids, Michigan (1959-1962), I had found The *Reformed Journal* so stimulating that I went to the Eerdman's Publishing Company and bought all the available back copies, over a span, I think, of some ten years. I never did get them all read before I needed their space for other books and journals, but it had been an important vehicle on my theological pilgrimage. I offered the article. They accepted it and published it under the title, "Worship in the Reformed Church in America." That title, I think, was theirs, not mine, but since I have lost the original, I've given it a new name for this volume drawn from the original text.

The theological pilgrimage goes on, and today I would write one key paragraph very differently (paragraph 10 beginning "To some extent..."). I would not say, "The Word of God renews the church," but rather the Spirit of God. According to the Word, to be sure, but in the power of the Spirit, who is "the Lord and Giver of Life." Already then I mostly thought that, but apparently not yet firmly enough to challenge the safety devices of Reformed scholasticism that have so long subjected the Spirit to the Word—especially to the Word written. That subjugation I believe to be the major impediment to the renewal of the tradition. In the years that followed, I engaged it ever more sharply, as we have already seen particularly in the immediately preceding chapter and will see more explicitly in those that follow, particularly chapter 50.

The life and ministry of Jesus are presented liturgically in the New Testament. Indeed, the true meaning of his coming can be understood only in the frame of reference of worship. For example, the meaning of the cross is fully evident only in terms of a priestly sacrifice. Jesus' ministry, in turn, becomes the pattern for the worship of the early church: the central event in the worship of the church takes the form of remembrance of the central event in the ministry of the Lord of the church.

The glory of the risen Christ is also presented liturgically in the New Testament. It seems that only the hymns and prayers and songs of worship are adequate to speak of his glory. And at last the life of the age to come is portrayed as free worship (Rev. 22:3-5) without restriction of space or time.

The New Testament thus speaks of worship in two spheres: the heavenly offering of Christ, which he celebrates in glory until the time of the world to come, and the earthly offering of Christ which he celebrated in his life, death, resurrection, and ascension.

The worship of the church takes place at the meeting point between these earthly and heavenly spheres. In J. J. von Allmen's words, Christian worship "is the moment of encounter...between the world to come and the present age...between the Lord...and his people...who give themselves to each other, receive each other, in the joy and liberty of communion."

The Lord and his people are truly present to one another in Christian worship. Neither in word nor sacrament is there any thought of merely informing people of past events; it is rather a matter of launching the worshipers on the "full flood tide of salvation." In Christian worship the Lord who stands beyond the boundaries of time and space is present with them, and we who are bound by time and space transcend them. "Christian worship is the most momentous, the most urgent, the most glorious action that can take place in human life," Karl Barth said.

All this is to say that worship is more important than we generally think it is. Its content and structure largely determine the function, and shape the form, of our devotion. We *become* the hymns we sing, the liturgies we follow, and the sermons we hear. There is a connection between the burden of guilt carried by countless members of my denomination, the Reformed Church in America, and that relentless reading of the law sabbath after sabbath with no prayer of confession or assurance of pardon. There is a connection between our dim and blurred vision of the kingdom of God and the regular round of dated hymns, escapist songs, and sentimental anthems. There is a connection between our inability to give a reason for the hope within us and the fact that Sunday after Sunday we do little more than listen to someone else speak of it.

The Reformed Church in America has, to be sure, made some progress on these problems. The widespread acceptance and use of a revised liturgy has helped to relieve some of the guilt; the publication of *The Hymnbook* and a burst of new and worthy Christian songs has brought the kingdom back into focus; and a resurgence of biblical study and expository preaching has strengthened our hope in Christ and given it voice.

But we have just begun. If worship is as important as the evidence of the New Testament, the Old Testament, and church history seem to indicate, then liturgical renewal must be one of our major concerns. Presently, that is not so. Most of us take the liturgy as a matter of course, following what we have received from the church of our youth, the denominational liturgy, and a scattering of other sources. There are a few who know several liturgical traditions and use them freely. There are a few who live within the hopes and fears of our contemporary communities and seek to meet them. There are a few who struggle to relate all of this to the renewal of the church and its liturgy. Our growth depends on the enlistment of more of us in that struggle.

Yet many of us are suspicious of liturgical renewal. To some, it seems to be mere formalism; to others, a passing fad. Unfortunately, these impressions are often accurate, for the movement of liturgical renewal is beset with false starts and loss of direction—among them introducing contemporary language as the chief source of liturgical renewal, conceiving of liturgical renewal as a recapture of the old traditions, secularizing the liturgy, and the like.

To some extent we can protect ourselves against these errors by remembering that the liturgy does not renew the church. It is the liturgy itself which must be renewed. The Word of God renews the church. There can be no substitute for what the Heidelberg Catechism calls "the lively preaching of His Word" (Question 98). But the liturgy gives voice to that renewed life, expresses it concretely in a congregation, and nourishes it. When the people hear the Word of God, the idols must be destroyed, the altars of Baal broken down, and the Psalms set to music, lest what begins as renewal degenerate into legalism, rationalism, pietism, activism, or some other "ism." As the liturgy shapes the community so the community shapes the liturgy, for the liturgy is "of the people." The liturgy and the life of the community stand in a reciprocal relationship. They live together or die together.

If we accept this reciprocal relationship of life and liturgy as the fundamental principle of liturgical renewal, then it follows that liturgical renewal is the task of each Christian community. There can be no imposed uniformity. Services of worship will flow from the lives of congregations, will be created in their culture. The traditional approach of the Reformed church to liturgical forms offers generous opportunity for such personalized worship, for we require the use of prescribed forms only for the sacraments.

However, it must also be noted that although the Reformed church has only a limited requirement for prescribed forms, it publishes other forms and resources for the official guidance of its congregations. These materials draw heavily on the liturgical tradition of other Christian communities—a practice which also follows from our fundamental principle of the reciprocal relationship of life and liturgy, for the life which creates the liturgy is the life of the Holy Catholic Church. The words in which that life has found expression across the centuries are full of deep insights and long visions which should be used to nurture, test, and discipline our worship. Those who were pilgrims before us also sought the age to come and met it again and again in their moments of worship. Their records of these meetings can enrich ours.

The reciprocal relationship of life and liturgy calls for the liturgy to relate to all of life. The liturgy is not to be reduced to the practice of a sacred rite. Baptism—to take one example—is not to be regarded merely as a cultic ceremony of initiation into the sacred fellowship; it is a celebration of life, of the ultimate end of life as we stand at its very beginning. It declares that the life which has just begun can be fulfilled by living in fellowship with God in his church.

Something like the same quality of meaning is celebrated in the marriage service and the funeral service. Regrettably, these latter two services are now celebrated apart from the congregation. We are the poorer for it. Even though it may be impossible to reincorporate them into the life of the congregation, the fact of their happening should somehow be incorporated into the liturgy; a notice in the weekly bulletin or parish paper will hardly do.

So the liturgy needs to be expanded to embrace life—all of life. Christian worship is more than a cultic ceremony. Passing through the poverty line, either way, or unemployment and re-employment are surely worthy of incorporation in a Calvinist liturgy. Drug addiction, alcoholism, illness, and divorce should be dealt with in the liturgy, as should health, recreation, achievement, and reconciliation. They are not mere addenda but are integral parts of the expression of our common life between the times of Christ's coming and coming again.

This life-embracing liturgy is to take place in the context of mission, for worship and mission cannot exist apart from each other. Mission without worship becomes harsh, aggressive, activistic; it is cut off from its divine source and loses its sense of the mission of Christ and of his power and authority in which the mission is carried out. Worship without mission ends in a cultic rite and a self-centered society, a religious club held together by social, economic, and psychological ties, caring only for itself.

The central acts of Christian worship, the sacraments, can be fully understood only in the context of mission. Baptism is a sign of God's covenant with us, and the covenant is an election to service, to mission. In baptism "we are called to new obedience," "engaged to confess the faith of Christ crucified and to be his faithful servants unto our life's end." In the Lord's Supper, "in the joy of his resurrection and in expectation of his coming again" (that is, in the context of Christ's mission), "we offer...ourselves as holy and living sacrifices" (RCA liturgy). Our sacrifice, like Christ's, is for the world.

From time to time this link between worship and mission is forged in public view in an unforgettable way. Who can forget the power of Martin Luther King's speech on the steps of the Lincoln Memorial when he invoked the old spiritual, "Lord, I'm free, free at last"? That act of Christian worship charged the whole event with power and authority. It pushed back the horizon so that the event grew larger than a struggle for civil rights in the USA in the 1960s, larger than life itself, as the bonds of time and space were broken and we stood together before God. That is the function of the liturgy—to provide an experience of the ultimate meaning of life.

And that is the function of the Christian community in the world—not alone its leaders. Its leaders are charged to equip and prepare and lead the community, but not to act on behalf of the community. It is the whole church, not only the clergy, who live on behalf of the world.

Our ability to be effective in mission is again inextricably linked with the renewal of the liturgy. J. G. Davies speaks to the point:

A laity which is passive in relation to liturgical revision and passive in the forms of worship in which they are expected to engage will inevitably remain passive in the world. Whatever they fail to be in worship, they will fail to be in mission because of the unity of the two. Active participation in the mission of God is only possible when there is active participation in the celebration of the liturgy.

[Worship] must be of such a kind that it opens to man a future which he is expected to create and, at the same time, assists him to find his present responsibility in the world as the crucial medium of God's presence (*Worship and Mission*, pp. 147ff.).

And, of course, worship must be intelligible to the outsider (1 Cor. 14:16ff.), not only to the initiate. The language used must communicate. But it is more than a matter of language. We are in the midst of a communication revolution. The fundamental question today is not "what did he say?" but "what happened?" So the revolution is nothing to fear. It can help us by reinforcing the discovery that Christian worship is essentially a happening anyway. It is the work of the people, not just the word of the preacher. Worship has to do with meaning experienced, not just preached....

In any event, a commitment to liturgical renewal demands no less of us than that we all offer ourselves in the liturgy. To do that perhaps every congregation should have at least one skilled liturgist. We have long held that every congregation should have at least one skilled preacher—the liturgy deserves equal attention. Most young pastors learn soon enough that they must learn to preach if they are to survive. We all need now to learn that the congregation must learn to do the liturgy if it is to live—much more, grow.

37
An Ecumenical Consultation

A Church Herald *column, March 7, 1980*

To begin with a confession, I didn't really want to have this consultation. Already overworked, I knew that planning it would make more work, much more work, and the follow-up more still. And then there was the risk of ecumenical retreat or of heading off in some direction I could not in good conscience follow, much less lead. But I went along and the consultation helped along. Ten years later, the points made in this column seem at least predictive—and perhaps here and there even prophetic.

A meeting of the steering committee at the ecumenical consultation. L to R: Glenn Bruggers, secretary for Asia; Laura Mol, consultation coordinator; John Hiemstra, executive secretary, Particular Synod of New York; Robert Bast, moderator of the General Program Council; Arie Brouwer; Charles Wissink, moderator of the Commission on Christian Unity and of the consultation; Donald Bruggink, professor of historical theology at Western Theological Seminary.

The Reformed Church in America entered the 1970s as a deeply divided denomination. Ironically, most of our divisions were related to differences of opinion about Christian unity. We nearly tore ourselves apart at the synod of 1969 over a defeated plan of union with the Presbyterian Church in the United States, a proposal to enter the Consultation on Church Union, and an evaluation of our relationship with the National Council of Churches. Little wonder that we have been hesitant to set out again on the ecumenical journey.

The vanguard of the ecumenical movement, the councils of churches, have themselves been badly shaken. Tossed about by tumultuous seas of social change—and a few winds of doctrine—and often under hostile fire, they have seemed unable to set their sails before the stirrings of the Spirit. When they have, the fleet has generally refused to follow.

The World Council of Churches had a particularly difficult passage during the late '70s in the storm over its grant to the Patriotic Front of Zimbabwe, but the issues have been there throughout the decade. The poor in Latin America, Asia, and Africa have called out again and again for us to demonstrate our unity with them in their suffering. Standing with them (particularly in South Africa) has often meant standing against others who also name the name of Christ and to whom we have been bound by familiar ties of color and culture. Amid all this confusion and controversy, pessimists have not lacked opportunities to bemoan unity as a hopeless quest.

Although the body is divided, Christ still wills "that they may all be one; even as thou, Father, art in me, and I in thee...that the world may believe that thou hast sent me" (John 17:21). Unity in the 1980s will probably be even more difficult than was unity in the 1970s.

The denomination's Committee on Christian Unity has therefore planned an ecumenical consultation....for April 20-24, 1980. The consultation will bring together some 60 people: members of the Committee on Christian Unity, General Synod officers, seminary professors, denominational staff, particular synod executives, missionaries, leaders of other churches, representatives of ecumenical agencies with which we are affiliated, and representatives of agencies with which we are not officially affiliated such as the Lausanne Committee on World Evangelization and the National Association of Evangelicals. This ecumenical consultation will be an opportunity to take our bearings and to adjust our course in the light of the shining hope of Christian unity.

A successful voyage through the 1980s will depend largely on our ability to meet three essential needs. First, we need a *common commitment* to the ecumenical vision of unity in the church and in the world. The urgency of such an ecumenical commitment is surely second to none. Prime Minister Margaret Thatcher of England has called the 1980s the "dangerous decade." Energy depletion, economic collapse, international disorder, and nuclear war are a few forms of the apocalypse which now threaten to set the people of the world against themselves. Our calling in Christ is to stand together against all these terrors so that the unity of the church may be a witness to the unity of humankind, which we perceive now only with the eyes of faith.

Such a common commitment does not mean automatic agreement with the positions and pronouncements of the councils or of other denominations or even of our own. On the contrary, a common commitment would enable the most vigorous disagreement and debate among us, because we would be free from the threat of separation. Every happily married couple knows that's the best way to settle differences!

Next we need a *community of interest*, a group of people who have covenanted together to foster unity. Such communities of interest have played important parts across the centuries in many churches, including our own. The Society of Inquiry founded at New Brunswick Seminary early in the 19th century by the "father of the Reformed church," John Henry Livingston, was an important, nearly indispensable, influence in fostering an interest in mission within the Reformed Church in America. Why could not the ecumenical movement, which is after all a child of the missionary movement, be fostered in the same way?

Third, we need a *general involvement* in the movement toward unity. The Committee on Christian Unity reported to the General Synod of 1979 its intention to emphasize local unity. This emphasis, affirmed by the General Synod, is heard from many quarters today and signals a growing awareness that all the great issues of our global village must be lived out locally. One objective of the Ecumenical Consultation is to lead the way toward such a general involvement of our members in the ecumenical movement. Could there be a better way for us to live out that ancient motto of the Reformed church emblazoned on our denominational emblem, "Eendracht Maakt Macht" (In Unity is Strength)?

38

A Denominational Priority

A Church Herald *column, April 4, 1980*

Establishing this priority was a long hard struggle: Enabling people to think about concepts and policies before actions and programs; giving visibility to all major aspects of denominational programs; including the outreach of world mission without eclipsing our need to receive. Finally, we reached a consensus—and it lasted through most of the decade. It was the center piece of my effort to build ecumenical values into denominational life.

Crossing Cultural Barriers in Christ: Reaching and Receiving

Cultural Barriers and Church Growth

For almost four years now, the General Synod Executive Committee has been scanning the horizon in order to identify the single most significant problem or opportunity on which we should focus our attention and energy during the 1980s. During most of this four-year scanning period, the Reformed church has been deeply involved in church growth....Both new starts and examinations of established congregations have revealed that in almost every case the most difficult obstacles to growth have been barriers between congregational culture and community culture.

In some cases, particularly in the cities, these cultural barriers were highly visible: great disparity in income, contrasts in color, differences in language. In other cases, particularly in the suburbs, the cultural barriers were more subtle. The new people in the community might look and sound much the same as the traditional residents. The newcomers might even flock to the new churches in the community. But they could not be attracted to the established churches—at least not in significant numbers.

In case after case, church-growth examiners discovered that the very features which the members of the established churches treasured (their hymns, their style of worship, their sense of community, their organizations and activities), the things that made them "feel at home," that is, their *congregational culture*—these very things were barriers to the new people in the community. Ask any visitor!

In our mobile society, the pattern has become relentless: gradually the increasing number of new people changes the community culture; the congregation becomes a cultural island, shrinks, and dies with great loss of members, of meaning, and of resources for ministry. Crossing cultural barriers between congregations and communities is an urgent priority. Our life depends upon it.

Cultural Barriers and World Mission

Cultural barriers also loom large on the world mission horizon. During the three decades since World War II, there has been immense growth in cultural awareness and in cultural affirmation in those parts of the world to which missionaries have traditionally been sent. Colonial structures have been toppled, new nations created, histories rediscovered, and traditions reasserted. Missionary moratoriums have been declared—not only by governments but by churches which had received missionaries for generations....

Maintaining and increasing mission relationships across these barriers has demanded greater cultural sensitivity from the traditional sending churches like our own. We have been confronted with dozens of ways in which we have unconsciously exported our culture in the form of hospitals, schools, church buildings, technology, music, and clothing styles even while we have shared the Christ. We have also been made aware of how these cultural exports have sometimes become barriers between new

Christians and their own cultures, walling off the church and making it difficult for our brothers and sisters to evangelize within their own countries and cultures.

Bishop Sundar Clarke of the Madras Diocese, Church of South India, complains in his 1979 Christmas letter that the church is seen as "the most unpatriotic community in our country. We are still so pro-British and so un-Indian"—and this 32 years after independence from both church and nation!

Overwhelmed by these problems, some people have concluded that we should no longer engage in world mission. The gospel, however, is for the whole world—for every culture; therefore, we must instead face the harder task of freeing the church, its mission, and the gospel itself from cultural offense. We must reach across the barriers between our culture and another culture. At the same time, we must open ourselves and our churches to our brothers and sisters on the other side of those barriers so that we may learn and grow from the work of Christ among them. This twin task is our calling.

...the primary obstacle in the way of the church's world mission is remarkably similar to the primary obstacle in the way of the church's local mission. In both cases we are faced with cultural barriers. In both cases we must learn how to provide for two-way traffic across the cultural barriers.

Cultural Barriers and World Peace

What is true for sharing the gospel and opening the church is also true for healing the nations. During the sixth week of the captivity of American hostages in Iran, the New York *Times* headlined one of its stories "Impasse in Iran: A Gap Between Two Cultures." The article reported some of the immense cultural differences apparent in the political systems, moral values, and personal styles of the two countries and their leaders. These differences complicated the Iranian crisis beyond words because they are differences which are neither adequately understood nor appreciated.

So, here we are again—divided by cultural barriers. What has confronted us dramatically in the Iranian crisis is an everyday fact of life in our misunderstandings with many African and Asian and Latin American countries. The security and well-being of our world in the 1980s is directly related to our ability to cross such cultural barriers. Unless we can cross these barriers, we will experience increasing misunderstanding, fear, and anger....

Cultural Barriers and the Bible

Since this crossing of cultural barriers appears to be an urgent need in our local congregations, our denomination, the world church, and the world itself, it would seem almost to force itself upon us as a denominational priority. Before we draw such a conclusion, however, we need to examine this proposed priority to see if it is worthy in the light of scripture. We need to test this presentation of our calling in Christ and to see if it would be a faithful pursuit of our pilgrimage.

Human suffering as a result of cultural barriers is one of the oldest and most important themes of the Bible. In fact, the introduction of these cultural barriers is portrayed in the famous story of the Tower of Babel (Gen. 11:1-9) as the culmination of God's historical judgment on human sin and as a direct result of human alienation from God (Gen. 3).

The New Testament church struggled with the relationship of Christ and culture and the church from its earliest days. In Galatians, Paul was writing to churches in danger of succumbing to those who insisted on the old ways and resisted any cultural changes to accommodate the newcomers. He told them that "neither circumcision counts for anything, nor uncircumcision, but a new creation" (Gal. 6:15). In Corinthians, dealing with a church which had very nearly capitulated to the surrounding culture, he asked, "Has not God made foolish the wisdom of the world?" (1 Cor.1:20).

The whole matter came to a head in the Jerusalem council reported in Acts 15. The apostles and elders in that council decided that the old cultural barriers encoded in the law of Moses had to give way—but some enduring values had to be respected! The apostle Paul summed it up theologically in Ephesians by declaring that God in Christ "has broken down the dividing wall of hostility" and created "one body through the cross." The Gentiles are "no longer strangers" but "fellow citizens...and members of the household of God." At the center of this letter (Eph. 2:11-21) Paul portrays, in bold and sweeping strokes, a colossal jumble of broken barriers and destroyed divisions, all abolished in Christ.

All of these books, but especially Ephesians, show us that crossing cultural barriers involves not only what we do but even more who we are. Our first need is not for new programs but for renewed persons. As renewed persons, we will find the grace and strength to renew the corporate personalities of our congregations and our denominations so that we and they will be transparently open to persons of other cultures. We need nothing less than the personal transformation—the new creation—available to us all in Christ.

Naming a Priority

For some time now we have been searching for a way to express the heart of all these complicated interactions in a simple phrase. It's no easier than naming a baby! Denominational staff, executives of particular synods and denominational agencies and institutions, moderators of General Synod commissions, and the pastors and people of nearly 30 pilot churches have been among those participating in the search.

Most of the discussions concerning the name have been about whether the priority should be called *cross*-cultural mission or *inter*-cultural mission. A member of the Reformed Church of Willow Grove, Pennsylvania, suggested that "the vagueness and confusion lies in the word 'mission' which means only *task*. This must be defined according to who we are relating to: our next door neighbor, inner-city blacks,...Muslims, the Chinese,...etc." In other words, we had been discussing the first name when the problem was the last name!

In response to that insight, it is now proposed that...the urgency of outreach and the necessity of two-way traffic across the barriers both be expressed in the priority "Crossing Cultural Barriers in Christ: Reaching and Receiving."...Faithfulness to such a priority would:

Call us to share the gospel with people of every culture in the context of those cultures.

Lead us to open our congregations to people of different cultures in our communities and around the world.

Inspire us to work for the healing of the nations....

39

An Affirmation of Christian Unity

A statement by the General Synod of the Reformed Church in America, June 8-12, 1981

The ecumenical consultation described above in chapter 37 was an opportunity to build a broader, firmer base for our ecumenical commitment than that provided in the existing policy statement, "The Unity We Seek to Manifest," approved by the General Synod in 1966. I drafted, the Committee on Christian Unity reviewed and edited, and in 1981 the General Synod approved (*Minutes of the General Synod*, p.146).

In May of 1988, I adapted the affirmation for an ecumenical service of worship incorporating the understanding of God as mother as well as removing other sexist language, recognizing the political brokenness of the human community and casting it in an eschatological order (see chapter 33), as well as making a few other less significant changes. It is my adapted version that appears here.

An Affirmation of Christian Unity

L. We believe
P. that there is one Lord, one faith, one baptism,
    one God, Father and Mother of us all,

who is above all and through all and in all.

L. We remember
P.　that this one God did make from one family
　　all the peoples of the human race
　　now broken and scattered in many nations.

L. We confess
P.　that our sin has separated us from God,
　　from the earth and all living things,
　　from one another, and from ourselves.

L. We give thanks
P.　that God in Christ, who is our peace, has
　　　　broken down the dividing walls of hostility,
　　　　created one new humanity in place of many,
　　　　reconciled us all to God in one body, through the cross,
　　　　given us all access in one Spirit to God.

Unison: BLESSED BE THE NAME OF GOD FOR EVER AND
　　　　EVER!

L. We affirm
P.　that this mystery of reconciliation,
　　　　fixed in the eternal purpose of God,
　　　　realized in Jesus Christ, and
　　　　guaranteed by the Holy Spirit,
　　is being made known through the church.

L. We rejoice
P.　that we are members of this body,
　　　　gifted by Christ,
　　　　gathered in love,
　　　　growing in peace,
　　for the sake of the world.

L. We confess
P.　that we have not lived at peace among ourselves;
　　that we have separated ourselves from other Christians;
　　that our pride and fear and indifference have hindered the
　　　　search for unity.

L. We trust
P. that the church, in spite of its visible brokenness,
    is one in the Spirit;
    that the church is foretaste, sign, and instrument of a renewed
      human community;
    that God is working in all creation toward a new heaven and a
      new earth.

Unison: WE REJOICE IN THE GIFT OF UNITY, ALREADY
        REALIZED IN JESUS CHRIST.
        WE BELIEVE THE PROMISE OF UNITY, TO BE
        FULFILLED IN THE NEW CREATION.
        WE ACCEPT THE TASK OF UNITY, NOW BEING
        MADE VISIBLE IN THE CHURCH.

L. We therefore promise one another
P. to demonstrate our unity in Christ by
        maintaining the bonds of peace;
        speaking the truth in love;
        bearing one another's burdens.

L. We therefore pledge ourselves as a body
P. to seek the unity of the church through
        communing with other Christians in worship and in work;
        being with other Christians in councils of churches;
        uniting with other Christians in faith and order.

L. We therefore commit ourselves with all Christians
P. to serve the unity of the world by
        proclaiming the gospel of peace and reconciliation;
        sharing the earth's goods with the poor and hungry;
        seeking justice within and among the nations.

Unison: UNTIL THE UNITY WHICH GOD NOW SEES
        MAY BE CLEARLY VISIBLE TO ALL,
        SO THAT THE WORLD MAY KNOW THAT CHRIST
        WAS SENT
        TO DEMONSTRATE THE PERFECT AND
        EVERLASTING LOVE OF GOD.

40
Geneva, John Calvin, and the World Council of Churches

A Church Herald *column, October 31, 1980*

Membership in the WCC had been a touch and go business at the General Synod of 1979, as often before. I wanted to shore it up—particularly among the most Calvinist contingent of the RCA. Reporting on my second meeting of the Central Committee, and my first in Geneva, I drew therefore on my own mystical connection with the Reformer—most strongly felt on my first visit in 1968, but in later visits as well. All that seemed to me just right for a Reformation day column.

The presence of John Calvin was almost physical on my first visit to Geneva, Switzerland, in 1968. I vividly recall my afternoon wanderings through the streets of the old city. My imagination played over the walls and buildings, wondering what they were like in the sixteenth century when the father of the Reformed church preached and prayed and argued and berated the citizens of Geneva into a living faith and the reformation of the church.

I returned to the old city the next morning, Sunday, to worship in the cathedral where Calvin and his successor Beza had preached. Since the service was in French (which I did not understand), I went next to worship with the Scottish Presbyterian church in "The Calvin Auditorium." This simple, even austere, building only a few hundred feet from the cathedral was the scene of Calvin's weekday lectures. On Sundays it was the place of worship for the English-speaking refugees whom John Knox, the Scottish Reformer, served as pastor.

I worshiped there again this summer while in Geneva for a meeting of the World Council of Churches' Central Committee. (The Central Committee is the continuing governing body of the World Council and is made up of 135 members from all over the world.) During the nine-day meeting in Geneva, I found myself reflecting now and then on the relationship between the spirit of John Calvin and the work of the World Council.

Several times during the meeting there were vigorous complaints that the World Council was unduly Reformed in its membership, theology, and general outlook. Such complaints are often heard, and the World Council tries to respond to them by providing for the full participation of other traditions. But the truth is that it (like the National Council of Churches in the United States) *is* largely shaped by the Reformed tradition.

Every student of Calvin knows that he mourned the divisions of the church and worked for its unity. The intensity of Calvin's longing is well expressed in his letter to Archbishop Cranmer of the Church of England in which he says that he would gladly "cross ten seas" in order to foster the unity of the church. His sons and daughters have tried to be faithful to his heritage by working to heal the brokenness of Christ's body. Our own Reformed church missionaries have often been in the vanguard of that movement, helping to give birth to councils of churches and united churches in many lands.

Concern for unity in the World Council extends through and beyond the unity of the church to the unity of humankind. This vision of God's plan for the unity of the whole world (Eph. 1:9-10) is at once the beginning and the end of the World Council's commitment to programs of justice, freedom, and peace. In this also the World Council is faithful to the teaching of Calvin, who insisted upon justice as the basis for a unified society in the city of Geneva.

The Reformed character of the World Council of Churches is due in part to the life and work of a famous son of the Dutch Reformed church, W.A. Visser't Hooft. This ecumenical pioneer was general secretary of the World Council from before its founding in 1948 until his retirement in 1966. The celebration of his eightieth birthday during the Central Committee meeting provided a festive moment and an occasion for him once again to trumpet the call to Christian unity:

According to the New Testament, unity belongs to the nature of the church. And not merely some Platonic unity, but the unity which is visible and tangible enough to convince men that these united Christians know about the secret of reconciliation and have overcome the separation and estrangement in the life of humanity.

In protest against those who have said that the church's history was a "hodgepodge of error and violence," Visser't Hooft sided with Calvin in claiming that "church history was a story of resurrections." This grand old man then went on to remind us that:

As men and women of the ecumenical movement we have special reason to speak with gratitude about the churches. They have to a considerable extent responded to the call to come out of their isolation, to enter into dialogue, to assist each other, to take common action in meeting human need, to speak out together against oppression and injustice. It is in our time that many names have been added to the names representing the great cloud of witnesses, of churchmen and churchwomen who made every possible sacrifice for the sake of the faith. I count it a very great privilege that I have been allowed to share in the life of such a company. I know that many of you have the same feeling.

Yes, I do. And I could not help but feel that Calvin, who himself "made every possible sacrifice for the sake of the faith," would have been glad to see that his sons and daughters were part of such a company.

41

Communication in Communion

A presentation to the NCC's News and Information Committee, New York, NY, February 4, 1981.

My policy as a denominational executive was to interpret to family, friends, and the whole church what I was doing and the directions in which I was leading. I wanted them all to know and, ideally, to understand. Indeed, the *Church Herald* column, where several pieces in this volume first appeared, was initiated precisely for that purpose. I wanted to be in direct communication with the members of the denomination.

Through most of my fifteen years on the denominational staff, it was the councils of churches that were most likely to be misunderstood—or understood and disagreed with! I have long believed that most (not all, but most) of that misunderstanding and disagreement would disappear if the information available to the councils when they made their decisions was available to all. I believed that because I had found it true myself. Because of their unique access to movements within the churches as well as to the churches' institutional leadership and because of the trust developed by the long history of the council's advocacy for the poor and oppressed, the councils often received information not available to the general public. Decisions made on the basis of such information would naturally seem to be against the facts—the generally known facts that is. So I worked at spreading the lesser known facts, explaining the reasons and harnessing the institutions I headed for the same purpose.

It seems that my commitment to communication was generally thought to be somewhat higher than that of other persons in similar positions in other churches. That at least was the reason offered by Warren Day, assistant general secretary for news and information of the NCC, when sometime late in 1980 he visited my office to invite me to participate in a panel on the role of church journalists. The other two panelists were Kenneth Briggs, then religion editor of the New York *Times* and James Wall, editor of the *Christian Century*. Each of us were to speak from our distinctive perspectives for an audience of church journalists, most of whom worked for the NCC's member communions and with whom we would enter into discussion.

I accepted gladly. Almost since beginning my work as general secretary of the RCA three years earlier, I had been engaged in an ongoing, mostly low-level conflict with the editor of the *Church Herald*. This invitation seemed to be an opportunity first to think through and articulate carefully and systematically my own views of that relationship. Discussing those views with the broad spectrum of church communicators, I thought, would further help me grasp that point of view free from the confines and conflicts and constraints of the structures within which the editor of the *Church Herald* and I were necessarily bound. And there was always the chance that I might discover a few alternative views as well.

The presentation was well received and the discussion great fun. I later distributed my statement in writing to the General Synod Executive Committee as background for our continuing discussion of communication issues. Abbreviated and modified, the statement also appeared as a column in the *Church Herald* for March 20, 1981.

The title of the presentation reflects a proposal then before the NCC to declare itself "a *communion* of Christian communions." A few months later, the council's Governing Board scaled that back to "community of communions." A few years later, the council was to confess that even that was overreaching.

Rereading this presentation ten years later, I am struck by the warning about the loss of denominational significance in the paragraph describing the first function of nurturing and training. Denominational publications are in far deeper trouble now than they were then—as are the denominations themselves. The future, it seems, cannot be other than ecumenical if it is not to be sectarian.

The task assigned to me is to look at a church journalist from the perspective of a denominational chief executive. I think I can serve you best by speaking concretely out of my personal and professional experience, opinions, and practice. That approach also gives me an opportunity to test those opinions and practices with an informed and tough-minded audience outside of our denominational system.

For various reasons, I have from time to time been asked to list my most satisfying work experiences. Editing a college newspaper always appears on that list. I loved it—choosing, writing, and editing the stories; composing the editorials; doing the paste-ups; and seeing it through the press. There was even a certain exhilaration in being summoned to the president's office when he did not approve of my headlines or cartoons or editorial opinions!

At seminary, I found there was not a student paper, so I started one with the mildly provocative name of "The Ventilator." The administration was again attentive, and an occasional rumor suggested that our publication sometimes caught the angry attention of our denominational offices at "475."

For most of the twenty years since, I have been a regular contributor to our denominational publication, the *Church Herald*—

for some time as a contributing editor and for the past year as a monthly columnist.

As for my exposure to the public media: WQXR wakes me in the morning, but after that it's mostly print. the New York *Times* has sustained me through thirteen years of carpooling. I receive and read dozens of magazines and journals—to say nothing of a complete subscription to World Council publications. I have been glued to "Masterpiece Theater" for all of its ten years and see a few other things on Channel 13, which is one of my long-term preferred charities. I watch very little other television, although over the holidays my college kids did stir my interest in "M*A*S*H." This lack of television exposure I freely confess as a limitation—but I do read about television!

In the days before I joined the Reformed church's national staff, I had tried, with as little success as others before me, to begin an independent journal of opinion in the Reformed church. As a denominational staff member, I have helped to start one newsletter and three journals, all but one of which are still going strong.

From the beginning of my tour as a denominational executive, I have insisted that our communications officer be a part of our planning and policy staff. I have involved myself deeply in the work of the department, have regularly increased the communication budget far beyond other increases (and sometimes in the face of decreases elsewhere), and have at least tried to be a fountain of information in an effort to withstand the desertification of the bureaucracy.

Why? Because I am convinced that today more than ever the quality of our community life is dependent on the quality of our communication. (I doubt if I have to prove that to you, but I thought you should know that you don't have to prove it to me!) Perhaps we can agree that common roots, ethnic identity, institutional affection, distinctive confessions, dominant leaders, judicatorial authority, and whatever other powers there be or have been will no longer suffice. Communication is at the center.

Little wonder then that the church journalist's passion, sense of meaning, and experience of vitality should be closely linked with the quality of life in the communion served. And little wonder that there should be conflict between the communication department and the general secretariat; they are both at the center of the church's life.

Yet such conflict, at least constructive conflict, can contribute significantly to the well-being of both executives and

communicators and of the church at large. Bureaucracies are
always in danger of serving themselves: their people, their
programs, their policies, their power. It would seem that journalists
run similar risks: increasing circulation, telling and selling a story,
earning a reputation, maintaining their independence. (You know
your temptations better than I.) These two self-centered tendencies
can be offset by structured conflict.

The effective enlistment of the church's members in serving the
world, in fact, requires the close cooperation—and thus the
conflict—of church executives and church journalists. If such
cooperation is to be meaningful, it must begin at the beginning—
when and where policies are conceived and developed—not only as
they are implemented and surely not after the fact. John Bluck puts
it precisely in his essay, "Beyond Neutrality":

> ...media strategy must be towards informing, educating, and
> equipping the thousands to do the job, preparing them
> beforehand with news and resources, listening to their responses
> and *if necessary delaying or altering Council actions* according
> to whether those actions can be adequately interpreted and
> understood by the network of communicators. (Emphasis mine)

Such participation of the communications staff rests on the
assumption that the particular gifts of communicators include seeing
with the eyes, and speaking with the voice, of the people. Of course,
that implies a more fundamental assumption; namely that policy
and program cannot be developed apart from the people. The
irrelevance of many of our policies and pronouncements is, I think,
directly due to their being formulated apart from the people and in
an alien tongue never adequately translated. Participation of
communicators could help correct that.

Participation in the planning and policy councils of the
denomination, of course, works two ways. Policy and programs are
influenced, but so are publications. Yes, there are risks involved in
such participation. Journalists may feel less independent of the
bureaucracy and executives may feel restrained by public opinion—
and both may feel somewhat less prophetic and righteous! To borrow
John Bluck's words again, "...this personally engaged, relationship-
based style of communication is enormously demanding on its
practitioners. [It is] much easier to retreat behind the defence of
objectivity and the claim to be above personal interest or
institutional bias." However easier such presumed objectivity may

be, I am convinced that the community will benefit from cooperation and the structured conflict that goes with it.

In all this, I assume that a church journalist is not merely a journalist working for the church but rather a journalist committed to the service of the church in its service to the world. I look for the fulfillment of that vocation through at least six different functions.

First—nurture and training. The formal educational programs of most congregations rarely determine the piety of their parishioners. Many other influences play a part—among them the hymnbook, religious radio, the electronic church, and the religious journal. Independent journals seem to have taken over most of the print market. Church journalists need somehow to recapture it, or at least to play a larger part in the lives of our members, if the formal communities of faith we call communions are not to lose their significance. For all but a few of the giant denominations which can effectively use the electronic media, church journals are our only effective way of communicating directly and regularly with our membership on matters of current interest.

A second function, and one which may be of particular interest to this committee, is reporting the news and information. I am convinced that the opinion gap between "475" and the people in our churches is due in large part to the personal relationships we professionals are privileged to develop across cultural barriers and to the differences in the news and information we receive through such relationships. Information available to church executives and church journalists through private networks is, of course, often difficult to publish. Even when these obstacles can be overcome, our limited means are easily overwhelmed by the secular media which usually relies on more conventional sources of information.

These external difficulties are compounded by internal obstructions. Yes, there is a tendency for church executives to cover their tracks and tell only the good news; and, yes, it is appropriate for journalists to dig out the facts and tell the whole story—if it serves the common good, "the integrity and the life, validity, the health of the body of Christ" in the words of *Sojourners*. Our hope for open channels lies in church journalists keeping that commitment to the community clear and consistent and in church executives accepting church journalists as partners in mission; in church journalists cultivating a continuing sensitivity not only to the media's capacity to wound, but also to the difficulty of healing the wounds; and in church executives trusting church journalists to get the story straight and daring to believe that the people will accept bad news—it's cover-ups they don't like—and that there is, therefore, value in church executives telling the bad news themselves. Only by telling both the good news and the bad news can we together preserve the distinction between news and propaganda and keep the community credible.

A prerequisite of such a partnership in mission is freedom from fear of cooperation either in the name of program integrity or freedom of the press. The partnership itself requires that we protect, preserve, and seek these freedoms in community—a community regularly strained and strengthened by our common effort.

Third—discussion and development of policy. No organization, and certainly not the people of God, should depend entirely on its formal leadership. The participation of the people is essential. No one is in a better position to elicit ideas and stimulate discussion than church journalists through their regular contact with the people of the church.

Fourth—interpretation and advocacy. Official church journals must not be limited to the expression of official views. Such limitations are damaging to both the journal and the church. Official denominational publications may, however, be required to insure that official policy and program is fairly reported, interpreted, and advocated. They may also ordinarily be expected—but not required—themselves to represent denominational policy while at the same time providing for and actively seeking a faithful, free, and open expression of dissenting opinions. One should, as Dennis Shoemaker has argued, be able to find the best discussions—pro and con—about denominational issues in the pages of the official denominational magazine. No mean task that, but essential for the well-being of the community.

Review and criticism is a fifth function. Denominational policies are, of course, not infallible decrees. Reporting both the good news and the bad news will help keep that clear and thereby serve both the journal and the communion. Editorial and other comment on events, developments, and directions may serve to strengthen or change denominational policies, improve agency performance, and enrich community life. The quality of these results depends largely on integrity of relationships and style of operation and can hardly be regulated. They may, however, be judged in the light of David Halbertstam's description of good and bad newspapers:

> ...a newspaper at its best reflects and hears all factions of the
> community, letting them play their will out as openly as possible,

examining the legitimacy of each case on its merits, trying to limit the emotions and passions...

Halberstam judges a certain newspaper unfair because "it appealed to ignorance and prejudice and it fanned passions" (*The Powers That Be*, p.117). Similar judgments may be laid upon some of the independent publications with which most communions are both cursed and blessed. Now and then our official publications also fail to measure up. Opinion, including angry, opposing opinion, should not be suppressed, but this need not entail lapses in integrity and style which tend to lower the level of debate in the church.

Finally, promotion and enlistment in the mission of the church. Yes, I think there is an important place for promotion and enlistment in the work of church journalists as long as it is clearly identified and kept in balance. Presently, we do not, I think, do enough of it. We fall short largely because what we do is too often institutionally self-serving and therefore somewhat embarrassing. What more might we do in promotion and enlistment? I offer one example which I know some of you have already done—at least in part.

Last fall I found myself growing more and more frustrated about the bloodletting in Latin America. I, therefore, welcomed the request to sign a letter of protest to President-elect Ronald Reagan. I welcomed it the more because I have rarely, if ever, received a letter drafted for group signature which was so well stated. A few days later I was gratified to see the letter reported on the front page of the New York *Times*.

I would be even more satisfied, much more satisfied, if the church in this year of study on Latin America had better nurtured and trained its members, reported the news and information, discussed and developed ways of addressing the situation in Latin America, interpreted such policies, subjected them to review and criticism, and been in a position to promote the signing of countless letters by church members, which might then have made such a difference as to cause a change in policy and protect and preserve the lives of our brothers and sisters in Latin America. If the people of God could be so enlisted around issues of deep concern to all people, then I am sure we would also make more news of interest to the secular media at the same time.

Finally, this word of perspective from Trevor Beeson:

The Christian faith has never been effectively communicated by a corrupt church. There have been periods in history when the church has produced monumental buildings and theologies. There have been times when the church has exercised extensive temporal power and taken possession of the consciences of individuals. But, on the whole, these have not been eras of effective Christian communication. *It is when the love of God has been revealed in the lives of individual men and women, and in the life of the church itself, that the world has been moved to enquire whether the Christian Gospel might have light to throw upon the human condition.* (Emphasis mine)

However we may judge the life of the church, we have a job to do together in mission. Requiring church executives to think through their prejudices and perspectives concerning church journalists, as you have done by inviting me to speak to you today, is one way to help us do a better job together. Over the years, perhaps nothing has helped me more than regular conversations with church communicators in an atmosphere of cooperation and mutual respect. I anticipate your questions, comments, and grievances.

42
Ecumenical By Accident
and Incident

A Church Herald *column, January 22, 1982*

One of the follow-up projects to the Ecumenical Consultation discussed in chapter 37 was a survey of ecumenical activity in Reformed church congregations, classes, and particular synods. In the torrent of data, much of it deadly dull, were these pleasant surprises of accident and incident.

...The reports from the congregations contain a good deal of information about local ecumenical interests. Some indicate that they have become ecumenical by accident. They may have begun relating to a congregation of another denomination because one or another's building was destroyed or damaged by fire or made unusable for some other reason. In other cases, tragedies affecting the families of pastoral or lay leaders of another congregation have led to personal relationships which have then blossomed into relationships between congregations. These new relationships were sometimes cited as "compensation" for the tragedy....

Joy in new relationships is even more prominent among those who may be described as having become ecumenical by incident. Pastor's conferences are likely places for this to happen. A pastor may attend in order to study worship or preaching or counseling and leave having found a new kindred spirit. In urban areas, this new friend may be another pastor from the same community but unknown before the conference. That personal relationship then easily becomes a bridge for congregational relationships.

Lay people often have similar experiences in their own communities. They may attend a cooperative teacher-training class or an issue seminar, or they may help in a local cooperative ministry. Bonds may be formed with one or more people from other churches and yet another bridge is built.

Quite naturally, this ecumenism by accident or incident often leads to ecumenism by intent. A sudden illness or unexpected absence of the pastor may have led the consistory to invite a neighboring pastor from another denomination to fill in. They like him, so they do it again—this time as a planned pulpit *exchange* rather than merely pulpit *supply*.

Congregational prayers for a neighboring congregation in crisis may so enrich the worship service that prayers for other Christians become a regular part of the service. The joy of new relationships with other Christians may lead to a quest for institutionalizing these relationships in regular joint worship services, a minister's association, a local council of churches, or some other organization.

Ecumenical relationships, however they come about, can benefit church institutions as well as church members. In some cases such relationships have been the basis for united ministry or even united congregations that have drawn together two or more congregations and added new life to old.

Communities can also benefit. One Reformed church pastor writes:

> I am firmly convinced that it is this strong ecumenical association that gives the town its sense of "community." The clergy meet once a week and are actively involved in local and community concerns and seek to be of service both to one another and to the town as a whole. There is a warm feeling of love between all the churches in town and a deep belief that we are all serving and worshiping the same Lord and that the more we can do together the greater that service will be.

Many Reformed church congregations will celebrate their ecumenical pilgrimages during the week of Christian Unity from January 18-25....It's a good time for building on last year's ecumenical accidents and incidents.

43

CRC/RCA—Together on the Way

A Church Herald *column, February 18, 1983*

The CRC is the Christian Reformed church, which had its origins in schism from the RCA (the Reformed Church in America) in 1857, boosted by another controversy and a number of congregations seceding from the RCA in 1882. Here, I cite a few signs of convergence, and put them in the context of the convergence of our "mother churches" in the Netherlands—whose union is behind schedule, but they are still "together on the way."

Relationships between the Christian Reformed church (CRC) and the Reformed Church in America (RCA) were a stormy affair for most of the first 100 years of our separate lives. In 1878, twenty-one years after the first schism, a pastor's "undue familiarity with the Reformed church" was still an offense to his Grand Rapids CRC congregation. Decades later some Reformed church leaders still wrote of the Christian Reformed church as "an illegitimate church." Anger and self-justification abounded on both sides.

In the late '40s and early '50s, congregations in many small midwestern communities continued to regard marriage across denominational lines with grave concern—and with sharp eyes to see which church (and which dominie) would win the struggle for the denominational allegiance of new families. A special pathos surrounded the RCA man who followed his new bride into the CRC, thereby demonstrating to many in the RCA that he was "not master in his own house." Unhappily, the groom could not compensate for that chill in old RCA relationships by basking in the warmth of his new CRC relationships, for there the new member was often subjected to an informal but prolonged period of probation.

Post-war America was on the move, however, and old barriers were breaking down. CRC/RCA anger began to give way to self-deprecating, and sometimes gently prodding, humor as attitudes changed among the members of both churches.

This common storehouse of Dutch-American humor, artfully employed by representatives of both denominations as they exchanged greetings at one another's synods, gradually paved the way for steps toward formal reconciliation. In 1898, sixteen years after the second schism, the two churches had been unable to reconcile the *Reformed church's desire for "brotherly kindness"* with the *Christian Reformed church's emphasis on mutual watchfulness in clearly defined ecclesiastical relationships*— a difference that still characterizes the attitudes of the two churches toward a relationship with one another. During the next decades, both sides seemed content to probe old wounds now and then, while the Reformed church moved into ever-widening ecumenical relationships and the Christian Reformed church concentrated on the "mother church" in the Netherlands. As recently as 1944, the Christian Reformed church's offer to recognize the Reformed Church in America as a "corresponding church" (something short of a "sister church") was again declined.

Movement was continuing, however. In 1966, the two denominations' committees on interchurch relations talked together—about whether to talk together about church union. They decided not to. The Reformed church was then talking union with the Presbyterian Church in the United States.

When the Reformed-Presbyterian talks failed in 1969, the Reformed Church in America was temporarily preoccupied with internal tensions. On Reformation Day, October 31, 1972, however, the two interchurch relations committees opened a three-day joint conference for the purpose of exploring relationships between the two denominations. The conference was held in the historic Ninth Street Christian Reformed Church in Holland, Michigan, which had seceded from the Reformed church in 1882 and taken that very building with them into the CRC.

The "warm" spirit at this conference was, however, of a very different nature. Again stimulated by a generous outpouring of Dutch-American humor, the delegates proposed cooperation in a wide variety of areas along with several celebrations to foster the new spirit. Two years later, the Christian Reformed church abolished its old categories of ecumenical relations, and in 1976, not without some struggle, extended to the Reformed Church in America recognition as a "church in ecclesiastical fellowship." The General Synod of the Reformed Church in America, meeting in Madison, New Jersey, in that same year accepted the recognition unanimously and sealed its vote with a standing ovation in one of the most moving moments in recent synod history. As a consequence we are now formally committed to recognize one another's membership and ministry, to consult one another on issues of joint concern, and to accept each other's members around the Lord's table.

Those formal connections support an ever-growing web of relationships. In 1975, the two churches jointly developed an "Evangelism Manifesto." In that same year, the *Banner* and the *Church Herald* published a joint issue. The interchurch relations committees of the two denominations have long sustained a permanent joint subcommittee on CRC-RCA relationships. Western and Calvin seminaries are in regular contact. The colleges are members of the Association of Reformed Colleges (ARC). In 1981, the Christian Reformed church's synod formally approved a Reformed church minister as a fraternal delegate to the Education Committee of the Board of Publications in order to facilitate the growing cooperation in the development and use of the Bible Way curriculum. Many classes now regularly exchange ecumenical delegates. Joint denominational staff meetings have facilitated growing cooperation in church planning and development, in world mission, and in the ministries of "Words of Hope" (RCA) and the "Back to God Hour" (CRC). And we find ourselves now with a deepening common conviction about the relationships of the black and white Reformed churches in South Africa.

In the course of these developments, both denominations have celebrated anniversaries: the RCA its 350th in 1978; the CRC its 125th in 1982. Both anniversaries have provided significant opportunity for reflection and self-discovery, along with the typical pomp and circumstance and celebration, including a special birthday party for the CRC held in Holland, Michigan, in 1982 and sponsored by the joint committee of the two churches.

The *Banner* published a number of reflective articles during the CRC's 125th anniversary year and on January 10, 1983, an entire issue was devoted to RCA-CRC relationships. The dominant motif in the CRC reflections on the relationship between our two denominations seems still to be that employed by Dr. John Krominga, at the 1972 joint conference: "The relationship between the two denominations is peculiar, if not unique. Perhaps the most useful image is that of a divorced couple who keeps seeing each other. No matter how many people are in the crowd, the estranged mate is the first person they recognize." I remember hearing him speak those words and shared in the general feeling of the conference that it was a strikingly apt image. But that was 10 years ago. In that intervening decade, we have passed through the feelings of several generations. In 1972, there were still quite a lot of people who were acting out the anger of their great-great-grandparents who had carried out the schisms of 1857 and 1882. Most of us no longer feel that we are the divorcees. We are at most the descendants of divorcees—separated brothers and sisters who in varying degrees regret the separation.

Reading some of the anniversary reflections in the light of my own reflections on our interdenominational relationships, the conviction crystallizes that we have a great deal to learn about ourselves *which we can only learn from one another.* That conviction springs in part from some experiences of a very different kind of separation in a much smaller family. All my adult life, I have lived something like a thousand miles or more away from my family home and continuing family center. So I have visited. Since the death of my last parent two years ago, those visits have been mostly with brothers and sisters and they have been filled with reminiscing and reflecting. Each time I have come away from those gatherings having learned something new about myself— stemming from the differences in the way my brothers and sisters view our parents, the things they (older than I) remember about me that I've forgotten, the insights that come from new experiences interacting with renewed memories. Each time I have learned something about myself from my brothers and sister, *which I could not have learned without them.* All this is to say nothing of the opportunities provided for healing old wounds, sharing the joy of nurturing the next generation, and simply enjoying one another.

I think something like that is true of the relationship between the Christian Reformed church and the Reformed Church in America. Neither of us can truly know ourselves without the other. Could *anyone* from the Reformed church have challenged us last year at General Synod as Stanley Wiersma did in his tribute to B. D. Dykstra—and in his pressing questions to the RCA? (Reprinted in the *Church Herald* of October 15, 1982.) *We are sisters and brothers connected by special ties and a common parentage who need one another to be whole.*

Take, for example—and I choose this example because it is one of the most critical needs we have in common—our attitude toward the tradition. I refer especially to our particular tradition of being Dutch Reformed in North America. The CRC more than the RCA has struggled to come to terms with it. We (the RCA) have too much let that tradition ooze away as we succumbed to the culture. On the other hand, they (the CRC) have sometimes clung to the forms of the tradition long after those forms were emptied of meaning and thus sealed themselves off from the culture—and just as surely let the tradition slip away. Of course, each church has done some of each.

The tradition, however, is longer than either 125 or 350 years and larger than these shores. Neither of us can understand ourselves or one another apart from our common, but very different, origins in the Netherlands. While the roots of the eastern RCA are deep in the established church of the Netherlands, the western RCA and the CRC both spring from secessionist groups in the Netherlands. The details are too complex even to outline here, but the dynamic needs to be noted. It was important in both the schism 125 years ago and the schism 100 years ago and is still important today. Christian Reformed historian Herbert J. Brinks' comment about ignorance of denominational history in general is particularly true of ignorance about our Dutch heritage. Without it, "...we flounder about like cultural orphans. Continuity depends, then, on dogged traditionalism rather than on a knowledgeable understanding of how we came to where we are."

Among the factors stimulating me to write this review of CRC-RCA relationships is the news that the separated sisters and brothers in the Netherlands are talking about getting back together again and are trying to do it by 1986, exactly one century after the secession led by Dr. Abraham Kuyper. The theme for their union effort is "Samen Op Weg" or "Together On the Way." The main obstacle to the union appears now to be the conservative Reformed Alliance within the church that Kuyper left because of its alleged liberalism! The alliance now objects to alleged liberalism within the church that he founded!

Our RCA/CRC anniversaries have not led to anything so dramatic or so complicated, and to this writer the prospect for union between the RCA and the CRC appears to be still beyond the horizon. We can talk together on the way, however, and learn about ourselves from one another as we go.

Since "Together On the Way" is the literal meaning of the word "synod," our two general synods seem good places to keep cultivating the relationship. This summer the RCA synod will again receive ecumenical greetings from the CRC—the only denomination invited to bring such greetings annually. We will also celebrate the history and ministry of the Christian Reformed church in our Sunday evening festival service. Nothing dramatic there, but the anniversary stories have reminded us that we have had enough drama to last us quite a long time. For now, we will do well to continue our movement toward one another as we walk together on the way.

44

The Lordship of Christ in the Reformed Church in America

A sermon at the Synod Festival prior to the 177th Regular Session of the General Synod, Pella, IA, June 5, 1983

At the 1983 synod in Pella, Iowa, we began the practice of holding a Synod Festival prior to the formal opening of the business session. The theme was "The Lordship of Christ," and three different speakers treated three different aspects of the theme. Since this was my last synod as general secretary, I was invited to preach at the final service of the festival on Sunday evening to an open-air congregation of Reformed and Christian Reformed church members from the area as well as the synod delegates in attendance. The sky was dark and the winds strong, but the rain held off. An hour or two later, most of us were crowded into the First Reformed Church to dedicate the completed but not yet published hymnal, *Rejoice in the Lord*, which I helped to launch five years earlier as the denomination's 350th anniversary project.

Rereading this sermon now, I recall that I was even then uncertain about the expression "translate the tradition." In the end, its alliterative appeal and linguistic (Dutch) allusion won out. Today I would say "fulfill the tradition"—as did our Lord! Translate suggests that the substance is already there; fulfill suggests—as does the sermon—that it is not complete as it is.

Text: Luke 4:18-19

My sisters and brothers, in the last twenty-four hours many of you have said to me, "So, you're leaving us." I have been quick to respond, "No, I am not leaving you, only my work as general secretary," but this is a sort of farewell and a turning point in my own life. I am, therefore, deeply grateful for the opportunity to reflect with you on some fifteen years of official leadership in the denomination. I want to do that not only against the background of fifteen years of work in the denomination but in the light of our longer history as a church.

The lordship of Christ over the church is a treasured part of our Reformed tradition. It was the main impetus of the Reformation, and it was the hope that sustained our fathers and mothers in the face of hangings, burnings, and drownings during the struggle for the Reformation in the Netherlands. Hundreds, even thousands, of people sacrificed life itself because they would render allegiance to Christ alone—and not at all to any other. Two hundred years later, John Henry Livingston pursued a vision of unity in Christ strong enough to bind together the warring factions of our church deeply divided against itself. In the middle of the last century, Dominies A.C. Van Raalte and H.B. Scholte led their people to settle in the forests of Michigan and on the plains of Iowa in order that they could honor the lordship of Christ in accord with their own consciences. I myself, as many of you, have heard from my own parents and their families and friends of the struggle against the plagues of locusts and hail and drought which left the fields barren and the granaries empty. I have been at once sobered and thrilled by the knowledge that though their faith may have faltered, it did not fail; that however meager the harvest, the first fruits were offered to the Lord.

Now the task of honoring the lordship of Christ in the Reformed Church in America is ours, and I invite you to look with me at the words which our Lord used to introduce his ministry. I have chosen them because the ministry of Christ is the supreme model for the ministry of the church which would honor him as Lord.

I invite you to notice first that the ministry of Christ and the ministry of the church is the ministry of the Holy Spirit. The first words of our text, the words of Isaiah and of Jesus are: "The Spirit of the Lord is upon me." The ministry of the church of Jesus Christ is a ministry of the Spirit.

For several decades now, the Reformed Church in America, along with many other churches in the United States and indeed around the world, has been challenged to pay more attention to the Holy Spirit. A few of our congregations have been deeply disturbed and some even divided over the so-called charismatic phenomenon and its interpretation. Sometimes we relish the stories of excess and error, which are not hard to find, because they reassure us that our old way of reliance on the written Word, and the written Word alone, is the best way.

But this movement is calling us to reexamine that heavy emphasis on the written Word. It is surely one of our greatest strengths, but a strength may become a weakness. We have all seen people who have turned strength into weakness by depending on it to the exclusion of other personal qualities. Our Reformed emphasis on the written Word may become just such a weakness by stifling the Holy Spirit.

Perhaps now that the charismatic movement has quieted down a bit and isn't quite as threatening as it was a decade or two ago, we can somehow muster the grace to confess that *errors of over emphasis* are frequently compensations for *errors of under emphasis.*

Most people now agree that the Pentecostal movements in Latin America in an earlier generation were indeed movements of the Spirit to free people from the powers of the world, which had crept far into the church. I believe that the charismatic movement is mostly staying within the churches and it may therefore be a means of renewal for us all.

Our need for the renewing power and presence of the Spirit of Jesus Christ is urgent. In many places it is desperate. In many of our congregations, the Spirit seems at best to be a peripheral presence. Pastors and people labor, and I mean *labor*, to maintain the *forms* of life. But the *spirit* of life is absent. Forms of worship are observed, necessary duties are performed, but they are dull and labored and lifeless, or they are artificial, sensational, and sentimental. In such places, joyful, Spirit-filled worship, witness, and service are hardly known.

But where the Spirit is, there is life. I have seen such life in the congregations of the Reformed Church in America. I have known the presence of the Spirit in those congregations in the love of the

members for one another and for the world, in their open
acceptance and celebration and offering up to God of one another's
gifts as well as their own, in their willingness to forgive one
another's faults, in their joy in worship, and in their willingness to
work.

I am not suggesting that we should all seek the gift of tongues.
And I am certainly not suggesting some sort of spiritual narcissism
which concentrates on the inner workings of the Spirit. I am
suggesting that we should all open our lives to the working of the
Holy Spirit and use no defense, theological or otherwise, to protect
ourselves against the working of the Holy Spirit. I am suggesting
that we take seriously the apostolic admonition to be filled with the
Spirit and earnestly to desire the gifts of the Spirit because the Spirit
of God is the only source of meaning and the gifts of the Spirit the
only means of ministry.

To minister in the Spirit is to demonstrate the fruits and gifts of
the Spirit. To be full of the Spirit is to be full of life. We do not
decide if people are full of life by taking their blood pressure. We
say someone is full of life when that person overflows with life. To
be filled with the Spirit is to overflow with the fruits of the Spirit—
love and peace and joy. To be filled with the Spirit is freely to use
the gifts of the Spirit for building up the body of Christ.

Instead of stifling the Spirit, our Reformed emphasis on the Word
of God can free us to be open to the Spirit.

We trust in the Word and, therefore, we can find the confidence
to take the risks of openness to the Spirit. We can trust ourselves to
the Spirit because we trust ourselves to the Word, and we can
therefore test the spirits to correct our errors. We who can claim to
be Reformed according to the Word of God need have no fear to set
our sails to catch the full winds of the Spirit. We have the Word of
God to keep us on course. The ministry of the church of Jesus Christ
that would honor the lordship of Jesus Christ is such a ministry of
the Spirit.

It was precisely such an openness to the Spirit that led to the
renewal of our denomination at the Festival of Evangelism in 1970.
When a member of the planning task force tried to stop a certain
unplanned movement that was taking place at a critical point in the
festival when he thought it might make everything go wrong, Pastor
Adrian Tenhor said, "The Spirit says 'Go', man." And the
unplanned movement went forward and became the turning point in
the Festival of Evangelism. When it seemed that all our expert
planning wasn't going to work after all, the Spirit gave us the gift of

life. The way of renewal is always the way of the Spirit because the Lord is the Spirit and the Spirit is the presence of the risen Christ among us. So, if we would honor the lordship of Jesus Christ in the Reformed Church in America, our first responsibility is to follow the Spirit.

Our second responsibility is to translate the tradition. That is part of following the Spirit of God because the traditions that we cherish, which we have honored in banners, in hymns, in songs, and in our words together this week, those traditions are a gift of the Spirit of God, and it is our responsibility to translate those gifts of the Spirit of past generations so that the lives of today's people can be enriched by those same gifts.

A constant concern during all these fifteen years that I have worked in the denominational offices has been our denominational identity. We have always had trouble with our denominational identity. During all our 350-plus years, there seem to have been only a few short times when we have been certain of our identity—and when we have looked back at those times, we have recognized that we have often been wrong! We have rarely felt confident that we have known who we are. Sometimes we have seemed to lose our identity before we had found it again after the last time we had lost it!

To translate our tradition is absolutely essential to the renewing of our denominational identity. Tradition, as Tevye in *Fiddler on the Roof* reminded us, tells us "who we are." Without tradition, he sings, our lives would be "as shaky as a fiddler on the roof." We cannot ignore our tradition. As we prepare ourselves for the General Synod, to ignore our tradition may be compared to those of us who landed at the Des Moines airport in the last few days saying that we have come to Pella from Des Moines. But that statement, even though it is true insofar as it goes, will not shed very much light on the General Synod and its debates. We can understand ourselves, we can know who we are, only in terms of our journeys from New Brunswick, New York, Grand Rapids, Detroit, Chicago, Denver, and Los Angeles, as well as Canajoharie, Carmel, and Corona. Those longer journeys and our longer histories are absolutely essential for understanding who we are. That is true for us within the Reformed Church in America. It is true for us, and particularly true for us, across the boundaries of our two denominations— Reformed and Christian Reformed.

But, if you remember Tevye's struggle in *Fiddler on the Roof*, you know he had a very difficult time translating that tradition. So have we. For much of our history, we have literally refused to translate the tradition by clinging to the Dutch language. But the refusal to translate applies to content as well as the language of the translation. In the *Centennial Discourses* of 1876, the Rev. Talbot W. Chambers, pastor in the Collegiate Church in New York, could boast that "for an entire century the truth has been held without the shadow of a change." (Well, he may have been exaggerating a bit in order to score a point against the Christian Reformed church.) But such a refusal to translate the tradition kills the tradition and stifles the life of the church.

It has stifled the life of the Reformed Church in America. Deprived of a living tradition, some of us have sought shelter in the rigid formulations of fundamentalism (from the days of Van Raalte's settlement in Holland that has been true): a few have wandered into the arid wilderness of angry social activism; others have turned aside into a kind of bland and colorless Protestantism or into an overly sweet evangelicalism. But none of these are true to the tradition. And none of them translate the tradition.

To honor the lordship of Christ in the Reformed Church in America (and, of course, in the Christian Reformed church as well), we must learn from our Lord how to come to terms with the tradition. You noticed that the text Jesus used at the opening of his ministry was not original with him. He used the tradition in the form of Isaiah's prophecy to announce his own ministry. From the beginning to the end of his ministry, even to the cross itself, Jesus concerned himself with tradition and translated it for the people of his own time. To those who were worried about the revolutionary nature of his teaching, he said, "Think not that I have come to abolish the law and the prophets; I have come not to abolish them but to fulfill them" (Matt. 5:17). Having said that, he went on to render all sorts of radical translations of the tradition. But he kept his word. He did not destroy the tradition, he fulfilled it. The commandment against murder, he translated to apply to anger. The commandment against adultery, he translated to apply to lust. The drive to legalism, he translated into an aspiration to righteousness. He pressed beyond and behind the form and letter of the tradition in order to seek the substance and spirit of the tradition and to make use of the ministries of the Spirit in the ages gone by.

Now, my sisters and brothers, the very name of our church and of our faith is drawn precisely from that way of dealing with the tradition. Our claim to being Reformed is not authenticated, it is betrayed by preserving the tradition untranslated. *Our claim to being*

Reformed is authenticated only as we follow the Spirit, who is always doing a new and unexpected thing among us and who is always calling us to translate the tradition given in ages past in accordance with the Word of God in order that we may meet the challenges of the new age.

More has probably been done to translate the tradition of the Reformed Church in America in the last thirty years than in all the 300 years before that. We have reshaped our liturgy and we are reshaping our liturgy to make it a vehicle for mingling our own expressions of devotion with those of our fathers and mothers. We have approved, after twenty years of debate, a restatement of our historic faith in the form of a "Song of Hope." And tonight we introduce a new hymnal—always the hymnal is the most powerful instrument for shaping our common life and translating the tradition.

Much has been done, but much remains to be done. I am persuaded that without such a translation of the tradition we will not find the way to the renewal of our denominational identity and witness. We need to be, my brothers and sisters, who we are and who we have been if we are to be what God wants us to be.

My third reflection, and our third responsibility in honoring the lordship of Christ, is to seek the kingdom of God. Beyond and above all else, we need to seek the kingdom of God. Our Lord says that he had been sent to proclaim release to the captive, recovery of sight to the blind, to set at liberty those who are oppressed, to proclaim the acceptable year of the Lord. That is kingdom language. There isn't any mistaking it.

During most of the fifteen years that it's been my pleasure to work for the Reformed Church in America, we have struggled in our congregations, classes, particular synods, the General Synod, the General Program Council, everywhere—we have struggled with the meaning of the kingdom of God. These have been times when we have been frightened and angered by social upheaval and international tension. These have been times when we have been worried about declining church membership. And we have been tempted, sorely tempted, to turn inward, to focus on our individual lives within the Reformed Church in America.

But the lordship of Christ in the Reformed Church in America and in the church of Jesus Christ has no meaning apart from the lordship of Christ in the world. It cannot be separated from the lordship of Christ in the world anymore than it can be separated from the lordship of Christ over our individual lives. The church is

God's chosen community to demonstrate the nature of Christ's lordship to the world. It is a partial realization of his kingdom of love and peace and joy and justice. It is given as a demonstration for all the world to see as the sign of that kingdom. The church is never an end in itself. It is always a community on the way to the kingdom.

So, my Reformed sisters and brothers, we must seek the kingdom. We must seek the kingdom by joining with those who struggle in the name of Christ for the healing of the nations: with Dr. C. M. Kao, general secretary of the Presbyterian Church in Taiwan (partner church in our world mission program for many years), who is now in his fourth year of imprisonment for seeking the freedom and human rights of the people of Taiwan—we seek the kingdom by joining with him; with Dominie Beyers Naude of South Africa now in his sixth year of banning because he has sought the abolition of apartheid; with Bishop Desmond Tutu and Pastor Allan Boesak, also of South Africa, whose lives are daily imperiled because they too oppose the evil of apartheid; with Kim Dae Jung, imprisoned, tortured, and exiled because he sought the freedom of the people of South Korea. We must stand with them and with the countless millions who worship Christ under the watchful eyes of those who rule in the name of Marx and Lenin.

We must seek the kingdom by insuring that the church never becomes an end in itself; by insuring that we will never seek the growth or the peace of the Reformed Church in America by sacrificing our unity and our solidarity with the people and churches just named or with others unnamed who witness and serve under the cross.

We must seek the kingdom by giving ear to those strange, unfamiliar, and even alien voices of the poor and oppressed, the tortured and martyred, which are sometimes echoed in the statements of our denominational staff; sometimes echoed in the teaching of our college and seminary faculties; sometimes echoed in the reports of our General Synod commissions, or echoed in the actions of the councils of churches.

We must seek the kingdom, my Reformed sisters and brothers, because without the kingdom nothing else matters—not church growth, not world mission, not Christian discipleship. If they do not point to the kingdom, they are all vanity and seeking after the wind. The kingdom (first, last, and always, the kingdom of love and peace and justice and joy) is the test of the lordship of Christ over the church.

That is my vision of the lordship of Christ over the Reformed Church in America. During these last fifteen years, I have seen this vision fulfilled again and again and again.

I have seen this church make its way back from the factional conflicts over the Consultation on Church Union, the National Council of Churches, defeat or merger with the southern Presbyterians, and, still on the same agenda of the same General Synod, the demand for reparations presented by James Forman and the Black Economic Development Conference at the synod of 1969. I was present again nine months later when the Reformed Church in America gathered at Cobo Hall in Detroit for the Festival of Evangelism trusting the Lord of the church to overcome our brokenness and bind us back together—and I saw the Lord do a mighty work.

At that same bitterly painful synod of 1969, I saw this church form a Black Council for the Program of General Synod because that seemed to be (even in the midst of all our hurt and anger and pain) what the Lord was requiring of us. And we did it. In the years after that, I have seen this church open its doors to Hispanics, American Indians, and Pacific-Asian Americans because this too seemed to be what the Lord required.

At the Festival of Mission in 1971, I saw the Reformed Church in America immobilized, traumatized for a little while, but then able to expand its vision of the kingdom of God as John Gatu of Africa and Jose Miguez Bonino of Argentina preached and pleaded before us *their* understanding of the lordship of Christ. I have seen the Reformed Church in America join with the Christian Reformed Church in North America to cast off the anger of generations of separation in order to recognize in one another's churches the integrity of our common confession that Jesus is Lord. I have seen this sturdy old church find the freedom to set aside centuries of patriarchal tradition in order to follow the Spirit who was calling our sisters, as well as our brothers, into the ministry of the Word and the sacraments. I have seen this Dutch Reformed Church in America free itself from decades of fruitless discussion with the Dutch Reformed churches of South Africa in order to open wide our arms and our hearts to our Black sisters and brothers in that conflict ridden land.

I have seen offerings gathered and churches built. I have seen the hungry fed and the discouraged filled with hope. I have seen and heard the gospel preached in many tongues in many lands. I have seen the people of God gathered into the church of Jesus Christ.

These are a few, only a few, of the joys I have known in the service of this church. My debt to the Reformed Church in America was beyond counting before I began this work. Pastors, professors, and parishioners without number had made me a debtor. Each year in this work has increased my debt. I can never repay it—but I have done my best to offer a fair return on your investment!

And I shall go on doing so. I leave my work as general secretary, but I do not leave the Reformed Church in America or its ministry. It is, in fact, the faith and witness of the lordship of Jesus Christ of this church that compels me now to take up the World Council of Churches' work for justice and service. I find my hope and strength in confessing Christ as Lord in that same tough-minded tradition of Scholte, Van Raalte, Livingston, Calvin, Augustine, and Paul—all of whom we here all call our fathers in the faith, all of whom knew and confessed only one Lord, and all of whom found strength in that confession to place their hope in God in spite of all the evidence against hope, and all of whom invite us all now in this General Synod, and in all the General Synods to come, to honor the lordship of Christ in the Reformed Church in America.

45

Some Reformed (and Reforming) Perspectives on Church Order

An article in the Reformed Review, *Spring 1985*

The *Reformed Review* is a scholarly journal published by my alma mater, the Western Theological Seminary of the Reformed Church in America at Holland, Michigan. The Spring 1985 issue was a tribute to Professor Elton M. Eenigenburg, then retiring and since deceased. I was asked to contribute a chapter on church order. I wanted to do it, because I had appreciated him greatly as a professor and honored him as a person. The difficulty was that I had long since found myself in sharp disagreement with the basic principles underlying his extensive reordering of the Reformed Church's *Book of Church Order* in the 1960s. Already in the mid-70s while writing the chapter on church order for my popular history, *Reformed Church Roots*, I had written a lengthy addendum criticizing that arrangement. I had not published it because I did not think we could reorder the *Book of Church Order* again, and I saw no point in risking the wounding of an old friend and mentor.

Confronted with this invitation, I found a way to say it all in ecumenical context—and in such a manner that he wrote to thank me for my comments as well as for the personal tribute with which I prefaced this article, but which is here deleted.

The issues addressed in this article seem more urgent for the ecumenical movement in the coming decade than they were in the one just passed—when they were already critical.

The Reformed Passion for Church Order

We Reformed are famous for stressing that all things be done "decently and in order." The historic solemnity with which our fathers spoke those words has mercifully eroded. (We then thought that decency and order required our mothers to keep silent!) One now more often hears the words spoken tongue in cheek. That's good. Evidence abounds that our "order" and our "decency" have been at least a touch heavy-handed in the past—ask our silenced mothers, or their daughters!

Paul's original admonition (2 Cor. 14:40), we may recall, was delivered in the midst of a bewildering outpouring of gifts of the Spirit and a confusing jumble of activity which people were claiming to be the work of the Spirit. All this had the church at Corinth in a frenzy. Paul urged that things be "done decently and in order" because without order they couldn't be done at all. Later Christians have sometimes clung to the phrase not so that things *can* be done, but rather so that they *cannot* be done. The first defence against that kind of heavy-handedness is often a lively sense of humor. But sometimes a passion for justice, moral outrage, ecclesiastical disobedience and adjudication, constitutional amendments—the whole catastrophe—is required.

But if overemphasis on order can be a problem, so can underemphasis. Church order, and civil order too, is important. Deciding *how* important is a matter of balance, a delicate matter in a world that is itself out of balance. Generally speaking, the formal structures of society (e.g., governments) today press the need for more "law and order," even to the point of oppression and repression which brings in its train the disorder of resistance and sometimes civil war. Meanwhile, the informal structures of society (e.g., neighborhoods and other communities) are generally becoming ever more disorderly. The two tendencies are indeed bouncing off one another, each aggravating the other. Our "passion" for church order is quite naturally affected by, and also interacts with, this order and disorder in the world. The current rash of ecclesiastical legalism in public policy—which reached epidemic proportions before last fall's election—is only one of many current examples.

Calvin also lived in a time of great disorder in the midst of which people were quite naturally preoccupied with order. Eugene Osterhaven has argued, and I would agree, that Calvin's times, temperament, and training combined to make his delineation of a Spirit-filled church order his "major contribution to the faith of the Church." Among the various authorities cited, Osterhaven includes Josef Bohatec who speaks of Calvin's "passion for order" and A.M. Fairbairn who judged that "Calvin was greater as a legislator than a theologian...his polity is a more perfect expression of the man than his theology."[1]

Its Ecumenical Urgency

But this "passion for order" is not so much a Reformed idiosyncrasy as it is a Reformed contribution to the ecumenical movement. The issue is no less urgently on the ecumenical agenda in our time than it was in Calvin's.

In many places around the world today, there is a visible movement toward consensus in matters of faith and doctrine, as there is on the sacraments. Even the barriers around the separate tables of the eucharist show signs of being lowered. The liturgies of the churches which gather up the offerings of the various historical experiences of their respective communities are inherently drawn together as they are lifted up before the one God. And the doctrines of the church, which sometimes absolutize various historical conflicts, can be, and are, reinterpreted, recast, reformed, or rejected in accordance with the methodology of our different traditions. But when we come to the questions of order and ministry, we are in a quagmire. In all the relations with Rome— Orthodox, Anglican, Protestant, Evangelical—it is *the* issue, and in most of the relationships of the churches with one another in the WCC or in the NCC or in COCU, it is *the* issue. For in the orders of the churches these historical conflicts are variously embodied in the very offices (and frequently identified with the very persons) of those who most represent the contemporary historical institutionalizations of the church—deacons, elders, ministers of the Word, bishops, metropolitans, patriarchs, and popes. Little wonder that church order is among the thorniest thickets along the way toward the unity of the church.

It is therefore of considerable surprise that the ecumenical movement has worked only sporadically on the broad principles of church order, i.e., on the the church as institution. The most comprehensive effort resulted in the "Report on Institutionalism" presented to the fourth world conference on Faith and Order held at Montreal in 1963. The report, however, apparently received only scant attention since the conference record hardly refers to the issue. Nor has the matter been taken up again in the formal program of Faith and Order.

Much of course has been written, and even more has been spoken, about ministry and offices—the most important current conversation piece being the WCC Faith and Order document, "Baptism, Eucharist and Ministry." Over the decades, the Faith and Order movement has devoted considerable attention to the methodology of these discussions.

Writing on "reconciliation in ministry," Geoffrey Wainwright cites Faith and Order pioneer Edmund Schlink's observation that an ecumenical dialogue which limits itself to a comparison of canonical and dogmatic statements on matters of church order

> will remain stuck in fruitless confrontation. These differences, however, appear in another light and can be largely eliminated *if one considers the service* which is actually carried out through those ministries and relates it to the service committed to the apostles. Only if they are *translated back into the elementary functions of church life* can canonical rules be compared in fruitful dialogue. For those elementary functions have their centre in the worshipping community (emphasis added).

Wainwright further notes that he himself has used this theological method extensively in his book *Doxology* and suggests that the church's "'ways of worship'...already confirm what is expressed in theological mode in the Faith and Order texts on Eucharist and on Ministry." He then suggests that "to recognize and promote convergence in liturgical practice could become the most effective factor in the process towards the mutual reconciliation of churches and ministries."[2]

These three ways or "modes" of approaching the issues of church order—the service or functional mode, the liturgical mode, and the theological mode—are surely all essential. But the core of the issue remains the canonical or institutional mode. The liturgical, functional, and theological modes may be said, in a manner of speaking, to be over, around, and under the canonical core, but they do not address it directly—and sooner or later we shall need to.

The issue is not academic. In the international bilateral conversations with Rome, for example, the canonical issue of the role of the Bishop of Rome is *the* issue common to them all. Denominationally, the role of bureaucracies and their relationship to (or distance from) the pastoral structures of the church is primarily a canonical or institutional question, i.e., a question of order. Locally, the conflict over the base communities in Latin America, for example, is at bottom a canonical conflict over the role of the people and of the hierarchy in the life of the church.

In addition then to the theological, liturgical, and functional approaches to issues of order and ministry, we need also to address directly the core of the issue, i.e., the institutional embodiment of function, doctrine, and liturgy variously consolidated and variously weighted with tradition. For in the end functional symmetry, liturgical convergence, and doctrinal agreement must be embodied institutionally, i.e., canonically, through juridical decisions which will bring into harmony (not conformity) the various orders of the churches.

We will, I think, be helped toward that end if we can agree on a common set of perspectives within which we can address the issues of church order. Those which I venture to suggest may be summarized as a recognition that *church order is a historically conditioned directory of mission for the whole church in the service of world order.*

Historically Conditioned

All the structures we have inherited were developed in historical situations and have therefore been historically conditioned. To claim suprahistorical absoluteness for any structure or office is to contradict the meaning of the Incarnation and to attempt to restrict the freedom of the Spirit. The bewildering variety of apostles, prophets, evangelists, pastors, teachers, elders, deacons, etc. in the New Testament are best understood "as the biblical picture of the response of the Early Church in thanksgiving and service to the 'varieties of gifts' and the task given by God through Christ, or as the 'ordering' of the work of the New Testament churches as they labored to be obedient to the commission of their Lord."[3] Applying this perspective to the present situation, we will not ask ourselves which New Testament, or Reformation, offices are relevant for today's ministry. We will rather ask: What is the mission before us today, and what gifts have we received to do our work? And how, in faithfulness to the Word of God, can we best organize (order) them to do our work? In so doing, we shall quite likely experience for ourselves the tension and complementarity of charismatic liberty and institutional order so familiar to the New Testament church. Just such questions concerning mission, gifts, and order led John Calvin to establish the office of teacher in Geneva. That office met precisely the need of the time for instruction in the faith while, at the same time, giving official recognition to those with gifts for the task of teacher but lacking those additional gifts required for pastors—who were also teachers.

The precise shape of a church order, wrote Calvin, depended on the state of the times and "ought to be variously accommodated to the customs of each nation and age" (*Institutes* IV.x.30.). Consequently, church orders with or without bishops both met his approval, as did other orders with lesser variations.

The situation today is unhappily much less flexible. Centuries of polemic (and privilege) have called forth elaborate systemic doctrinalizations of church order grounding all manner of structure and office in scripture and tradition, thereby making them non-negotiable. It seems that we have quite forgotten that many of these structures and offices were originally nothing more than creative responses to practical need. The story in Acts 7 concerning the appointment of the first deacons is precisely such a response.

That same story illustrates another aspect of historical conditions: The churches and their various orders are frequently modifications of previous arrangements. The office of deacon, as well as that of elder (and of course rabbi and priest as well), were all present in the Jewish tradition. From the beginning the churches have drawn on such arrangements and offices as were available to them in their own time and place.

Underlying all this is the doctrine of the church which views it as the central sign and instrument of God's kingdom in history. The church is a historical movement constantly following the Spirit in adapting to changing needs and means but held steady by the Word to which it is bound. This is the heart of Calvin's teaching concerning the church and its order.

A Directory of Mission for the Whole Church

It follows that church order is a way of directing the actions of the body. As we speak of a directory of worship which guides us through the liturgy, so church order is a directory of mission which guides us in our work.

Paul's admonition "that all things be done decently and in order," you recall, was addressed to a body flailing about every which way. The word he uses for order is *tasso*, a word with a military background originally used to describe "the swift deployment of a fighting unit from a marching to a battle formation." It later came to mean the overall plan of battle as well as the appointment of soldiers to battle stations or to rank or to offices.[4]

Church order is then a directory of mission—which we amend when we want to change strategy. Ordination is an appointment to a task or office to carry out that action. Order and ordination are both for the purpose of carrying out the church's mission in the world.

The importance of this dynamic quality of church order can hardly be overemphasized. The church is an institution; it must be an institution if it is to do its work. Yet this institutional machinery has an inherent tendency to consume more and more time and effort and to become more and more self-important, thus turning *a means* into *the end*. The ultimate question to be asked of church order is always therefore whether it helps the church to do God's mission.

But there is also a *penultimate* question. The church is surely not itself the *end* of God's work in history, but neither is it merely a *means*. The church is sign (i.e. realization) as well as instrument, of God's kingdom. Church order is therefore concerned with the *being* of the church as well as with its *doing*—hence the importance of the sacraments in the order of the church. In our Reformed tradition, the sacraments are in fact second in importance only to the Word itself. And both Word and sacraments are means of calling the community together as well as of sending it out. Being and doing are inseparable in the church's mission. We must therefore also ask whether church order helps the church to be the church as well as whether it helps the church to be in mission.

Church order must therefore provide for and invite the participation of the whole people of God in the church and its mission. The formal offices, which occupy so much of our discussion, are after all legitimate only as they serve to build up the whole body. The function of church order is to provide for the harmonious and purposive growth of the whole body in mission.

In the Service of World Order

The full significance of church order, however, can finally be understood only when it is viewed as a means toward world order. Calvin (again) himself taught that church order was a vehicle for the renewal of the order of the whole world. Closely connected with church order in Calvin's thinking is the political order—which is identified with justice which Calvin defines as the "best constituted state of public affairs, in which everything is administered rightly and in order." Elsewhere Calvin says that God's purpose is "to reduce the whole world to order and subject it to his government." On this basis, Benjamin Milner suggests that "Calvin's political activism, then, may be traced directly to his conception of the church as that movement which stands at the frontier of history, beckoning the world toward its appointed destiny."[5]

A similar concern may be seen in Karl Barth's teaching. Barth portrays the relationship between church order and civil order in terms of two concentric circles. The church is represented by the inner circle and the civil order by the outer circle. Both are centered in Christ the Lord and both point to the kingdom of God. The outer circle is by no means an extension of the inner circle. Nor is the inner circle a smaller version of the outer circle. The church and the state have different roles in history. The church is to serve as *witness* to the state but not as its *guardian*.

The real Church must be the model and prototype of the real State. The Church must set an example so that by its very existence it may be a source of renewal for the State and the power by which the State is preserved. The Church's preaching of the gospel would be in vain if its own existence, constitution, order, government, and administration were not a practical demonstration of the thinking and acting from the gospel which takes place in this inner circle. How can the world believe the gospel of the King and His Kingdom if by its own actions and attitudes the Church shows that it has no intention of basing its own internal policy on the gospel? How can a reformation of the whole people be brought about if it is common knowledge that the Church itself is bent only on self-preservation and restoration—or not even that? Of the political implications of the theology which we have enumerated, there are few which do not merit attention first of all in the life and development of the

Church itself. So far they have not received anything like enough attention within the Church's own borders.[6]

Calvin's perception of the relationship of church order to world order was surely influenced by the social disorder of the 16th century. Barth's ideas were worked out in the midst of the church conflict in Germany in the 1930s and 40s. Just so the increasing oppression and disorder in our world underscores the urgency of our contemporary ministries of order. The church's life is intended to be a demonstration of God's order for the world rather than a reflection of human disorder. The struggle within the churches concerning the role of minorities and women, and the divisiveness of national boundaries and political and ideological barriers and other similar issues is therefore not only an internal matter. Nor are these issues to be regarded as barely legitimate questions on the church order agenda. On the contrary, they are issues of central meaning for the role of church order as sign and instrument of world order.

The Spirit is of course neither bound nor confined to the church. The church sometimes fails to serve as sign and instrument of the kingdom and is therefore itself disorderly. The Spirit may then work outside the church (or inside it in extraordinary ways) toward the renewal of world order and to call the church back to order so that it may again pursue its mission of renewing the world order.

In this light it would seem that Elton Eenigenburg's interest in biblical ethics and church order commemorated in this festschrift are essentially one interest. Church order is not merely a matter of arranging the ecclesiastical machinery. It is a means of ordering the life of the Christian community so that it may demonstrate the biblical ethic for the sake of the world. I salute him for helping us follow that way.

[1] M. Eugene Osterhaven, *The Faith of the Church—A Reformed Perspective on its Historical Development*, (Grand Rapids: Eerdmans, 1982), pp. 163, 240ff.

[2] Geoffrey Wainwright, "Reconciliation in Ministry" in *Ecumenical Perspectives on Baptism, Eucharist and Ministry* (Faith and Order paper 116, edited by Max Thurian, Geneva: World Council of Churches, 1983), p. 137.

[3] Robert Clyde Johnson, editor, *The Church and its Changing Ministry* (Philadelphia: Office of the General Assembly, UPCUSA, 1961), p. 99.

[4] *Ibid.*, p. 20

[5] Benjamin Charles Milner, Jr., *Calvin's Doctrine of the Church* (Leiden: E. J. Brill, 1970), pp. 29; 169, 195.

[6] Karl Barth, *Community, Church and State: Three Essays* (New York: Doubleday, 1960), pp. 186ff.

46
Theological Education and Ecumenical Learning

An informal address on the occasion of the inauguration of the Rev. Robert A. White as president of the New Brunswick Theological Seminary, New Brunswick, NJ, February 23, 1986

As minister of social witness for the Reformed Church in America, Robert White had been a highly valued colleague while I served as general secretary of the RCA. Sometime after I left for Geneva and the WCC, Bob was invited to become president of one of the denomination's two theological schools, the New Brunswick Theological Seminary in New Brunswick, New Jersey, the oldest such institution in the country. I was pleased to be a part of the inauguration ceremonies.

The "professorial certificate" to which I refer in the first paragraph is an official RCA document in which the professors of the seminary testify to "the fitness for ministry" of the seminary graduate, thus complementing the intellectual achievement recognized in the academic degree.

In the first section, "The Bible is Basic," I had the nagging feeling that I was leaving something very important unsaid. Later I found a passage I had marked many years before in Ernst Lange's *And Yet it Moves*,

The Bible is not a book but a library. It is not a closed collection of Christian axioms but many voices in open struggle for the truth....Among those engaged in the struggle there is a consensus—the event of Christ to which they all appeal, and the Christian experience which binds them together—but this consensus is only realized in controversy among the biblical...witnesses (p.40).

My insistence in the second section on "not leaping over the centuries—but rather tracing our way back through the tradition to its source," was a word to all those from the western part of the Reformed church who came east to escape the tradition—thereby impoverishing both the East and the West.

The third section, "Encounter Among Communities," I would today cast in a very different light. I have discovered that "the energy required to forge a common vision and vocation," is not to be found there, but in the Church beyond the churches and in the Tradition beyond the traditions. I spoke of that in the Western Seminary lecture that closes this third part of these ecumenical testimonies.

In the weeks following this lecture, I expanded it for my report to the Governing Board of the NCC presented at its meeting in New Orleans, Louisiana, in May 1986 under the title, "Ecumenical Formation in the Community of Communions." On the urging of several who heard it there, I offered an edited version of the report to the *Christian Century,* which published it later in the year under the title "Ecumenical Formation."

When Bob first invited me to give this address in connection with his inauguration, I thought of it as a rather formal occasion and, therefore, gave it this formal title of "Theological Education and Ecumenical Learning." As the time for the occasion drew nearer and I began to work on the speech and reflect on the fact that it was a late Sunday afternoon event, I decided to give it a subtitle: Ecumenical Formation—A Personal Testimony. And as I stand here now in this after-dinner atmosphere, I am inclined to think that still another subtitle might be: Coupons I have Clipped from my Professorial Certificate.

Whatever the title or the style, the subject is the same: the relationship between theological education and ecumenical learning. By theological education I mean the more or less formal study and reflection which is conducted in an institution such as this. By ecumenical learning I mean the more-or-less *in*formal experience and encounter which happens everywhere. Although I do thus distinguish between the two, my purpose is not to contrast them, but rather to reflect on their relationship and interaction. To my mind they are best brought together in the idea of "formation," by which I mean the creating, shaping, nurturing, and developing of Christian persons. Formation is thus one way of stating the meaning of our Reformed church tradition of the professorial certificate.

I have chosen to speak personally on this subject partly because I am not a theological educator and do not wish to pretend to be one and partly because I have had some experience—sharply accelerated in the last three years—of ecumenical formation. Throughout the last two decades of that experience I have seized opportunities to share as much of it as possible with as many people as possible and particularly with the people of the Reformed Church in America. This occasion is an opportunity to do that in some systematic way. I therefore offer four reflections on my personal experience of ecumenical formation.

The Bible is Basic

First, I wish to affirm the Bible as the foundation for theological education, the gateway to ecumenical learning, and the rule and guide for ecumenical formation. Speaking theologically, the Bible is the primary source book for our faith. Speaking ecumenically, it is our broadest common meeting ground. In terms of ecumenical formation, it is the fundamental historical nature of the Bible itself that is of primary importance.

The Bible is a wonderful mixture of story and history; prose and poetry; vision and prophecy; instruction and reflection. It is like an art gallery with paintings, sculptures, tapestries, mosaics, illuminated manuscripts, and other works of art arranged in some form of proximate historical continuity along a corridor that stretches from the dawn of creation to the beginning of the Christian era. Yet the quality and sacredness of the text combine with our repeated readings of it—our living with it, one might say—to make the people in these works of art seem all to be alive.

It is that fundamentally living historical quality of the Bible which makes it such a powerful instrument of ecumenical formation. The Bible is the story of the formation of a people—the Jews—and of another people—we Christians—sprung from that people. Within those stories of two peoples are set the particular stories of particular people being sometimes formed and sometimes de-formed in their experience with God and with other humans. The Bible is therefore a richly human and experiential book; it is a book that refuses to be codified or intellectualized or systematized. By its very nature as the living Word of God, the Bible is always drawing us into the process of ecumenical formation. That is why a theological education founded on the Bible is ideally suited to be an instrument of ecumenical formation and why a theological education founded on the Bible is the best preparation for ecumenical work and witness. And why a theological education at a Reformed church seminary is worth having!

A Critical Appreciation of Tradition

Experience with the Bible as the living Word of God leads quite naturally to a critical appreciation of one's own tradition, which is an essential second step on the way of ecumenical formation. In our Reformed tradition we hold that the Bible is the normative part of the tradition by which all else must be judged. This judging we also do historically, not leaping over the centuries, but rather tracing our way back through the tradition to its source. Just as the Bible can be properly understood only as a revelation in history unfolding over the centuries, so also the traditions can only be understood in terms of their historic development. For example, to trace our way back through the scholastic thickets of the Reformed tradition to the dynamism of Calvin himself is to use the tradition to set the tradition free and to open the way to ecumenical formation.

This digging back to the source is essential to the critical appreciation of one's own tradition. The more deeply we dig, the closer we come to the original vision. And the closer we come to the original vision, the less likely we are to cast it off. The closer we get to the source the more we find ourselves in touch with the original motivating force that gave the tradition the power and authority to mold the human spirit—and thus to become a tradition!

Without such historical discipline in approaching the tradition, persons too often—and too easily—choose one or the other of two false alternatives. Some cast off the tradition because of various "accidental" qualities which are not intrinsic to the tradition—and may even be distortions of it. Others cling to these culturally conditioned additions to the tradition and even move them from the periphery to the center, thus eclipsing the true light and power of that tradition. An historical understanding of both the Bible and tradition, however, serves to relativize all human formulations of the faith and thus to open the way to a dynamic experience of ecumenical formation.

This relativizing of one's own tradition by testing that tradition historically serves also to open the way to the testing of that tradition in the light of other traditions. Historical analysis of our own tradition frees us to engage in encounter and dialogue with others, clear about what is at stake. It is a truism of ecumenical dialogue that a person who knows only one tradition knows none. Yet too often in the course of theological education—and it is a special temptation in denominational or conservative or evangelical seminaries (which makes it somewhat of a triple threat for Reformed church seminaries!)—other traditions are introduced to demonstrate, directly or subtly, the superiority of one's own tradition *rather than* to test and complement that tradition.

(Of course in seminaries interdenominational, liberal, and tolerant, other traditions are sometimes introduced to demonstrate the *inferiority* of their own tradition—an opposite but equal shortcoming that need not concern us tonight.)

For example, some of the more ancient traditions, such as Orthodoxy, may be introduced as part of the historical development of the church and its doctrine—as an episode which has long since been passed by. I will, myself, never forget my own encounter with Orthodoxy as a living faith. What I had studied as an historical antiquity I encountered as a present-day reality by which millions of people were living and dying.

Encounter Among Communities

This leads to my third milestone in the pilgrimage of ecumenical formation—namely firsthand experience with other communities of faith—beginning with the communities within one's own community. For a small denomination, the Reformed Church in America provides a remarkable opportunity to grasp a very wide range of Christian experience in the United States. Small as we are, we are not so much a community as we are a community of communities (formerly two, East-West—now more nearly three, East-Midwest-West). Openness to this full range of one's own family of faith may serve as an introduction to experiences with communities of other traditions and cultures. Indeed openness to the communities within one's own community is a prerequisite to meaningful ecumenical engagement with other communities. The absence of such openness within one's own community tends to reduce ecumenical engagement with other communities to mere escapism.

Another essential requirement of genuine ecumenical experience with other communities is that each community be free to define itself and that they meet one another on more or less equal terms. This interaction of communities is very different from the interaction of persons of different traditions. It is in the meeting of communities, with all their weight of tradition and with their strengths and weaknesses, that we come closest to the heart of the ecumenical movement. Indeed, I find myself increasingly hesitant to apply the word ecumenical to anything less than such encounter among communities. It is in this encounter among *communities* that the conflicting heritages of the past and the divergent hopes for the future are most powerfully experienced, thereby providing the energy required to forge a common vision and vocation.

Another means of ecumenical formation, in addition to encounter among communities, is the experience of immersion in another community. Those of us who come from culturally dominant groups (and even we Dutch Reformed should count ourselves among the culturally dominant groups) are particularly in need of an experience of immersion in another culture shaped by some other cultural norms. Without such immersion we are too easily inclined to think of our ways as normative and thus again to absolutize them and to judge all others by them.

These immersions and encounters should not, of course, be limited to communities within our own country. Ideally, there should also be opportunities for experiences with people of other cultures on other continents. I recognize that the financial realities of theological education today may make such overseas experience extremely difficult. But that does not make the need any less real.

And again a prerequisite for such experiences with communities of other cultures and other traditions is a solid grounding in one's own tradition and culture. An absence of such grounding linked with even an average dose of American guilt can lead very easily to uncritical adoption of another tradition or other cultural expression of faith—thus failing to see that each one of us must work out our own salvation in fear and trembling in the context of our own cultures, in dynamic interaction with the faith experiences and expressions of others, and through the vehicle of our own personal experience. We cannot take over any other person's or group's spirituality. *We must create our own.* That is the essential norm of authentic formation.

The value of this experience in faith communities shaped by other traditions and other cultures, is of course partly to be able to see ourselves as others see us. But more than that, it helps us better to know and to celebrate the centralities of our faith, thus saving us from a self-righteous emphasis on the peripheral peculiarities of our respective traditions. An undue emphasis on such peculiarities is a natural feature of closed societies, which tend with increasing vigor to emphasize those qualities which distinguish them from other communities. Ecumenical interaction, on the other hand, acts as a corrective to the natural inclination of closed communities to conceive of their partial vision as universal and to absolutize what are actually cultural accidents—whether that be frock coats in the pulpit, black stockings in the street, or Greek philosophical concepts in the seminary. Authentic ecumenical theology does not minimize the differences of the various traditions; it seeks rather to come to terms with them both by challenging the absolutizing of matters which are accidental and by seeking clarity, correction, concurrence, and common confession of the centralities of our faith.

A Passion for the Glory of God

Finally, I would emphasize the importance of a passion for the glory of God. The ultimate concern of ecumenical learning is not the unity (or formation) of the body of Christ, but rather our vision of God. The convergence through the ecumenical movement of the

various cultures and traditions in the Christian church is not finally
for the sake of the church or even for the sake of the world, but for
the glory of God. It is only as our vision of God is enlarged to
encompass both East and West, North and South, black and white,
male and female, and all the other wonderful diversity of the
human family and all of God's creation that the processes of
ecumenical formation reaches fulfillment and the image of God is
renewed within us. We know, of course, that this fulfillment is
eschatological, but like all things eschatological, we may know
some sample, foretaste, realization of it in the present age.

That eschatological gift is best received and the vision best
perceived in worship, and best of all in ecumenical worship. We
know and frequently confess that the present brokenness of the
church is the result of sin. It is therefore true that the different
traditions and liturgies that have developed in our brokenness each
only partially reveal the glory of God, and even then are seen as "in
a mirror dimly." The more therefore we are able to offer the
glimpses of glory revealed through each of these traditions at the
same altar, the more we shall behold the glory of God.

These four elements of ecumenical formation: grounding in the
Bible; a critical appreciation of one's own tradition; experience with
communities of other traditions and cultures; and a passion for the
glory of God are qualities of ecumenical formation that may be
emphasized within the context of any tradition. But since most of us
here tonight are particularly concerned with the Reformed Church
in America, I want to draw out two special applications for this
church.

First, ecumenical formation in the Reformed Church in America
requires an effort greater than that needed in the larger so-called
"mainline" denominations. We are, for one thing, assuredly a more
ethnic group than, let us say, the Episcopalians, the Methodists, or
the Baptists. But even more to the point, we are a small group.
Consequently, in all the history of the World Council of Churches
since 1948, the Reformed Church in America has not once had a
member on any of the commissions of the WCC. Only through the
active, faithful participation of Marion De Velder were we given a
seat on the Central Committee of which I was the grateful
recipient some years after he earned it.

The significance of this marginal participation can hardly be
overestimated. For example, in one of the perennial debates about
the RCA's membership in the Council of Churches—in this case
the World Council of Churches—by far the most convincing word

in the debate was spoken by William Hill-Alto, a delegate to the synod who some years before had participated as a steward in the Fifth Assembly of the World Council of Churches at Nairobi. The absence in our ecclesiastical assemblies of people with such firsthand experience of the World Council (and to some degree of the National Council as well) results in a serious lack of resources for those discussions and for the ecumenical formation of the denomination.

The second point of particular application to the Reformed Church in America is a word of encouragement for administrative and faculty leadership not to grow weary in the well doing which I am calling ecumenical formation. There is, to be sure, no substitute for people who seek out ecumenical experiences for themselves, but ecumenical learning need not be an entirely autonomous enterprise. There is a place for guidance, instruction, even direction from theological faculties and administration. (In our Reformed ethic the law is not after all abrogated!) I cite as an example my own experience as a junior at Hope College seeking to major in English but being also enthralled by history, philosophy, and theology, and failing to see the significance of required courses in novel. My request to be excused from such courses elicited from John Hollenbach, then dean of the college, a one sentence reply, "Mr. Brouwer, an English major at Hope College takes novel!" Those courses turned out to be among the most inspiring part of my academic experience. Just so the words: "Mr. or Ms. Whomever, a student at a Reformed church seminary is concerned with ecumenical formation!" may produce similar results among theological students.

47

An Interfaith Greeting

Presented to the Ninth National Workshop on Christian/Jewish Relations, Baltimore, MD, May 13, 1986

The National Workshop on Christian/Jewish Relations is a major event held every eighteen months. Begun as a Catholic-Jewish venture in 1973, it now enjoys the sponsorship of many faith communities and agencies concerned with interfaith relations and draws people from several continents. The invitation to bring this greeting was a part of my initiation to the National Council of Churches as general secretary. I gladly accepted, since I have long held interfaith relations to be of very great importance—and this particular relationship of prime importance because of our Christian roots in the Jewish tradition.

Sisters and Brothers:

It is my privilege to greet you all on behalf of the Christian community—Orthodox, Roman Catholic, and Protestant. I begin with a few words of personal greeting.

As some of you know, I consider myself a hyphenated American: Dutch-American to be specific. The Statue of Liberty had been standing in the New York harbor for a mere twenty-seven years when my mother arrived there in 1913 with her parents and siblings from the Netherlands.

I mention that now because my Dutch heritage has been very important in shaping my personal commitment to the Jewish people. The Netherlands is a small country, and we who love it must therefore make the most of whatever claim to quality we can find! I have myself chosen to celebrate the history of the Netherlands as a place of refuge for Jews, and many other peoples, in 17th century Europe. I wish I could claim that heritage for my Calvinist forebears—actually we owe it to the insight of Dutch merchants! However that may be, the historical fact is still personally meaningful to me partly because I owe my own first name to the enduring influence of that refugee community. But more meaningful still, because in my own childhood, hearing the terrible stories of Jews (men, women, and children) taken away to be slaughtered by the millions, I took some comfort in the stories of the Dutch (men, women, and children) who risked their lives to save a few. And I like to think that the old Dutch proverb that "God created the world, but the Dutch created the Netherlands," in its own way has given the Dutch a special empathy for the place of the land in Jewish tradition and hope.

I have myself been richly nurtured by the psalms in Hebrew, Dutch, and English. From the prophets I have a caught a vision of a world made whole in peace and justice which is undimmed even after 18 years in various denominational and ecumenical bureaucracies! And much of what I know about justice I learned first from your ancient prophets and their contemporary interpreters.

For this, and much more, I and many other Christians, are forever indebted to the Jewish people past and present. We are grateful that we, in the Christian community, Orthodox, Catholic, and Protestant, can join with you our Jewish sisters and brothers for serious study and reflection on issues old and new, and that we can do so together as persons of faith.

The more we Christians know of our history with the Jewish people the more we know that we must always come together with you in an attitude of continuing repentance. I do not say guilt. I say repentance. Coming to grips with our past means struggling with our guilt until we find our way through to grace and hope. Only thus can we forge a common future. By continuing repentance, I mean a continuing turning away from the anti-semitic prejudice and persecution which have characterized so much of our Christian history and a turning toward the peace and justice and love and mercy of the Lord God of history whom we also follow and whom we know through your history.

We are thus continually called back both to the Christian scriptures and to the Hebrew Bible to renew our understanding of God's covenant and its requirements of us in the contemporary world. Only by thus drawing deeply from the living streams of our own faith and from the ancient ever-flowing wells of the Jewish faith can we be faithful to you, our elder sisters and brothers.

We Christians have yet fully to explore in our contemporary context the meaning of this special relationship between our two faiths for our church life and for our own relationship to the living Jewish people. The fostering of Jewish-Christian relationships in the local communities across this land depends upon ministers, rabbis, priests, and lay leaders moving beyond the casual and social, so that our faith communities can be engaged not only in cooperative service in the community, but also—even most of all—in celebration of one another's traditions, separately and together. This week of reflection and workshops can help—and for a dozen years has helped—equip our people, both Christians and Jews, with resources for this essential element of our life and work. We Christians are grateful to the Jewish community for your collaboration with us and to the planners of the workshop for their care and energy in planning what does indeed promise to be an outstanding program. We look now to God for the gift of turning our history into hope and our hope into history.

48

An Ecumenical Greeting

Presented to the General Synod of the Reformed Church in America, Grand Rapids, MI, June 13, 1989

The invitation to present this greeting had arrived sometime early in the year. By the time I delivered it, I knew that I would be resigning from the NCCCUSA, so I had a number of things to wrap up and a few others to tie down.

Mr. President, Mr. General Secretary, Delegates and other Friends, Sisters and Brothers:
It's good to be home. I can hardly tell you how very honored, pleased, and delighted I am to have received this invitation from your general secretary and my friend, Ed Mulder. When the General Synod met in New York last year, I looked in for a few hours, but officially, I haven't been back in the six years since I said my farewells at Pella. It's *very* good to be home.
For precisely that same number of six years, I had the privilege of serving you as general secretary. They were rich and wonderful years and I am indebted to you for them. In fact, lately, I've missed you more than ever!
Altogether, I spent fifteen years on the eighteenth floor with some of the finest colleagues anyone could ever hope for. I remember that we sometimes allowed ourselves tentatively to think that we were one of the best outfits around. But being a small organization, experimenting with new ways of working as a community in the Big Apple, we weren't quite sure. Well, in the last six years, I've had a chance to see quite a lot of other outfits in

operation. So for the record, we were, and you are, among the best, the very, very best. You can believe it.

Because we were a small organization, most of us then, and most of you now, had to do more than one thing well. Somehow you did it, and you do it, uncommonly well, so well, that more than a few of you are second to none. You can believe that too...

The Reformed Family

It's clear by now I suppose that this is family reunion time for me. That's true for many of you as well. The General Synod is always a gathering of the clan. This year it's two clans mixing together. That's good. Congratulations. The Reformed Church in America and the Christian Reformed Church in North America need each other. Neither one of us can know ourselves until we know one another.

Reading the April 1989 issue of *Perspectives*, I was fascinated by Richard Mouw's observation that denominational humor is at the heart of denominational self-knowledge. I stopped reading and laughed aloud: First, because it seems that my life among you has contributed generously to the store house of RCA denominational humor! Second, because I recalled a rich evening of story telling and story listening enjoyed by a small dinner party one evening at the RCA-CRC meeting at the Ninth Street Church in Holland, Michigan, in the 1970s.

I mostly listened, but my predecessor as general secretary, Marion ("Mert") de Velder, is one of the world's great story tellers. In fact, he tells his stories so well that sometimes he himself enjoys them so much he can hardly finish them! The Christian Reformed church's story tellers were there in force as well. It was a wonderful, rich evening, and I left it knowing and loving the Christian Reformed church better—and knowing and loving myself and Mert better too.

The Christian Reformed church has, for good and ill, preserved the tradition better than we have. As they shared it that night, and on many other occasions as well, I have more than once said: "So *that's how* that got into our blood!" or "*That's why* that works the way it does!"

Those experiences are very like others I often have had talking with my older brothers. They know the family traditions better than I do. Their memories go back farther and they live in cultural settings that help keep the stories alive. Listening to them, I often have had new insights as to how our family was formed, and my own person too—and why we respond to this and that in such and such a way.

As we discover one another, we discover ourselves. Indeed, we can know ourselves only as we know one another. That is of course true for the Christian Reformed church, as well, but it's not for me, or for us, to tell them how. We each need to make our own discoveries.

The Ecumenical Family

By one more extension of the family, from the denominational family through the confessional family, we reach the ecumenical family. And again, it's a matter of discovery—of the other; and of the self.

Perhaps I can illustrate it from an experience of Orthodox Christians. When the Orthodox churches entered the ecumenical family in force in the early 1960s, one of their foremost theologians, Alexander Schmemann, wrote a little book called *For the Life of the World.* He wrote it to explain the Orthodox to the rest of the *Oikumene.* Do you know where it became a best seller? Among the Orthodox! They found that in introducing others to Orthodoxy, they had discovered their own selves in new and revitalizing ways.

That is very much my own experience. Each passing year within the ecumenical movement has led to some deepened sense of what it means to be Reformed. Think of it for a minute in musical terms. Think of the Reformed faith as a hymn tune. If we study that hymn tune together as a Reformed family, we will shortly find that we all more or less agree on the melody. We will therefore spend most of our time talking about the harmony—or perhaps those few fine points in the melody on which we don't quite agree. Just so in theology do secondary themes displace primary themes. We may focus, for example, on predestination and lose sight of the more important theme of God's sovereignty—or even of God.

If, however, the ecumenical family studies that hymn tune along side the hymns of the other traditions, we are all much more likely to focus on the melodies. We are more likely to see the beauty and strength of the major themes. That's one reason we need one another. We will only know ourselves whole, as we know ourselves in relation to the whole.

The National Council of Churches

All this I say and believe in spite of the fact that some parts of the NCC and I have not been getting along very well lately. As many of you know from news accounts and various grapevines, the issues came to a head a few weeks ago in Lexington, Kentucky. Hours of debate, focused on a motion to remove me, led finally to a tie vote. I mention that struggle now because you are family and the family needs to know. I mention it as well, because I want both to commend you and to exhort you concerning that struggle.

First, to commend you. I cannot recall a time when I was more proud of this sturdy, faithful old church or more pleased to be a member of it than I was in those days. Under attack from nearly all points of the ecclesiastical compass, there were quite a lot of people who stood with me for truth and for a shared vision and for love and for justice—particularly for justice. That meant the world to me—so much so that I do not think it would have mattered terribly if I had lost the vote. The trumpets of justice had sounded, and with a very certain note indeed, so as to lift the hearts of those who had ears to hear.

Among the voices that were crystal clear from start to finish of that debate were those of the Reformed Church in America. To my ear, there was a very special note in their speeches. In their words I heard justice mingled with familial love—for me, which warmed my heart; and for the whole ecumenical family as well, which made me proud—that even in the heat of debate during those days of distortion, they, and therefore you, could love the larger family as well—and so well.

I went to Lexington knowing that if I did what I believed I had to do, my job was on the line. Those of you who know me are not surprised that I would adopt such a stance. It has to do with my understanding of vocation.

As I was drafting these greetings last week, I was suddenly led to think of that in terms of decades. The spirit in which I went to Lexington in 1989 is not unlike the spirit in which I and others went, in 1959, (ironically, in the same week of May), to the Board of Trustees of Western Theological Seminary on behalf of the future students of that institution; and in 1969 to this General Synod on behalf of James Forman of the Black Economic Development Conference and the black membership of this church; and in 1979 to this General Synod again on behalf of women ordained to be ministers of the Word. And some of you will remember a few other times between the decades as well!

Those experiences were shocking to some and painful to all, but they had to be done. We had exhausted all other means and it seemed we were at the last possible moment of opportunity for a breakthrough which we desperately needed. I had to do them, because I was in position to do them. It has to do with vocation.

We got our breakthroughs. We followed the Spirit. In the midst of all that shock and pain and turmoil, this old ship steadied and righted itself and set off anew on a course more true.

Whether that will happen at the NCC remains to be seen. At this moment, my job is still on the line. Most of us know that when there is a fifty-fifty chance of *losing* one's job, there may well be more than a fifty-fifty reason for *leaving* one's job. My exhortation, therefore, is that if such a thing should happen, then I would wish you to go on loving the larger family, and to love it no less. They need you as much as ever—even more than ever. And, as I suggested earlier, you need them.

That is in fact the heart of the struggle at the NCC. In today's world we all need each other more than ever before. In the face of social, political, economic, and cultural *disintegration*, I, and others, have been calling the churches to stand against those destructive dividing powers, and to stand against them *together* through greater Christian *integration*, as a sign of wholeness, of salvation, and hope for the world. We dare not permit that dream to perish. I pray that you will help keep it alive—and more, that you will struggle to give it new life—for the life of the world.

A Closing Note

Finally, one more personal note. For a dozen summers, this Brouwer family has been spending as much time as it possibly can in Cape Breton, Nova Scotia. Cape Breton overflows with so much gentle beauty that a local poet has written that when God comes to call him home, God will have to wait awhile as the poet takes one more turn around the island, to linger at Mabou and Margaree, at Cap Rouge, Aspy Bay, and Ingonish—only then will he leave—and even then reluctantly.

I myself like to think that it was here God finished the work of creation...and as that great, gracious hand glided off the planet, it gave a last loving touch to Cape Breton.

I like to think
that it was here God stood,
to pronounce the creation good.

In many ways, Cape Breton is to Canada what the hills of
Kentucky are to the United States—great natural beauty and deep
human poverty. As in Kentucky, so in Cape Breton, they sing of
their land—sadly, proudly, longingly, lovingly. One of those
outpourings of the soul is now the official island anthem. These are
the words of its chorus:

We are an island, a rock in a stream
We are a people as proud as there's been
In soft summer breeze, or in wild winter wind
The home of our hearts, Cape Breton

The home of our hearts, that is what I want most to say to you this
morning. Wherever next my pilgrimage takes me—in the NCC or
out—this sturdy old church will always be the home of my heart. In
the deepest spiritual sense, this sturdy old church will always be the
home of my heart. I have found that I love you even more than
before. God be with you—always.

49

A Pilgrimage Toward Wholeness

An ecumenical exposition at the Western Theological Seminary, Holland, MI, March 26, 1989

Sometime during the summer of 1989, I received a telephone call from John Smallegan, an elder in the Second Reformed Church of Zeeland, Michigan. "You have," he said, "a story to tell, and we would like to hear it." He invited me to preach and lecture. I accepted with the understanding that he would arrange for some other speaking opportunities on the same trip. Western Theological Seminary, where my old friend and former colleague Marvin Hoff was president, responded with an invitation to lead chapel and lecture.

At Second Zeeland, I preached "A Movement for Life" (see chapter 30) in the morning. For the evening lecture, I created a blend of an analysis of my experiences at the NCC but focused on the hopes for renewal of the mainline as sketched in chapter 35 of this volume.

The Western Seminary invitation I took as an opportunity to witness to my personal formation in the ecumenical movement and to integrate my denominational and ecumenical experiences which I hoped would be of some help to others struggling still, as I had, with a heritage of theological exclusiveness and ecclesiastical separatism. The chapel talk that follows focused on formation.

A note on the text:

Perspectives is a fairly new "journal of Reformed thought," sponsored by the Reformed Church in America. It had just published a provocative issue on interfaith relations.

SCRIPTURE: Ephesians 4:1-16; John 16:12-15

Text: Ephesians 4:13 "...until we all attain the unity of the faith and of the knowledge of the Son of God, to (mature manhood) maturity, to the measure of the stature of the fullness of Christ..."

I have chosen a text from Ephesians this morning because it was the study of Ephesians here at Western Theological Seminary that led eventually to my ecumenical conversion. After seminary, the book kept growing on me. Its cosmic vision appealed to my Calvinist soul; its extraordinary development of that vision to my growing love for theology; and its beauty of style to my deepening interest in liturgy. Both at Corinth and at Passaic, I had to remind myself not to preach from it too often!

When I became an itinerant preacher, I stopped worrying about that! For the last decade especially, I have preached the message of Ephesians over and over again, to stimulate ecumenical commitment and to sustain ecumenical hope.

I am by no means the first to make this close connection between the Ephesian letter and the ecumenical movement. You who know your ecumenical history will immediately recall that the theme of Ephesians was the basis for the theme of the very first Assembly of the World Council of Churches at Amsterdam in 1948: "Man's Disorder and God's Design." So decisive was the Ephesian letter at that primal ecumenical moment and thereafter, that I think it legitimate to describe the ecumenical movement as an exposition of the Ephesian letter. That is how I want to present it this morning. I've not done that before, so this approach saves me from the sin of preaching a shortened version of an old sermon and you from being compelled, as a more or less captive audience, to atone for my sin.

There are, of course, many ways in which the ecumenical movement is a bad sermon. It is not always faithful to the text and more often falls short of the vision. That I recognize full well, and more than once I have spoken to the problem with some pointedness and some passion. This morning, however, I am interested in its congruence with the vision.

The ecumenical movement may be described simply as a movement toward wholeness. We have all, I suppose, heard the familiar ecumenical slogan: The whole gospel, through the whole church, for the whole world. Over the years, we have come to see that a fourth dimension of wholeness, which earlier had been assumed, now also has to be explicitly stated. That fourth dimension is the whole person. The morning lesson from Ephesians speaks of it as, "the measure of the stature of the fullness of Christ." But that fourth dimension of the movement is found in the fourth chapter of the letter and if we are to allow the movement to expound the letter, we need to begin at the beginning.

Ephesians is one of relatively few books in the Bible where the theme is stated with unmistakable clarity. The first chapter, the ninth and the tenth verses: God's purpose is to unite all things in Christ, things in heaven and things on earth. Like the letter, the movement, too, begins with the world. It is a truism to say that the word *Oikumene* is not a church word at all. It belongs to the world—meaning the whole inhabited earth. Its application to the church needs then rigorously to be understood in terms of the world. The church can be ecumenical only as it offers its life to the world. That has been the orientation of the movement from its beginning. The watchword of the modern missionary movement was, "The evangelization of the world in this generation." The spiritual brokenness of the world, people came shortly to see, showed itself also in social, political, and economic terms. To evangelization were added service ministries. From within those ministries, a few prophets were able to see more deeply into the human condition and the social situation and began to call for justice. In pre-World War II in Germany, the confessing church found itself face to face with naked evil and in hand-to-hand combat with the principalities and powers. After the war, through the ecumenical movement, the churches managed as well to slip back and forth through the Iron Curtain.

Preoccupied with divisions between East and West, they did not at first see the divisions between North and South. But these too were recognized as brokenness that it was God's purpose to unite. In the 1980s, we have seen played out in the hard realities of history, the backside of the prophetic vision that peace requires not only justice among and within the nations, but also harmony with the whole creation. We are looking now for ways in which we humans can be freed from our technological isolation and reintegrated with the rest of creation.

These barriers of brokenness have been found not only in the secular structures of the world, but also among the religions. As every reader of *Perspectives* knows full well, this particular ecumenical exposition of the Ephesian letter is very much under debate. Yet, it is a question not to be put off. The brokenness among peoples of faith is too deep and too pervasive and growing ever more serious.

In Ephesians, God's purpose for the wholeness of the world is signaled by Christ's gift of wholeness to the church. For Paul, and for Peter, and eventually for the other apostles and elders and finally for us all, the mystery of God made known in the church as a sign to the world was the unity in one body of Jew and gentile. For us Christians, that great divide is the archetype of all human brokenness which we know in many forms. East and West, North and South, rich and poor, black and white, male and female, these and many other brokennesses of the world and the church Christ died to reconcile to God, to bring the hostility to an end and to make peace.

Of this reconciliation, the ecumenical movement is also an exposition—perhaps most radically illustrated in the struggle against apartheid. In apartheid is focused the brokenness of North and South as well as rich and poor and black and white and, in a different way, male and female as well. Apartheid cuts across both church and world right down to the marrow of human existence, gospel truth and church integrity. That is why in our time it has become a matter not only of ethics, but of faith, just as the struggle against Hitler and the Nazis did in another era. To be a "German church" or an "apartheid church" is to be not the church. That was the hard word spoken by the Lutheran World Federation at Dar es Salaam in 1977 and by the World Alliance of Reformed Churches at Ottawa in 1982 and by our own General Synod in 1981.

You see why both the Ephesian letter and the ecumenical movement put the world before the church. To preserve the unity of the church by accommodating ideologies that justify and foster division in the world is to pursue a false unity.

That concern for truth takes us to the third dimension of the ecumenical movement, the wholeness of the gospel. The morning lesson makes it crystal clear that there is only one Lord, one faith, one baptism, one God. It is no less clear that all this magnificent, ultimate unity can only be perceived through diversity, for the very simple reason that no one's gift is great enough to grasp it all. Diversity, therefore, is not opposed to unity; diversity serves unity. Only through diversity can we begin to grasp the wonder of unity. That is why the squelching of diversity always results not in the unity of the faith, but in a series of partial gospels.

Did you notice the dynamism of the diversity in the passage?

There are the apostles, firsthand witnesses of the glory of God revealed in Jesus Christ, telling what they have seen and heard.

And there are the prophets, discerning the Spirit, saying, "Wait, there is more!" rounding out the revelation, guiding the community into all truth just as Jesus promised in this morning's gospel lesson.

There are the evangelists, bringing back to the community what they have learned about the gospel as they told it to the world.

And the pastors, bringing in their wisdom about the gospel acquired as they employed it in the cure of souls.

And the teachers, from their sifting of the scripture and the tradition.

The unity of the faith is not static but dynamic—not that of a stained-glass window, but of a kaleidoscope. This is not to say that we can find license here for a kind of vacuous tolerance or for an ideology of pluralism. Plurality is affirmed and diversity is celebrated, but all in the "certain knowledge and hearty trust" that source and end and vehicle of all this diversity and plurality are one. The ontological unity keeps the plurality interactive and makes the diversity dynamic.

Nor will we find in this passage the slightest suggestion that the unity of the faith is an achievement to be attained in history, anymore than is reaching the measure of the stature of the fullness of Christ. Both are eschatological realities of the now and the not yet.

Perhaps you have seen in this description of dynamic diversity how the ecumenical movement is an exposition of this passage. Can there be anyone in this room who has not experienced firsthand the joy of discovering something about the gospel from someone else's gift? Surely, you know as well, the experience of your own gifts being corrected and enhanced in the act of receiving another's gift. Once you have begun on such a journey, you know that it will never end. You do not want it to end, because then your growth into Christ would end. The unity of the faith is a unity hidden with God in Christ that we discover as we grow into Christ.

Our protection against being blown about by every wind of doctrine is then neither to find shelter from such winds nor to cast out an anchor at the first sign of storm. It is to learn how to sail amidst the winds, staying on course amidst the winds of doctrine, but catching full-sail the winds of the Spirit.

You can see how the ecumenical movement helps to do that, because there you will find these winds always blowing. You need not sail very long before the wind of another tradition, to know that it can take you to places of the Spirit that your own tradition cannot. And often you will see as well that some of what you thought was a wind of the Spirit in your own tradition may well have been one of those misleading winds of doctrine. It is only in community, as comprehensive a community as possible, overflowing with all the gifts Christ has given to the church, that we will find the fullness of Christ and be able to grow into it.

That takes us to the fourth dimension, the pilgrimage toward personal wholeness, or as Ephesians puts it, toward maturity, toward the full measure of the full stature of the fullness of Christ. From the beginning, the ecumenical movement recognized that the world, the church, and the gospel, all these were broken by our divisions. It was not so clearly seen that the persons in those churches were broken, too. Now, the whole world knows that the liberation of people of color and of women is also a liberation of white people and males. We know that broken structures break people too. We know that only in community, only as all of us together, can we each be made whole. And we know too that renewal in the first three dimensions depends in many ways on the mysterious renewing power of God operating in this fourth dimension of personal wholeness.

This too, I have know firsthand. In richly diverse gatherings of the ecumenical community, as nowhere else in my ministry, I have felt myself close to Christ, more in harmony with the New Testament church, its sense of wonder, its passion for mission, its discernment of the Spirit, its commitment to Christ, its struggle to be the church. Sometimes that experience has arisen because we have found ourselves gathered together as we were driven by the principalities and powers hard against the grinding face of evil; sometimes it has come from the sense of being different in nearly every way save one, a common commitment to an uncommon Lord; and sometimes from the wonder of discovering in one another's simple humanity the glory of the image of God in which we are all made and into which we are growing in Christ—who is both the Beginning of this pilgrimage toward wholeness, and also its Fulfillment.

50
On Being Reformed in the Ecumenical Movement

An article in Perspectives, *October 1990*

This chapter was written as the lecture at Western Seminary described in the introduction to the previous chapter. My old college and seminary friend, Richard "Dick" Rhem, heard the lecture and asked for it for *Perspectives,* of which he was an editor. It was published in the 1990 Reformation Day issue with responses from several other people of varying Reformed (including Christian Reformed) persuasions.

My primary purpose was to weave together my own Reformed and ecumenical experience as a basis for the ecumenical vocation of my own community. In the end, it emerged as a challenge to all the traditions.

In the lecture at the seminary, I remarked, "Lest anyone think that this view of our tradition is but another example of the brain-addling effect of ecumenical involvement, permit me to say that the subject has occupied me, sometimes even preoccupied me, since seminary days..." I noted as well that my concern with theological methodology arose from classes in Old and New Testament theology taught by professors Lester J. Kuyper and Richard C. Oudersluys respectively, who often took issue with the systematic methodology of classical Reformed scholasticism. The questions came to focus in a specially offered seminar in theological methodology under the leadership of professor M. Eugene Osterhaven, professor of systematic theology at the seminary, who was present at my lecture and whom I took occasion publicly to thank.

I also took the occasion to say (again) a public word of thanks to the Reformed Church in America in the following words:

> I am myself deeply grateful for all that I have learned from each part of this church. The most valuable of those learnings by far has come from engaging the diverse ways in which we are reformed, and from that interaction seeking always to forge a new understanding of what it means to be reformed. In retrospect, I consider that now to have been a wonderful school for ecumenical learning. It was a splendid way of entering into the life experience of people who were members of the same family, yet very different from me, thereby enabling me to learn something more about being reformed, as well as about being human, than I possibly could have by myself.

All these expressions of appreciation had unhappily to be deleted from the article for publication in *Perspectives* to meet the confines of space, so I am doubly glad to include them here.

Many believe that involvement in the ecumenical movement entails a compromise of one's own tradition. Once I thought so myself, but I have not found that to be the case. I do not say it does not happen. I hold rather that one need not do so, and further to do so is to fail both one's own tradition and the ecumenical movement. I claim rather that the ecumenical movement is best served by faithfulness to one's own tradition; and conversely that the tradition is best served by faithfulness to the ecumenical movement. I will therefore advance the thesis that *our ecumenical vocation is to be Reformed*.

On Being Reformed

By faithfulness to one's own tradition, I do not of course mean traditionalism, compliance with the way things have been or a mere repetition of what has been said before. Such an approach would be neither Reformed nor ecumenical. It would stand opposed to the very heart of the Reformed tradition. From the beginning, we Reformed have been clear about that. The church is Reformed, we say, because it is always reforming. So venerable is that slogan that most of us still like it best in Latin!

We who treasure that ancient formula, *Ecclesia reformata quia semper reformanda est*, will not be surprised at Greek Orthodox theologian Georges Florovsky's affirmation that

> loyalty to tradition means not only concord with the past, but in a certain sense freedom from the past....Tradition is the constant abiding of the Spirit, and not only the memory of words. Tradition is a charismatic, not an historical principle (*Bible, Church, Tradition*, vol. 1, p. 80).

Orthodox theology reckons with that "constant abiding of the Spirit" and practices that "charismatic...principle" very little if any better than we do, I think. But the principle is there right at the heart of the Orthodox tradition and therefore at the root of all our traditions.

For us Reformed, that charismatic principle of the presence of the Spirit is unmistakably clear. Calvin, it has been authoritatively argued, was above all else a theologian of the Spirit. The risks of a Spirit-guided theology he knew full well. Painfully aware of the enthusiasts on the left wing of the Reformation, Calvin warned regularly against their excesses and found at least two ways to guard against them in his own teaching. First, he insisted always that the reformation of the church be "according to the scriptures," and second, that all things be done "decently and in order."

Of course, following the Spirit was still a risky journey. That risk Reformed scholasticism did its best to reduce. The scholastics defended the *deposit* of the tradition but did not sustain the *dynamic* of the tradition. They stressed the *testament* of the Spirit, but neglected the *testimony* of the Spirit. They followed *past confessions* but did not lead in *present confessing*; they preserved the *Reformed faith* but did not pursue *reforming the faith.*

After several decades of drawing "the teaching of godliness into frigid speculations" (Commentary on 1 John 2:3), to use Calvin's own denunciation of an earlier scholasticism, the tradition congealed at the Great Synod of Dordt in 1618-1619. Immediately upon the conclusion of that synod, the Dutch delegates, meeting in separate session, froze the tradition solid, declaring that the creeds were "in all things conformable to the the Word of God." With that apparently troublesome question forever settled, it was expected that confessional questions would no longer be raised. Indeed, one risked one's life to do so. Instead, ministers of the Word and professors of theology and others too, elders, deacons, school teachers, and whoever else was in position to communicate a new idea, all these were required to "defend the statements of our faith" and "reject all errors which are contrary thereto."

To such a formula of subscription, I affixed my name after graduation from seminary as did every Reformed church minister and professor of theology until the formula was modified in the 1960s. Even then, and still today, the official declarations for ministers of the Word and professors of theology in the Reformed Church in America hardly read as words of encouragement for that theological reformation which is at the heart of our tradition and therefore at the center of our calling as ministers of the Word and professors of theology—and of which Calvin himself is a leading example in the whole history of the whole church. It will not do merely to chip away at the frozen forms of the tradition only where they too much chill our life. If we want the tradition to flow freely and clearly as the water of life for a thirsty world, we will need to thaw it out. For that, we will need to learn to live with the heat of Calvin's own burning heart and the sustained theological debate that flowed from it.

Our inability to do so has been disastrous for our life as a church. Sensing the difficulty, if not the impossibility, of building a meaningful contemporary spirituality on the basis of a virtually unchanging formal doctrine, many of our members, and some of our ministers too, have turned elsewhere for their spirituality—most too often to evangelicalism, but sometimes to other "isms" as well. Since no spirituality can long exist without a theological foundation, they have soon begun to adopt the underlying theology of the spirituality they have found satisfying—in hymns, in devotional literature, in worship resources, and in retreats and conferences.

Sometimes such theological change happens mostly unawares and with relatively little pain. Where awareness dawns, however, pain is sure to follow. No way can be found to incorporate the new insights into the old tradition. The tradition is fixed and frozen. We can chip away at it here and there. We can carve out niches for church growth theology, liberation theology, feminist theology, charismatic theology, and perhaps a few other theologies, but there is no recognized operational vehicle for integrating those theologies into the tradition in order to reform both the new insights and the tradition itself.

We are left with some painful choices. Some reject the tradition; some reject the new insights. Most, I think, create shadow traditions which become the real forces that shape our common life. Since they are officially nonexistent and mostly unarticulated, we feel ourselves being changed in directions we have not chosen, by forces we have not legitimated, through processes we cannot engage. That leaves us bewildered, suspicious, afraid, cynical, indifferent—generally resistant to reform and renewal—and therefore subject to periodic upheavals which make the situation worse. All this we can overcome if we can find a way to keep the tradition fluid, to keep it dynamic and alive, to be always reforming it. It is not too much to say that our life as a church depends upon it.

Nor should this call to reform the tradition be heard in any way as minimizing the significance of what we sometimes call the distinctive characteristics of our particular tradition. On the contrary, this approach requires us to know those distinctives better. We need to know them not merely as theological slogans but as gospel truth, as historic examples of our continuing task of reformation, as historical encapsulations of the everlasting gospel shaped in response to the cultural and spiritual crises of their times and therefore conditioned by them. This approach requires us not only to study the tradition, but to be steeped in the tradition by living within the traditioning community.

On Being Reformed in the Ecumenical Movement

Ideally, this traditioning community is first our families, then our congregations, our denominations, and the whole church of Christ. I am myself deeply indebted to all these circles of faith. My understanding of tradition, for example, has been much enriched by the ecumenical movement and particularly by my contacts with the Orthodox churches. Indeed, it seems to me likely that Calvin's emphasis on the Holy Spirit may have been derived directly from that very source, the writings of the fathers with which he was familiar and which he often cited.

Those experiences and many others have long since persuaded me that the first fruit of being Reformed in the ecumenical movement is to be ourselves reformed by the ecumenical movement. It is to know ourselves more fully; it is to see more clearly the radical core of our essential being in Christ, deep within the various overlays of our particular historical experiences which in isolation from the larger Christian community unavoidably obscure in part our common and primary identity in Christ. (The pages of our history are filled with people who were more clear about belonging to Calvin than to Christ!)

Some may feel that they have long ago dealt with any such peculiar historical overlays simply by shucking them off. But it will not do merely to shuck off the past. The past has to be threshed and winnowed over and over and over again to find within it those signs and foretastes of the future which God has been revealing over the ages. To shuck off the past is to throw away those promises. To reform the tradition is to claim those promises for our future.

Moreover, it is dangerous to shuck off the past. Reformed scholasticism, for example, has a way of coming back, particularly in the form of its linear descendent, evangelical rationalism. If it has been merely shucked and not threshed and winnowed, we may not even know it well enough to recognize its rationalistic offspring. All unknowing, we may again embrace the old errors or, more likely it seems, equating rationalism with theology, reject all theology as rationalistic in favor of some form of pietism.

From such errors as these, the ecumenical movement can help protect us by providing us with the perspective of the length, the breadth, and the depth of the whole tradition of the whole church in which light we can more easily see the partial, and therefore incipiently heretical, nature of rationalism, pietism, and a whole host of other "isms"—including, of course, Calvinism and ecumenism.

That practical advantage of being Reformed by being ecumenical is also a matter of principle. From the beginning, we Reformed have understood ourselves as a reform movement in the one church of Christ—not as something separate and apart. Our calling to reform the tradition then can be accomplished only by engaging the whole tradition of the whole church in its mission to the whole world. To that understanding Calvin remained true against all manner of opposition. We follow it still, and nowhere more so than in the ecumenical movement which in many ways is itself a continuation of the Reformation. In that spirit, the 1982 Ottawa General Council of the World Alliance of Reformed Churches declared, "[T]here is for us no alternative to involvement in the ecumenical movement."

The Practice of Our Ecumenical Vocation

If our ecumenical vocation is part of our calling to be Reformed, then the place to begin is in our own life as a denomination. The ecumenical reformation begins at home—and particularly in how we deal with our internal differences.

Most of us, like most other humans, find ourselves most comfortable with familiar truths. Differences are often barriers to knowledge and understanding. What and whom we do not know, we often fear. And what and whom we fear, we avoid. Happily, in a church like this, we cannot avoid one another forever. Unhappily, diversities unengaged too often become divisions confronted, producing unnecessary and frequently destructive conflict. That is sometimes so painful that we build up structures to keep it from happening. Sometimes those structures do permit us each to do our own thing separate and apart. They also prevent us from claiming our unity, or even from learning very much from one another. We are all the poorer for it—each and every one.

If ecumenical reformation is first of all a matter of denominational renewal, then it follows naturally that our second ecumenical responsibility is toward our own confessional family. Virtually all that has been said about engaging diversity in our life together in the Reformed Church in America may also be said of our participation in the World Alliance of Reformed Churches (WARC). Sometimes in our history, and in WARC itself as well, it has been argued that the alliance is counter-ecumenical, that the gathering of families of churches within a common tradition is actually a divisive factor in the larger ecumenical movement. History has shown that the fear is not unfounded. It has also shown that of all the bodies among the Reformation family of traditions, WARC is among the most sensitive to this danger and the most unequivocal in its commitment to foster the ecumenical movement as a whole—and this even though many of its members do not participate in the wider expressions of that movement.

That call to be Reformed in the ecumenical movement extends as well to those Reformed churches that do not participate in WARC. For us, that is especially important in our relationship with the Christian Reformed church. I rejoice that the wounds of this most painful separation are being healed, and I would have us do all that we can to bind them. This past, too, needs to be threshed and winnowed to find the signs of God's future within it. Especially *this* past. It is among our first duties. Neither of us can be whole without the other. Yet, precisely because of the pain in this relationship and the special longing for restored relationships that accompanies it, we must take extra care not to change the questions and short circuit the search for unity. We must resist the temptation to ask merely, How can we be Reformed together? Even here, and always, the question must be How can we be Reformed together for the reformation of the whole church of Christ? That will protect us from making the mistake of trying to restore our particular past; it will keep us focused on our common future in the whole church of Christ.

A third and larger circle of ecumenical relations is to be found in the councils of churches. These as all of us know, constitute our most consistently conflictive ecumenical commitments. Yet our membership in the councils is also, and even preeminently, a matter of being Reformed, of being a reforming movement within the whole church of Christ, and not merely something separate and apart. It is an indisputable fact that the councils are the most inclusive and comprehensive gatherings of that church. Since in the councils, more than in any other place, we are in community with that whole church of Christ, those relationships are arguably our most important protection against sectarianism and therefore essential to the fulfillment of our vocation. Membership in the councils is to be based more on faithfulness to ourselves than on loyalty to the councils.

In a recent *Ecumenical Review* article, circulated as a reprint in our denominational ReSOURCES mailing, Lukas Vischer reports, "Historians of religion have pointed out (I believe correctly) that the convocation of councils is a typical feature of the Christian tradition." Then, in terms congruent with those I have been advancing here, Vischer goes on to state:

In order to remain true to its origins and to carry out its mission, the church needs to meet again and again in assemblies. These are used as instruments by the Holy Spirit whose purpose is to lead God's children into all truth. These assemblies are not chance events but have their roots in the very nature of the church....In order to understand the directives of the Spirit, the church needs to assemble, to invoke the Holy Spirit, return to the sources, and make room for the truth through the confrontation of different insights. Councils are therefore an integral part of the church's journey through history (Oct. 1989, pp. 504ff).

To be sure, Vischer is speaking of councils far more expressive of the fullness of the church than are those which we know today. But the principle holds even though the practice is not yet possible in the fullest sense.

The deep-rootedness of this principle of conciliarity in the life of the church is clearly evident in our denomination. We know it best in our classes, which are for us conciliar bishops, companies of pastors and elders "called out" (the root meaning of *classis*) to exercise mutual care and oversight. From time to time, the classes "come together" in synods (again a root meaning) for the same purpose on a larger scale. Of these, the councils (of which word the root meaning is *called together*) are an extension and as such no less essential to our life as *church* than are our classes and synods to our life as *denomination*.

A fourth set of ecumenical relationships are those with the evangelical community. Does being Reformed encompass them as well? Indeed it does. The evangelical community is an inherent part of our ecumenical commitment and vocation. To a considerable degree, it sprang from within the Reformed tradition. To an even larger degree it may be itself understood as a reform movement within the churches of the Reformation, much as those churches arose as reform movements within the Roman Catholic church. The widespread scholasticism, rampant rationalism, and tired ritualism in many of those churches needed some kind of an antidote. Many found it in the revivals and renewals.

Like the Reformation two or three centuries earlier, those movements too, began within the churches. Usually, however, their leaders were far more ready than were most of the reformers to break out of the churches when the old wineskins did not accommodate their new wine. Cut off from the body, again like the

Reformation churches before them and usually even more so, they hardened their positions, organized separately, built up walls, and frequently succumbed to rationalism or pietism in yet another painful example that schism always deforms the body. It is simply not possible for the churches to live their lives whole in continuing separation, any more than it is possible for a severed arm or the body from which it has been torn to be healed without reconnecting them.

All these relationships point to a fifth area of ecumenical fulfillment: church union. In a certain way, the consideration of church union is even more deeply disquieting for us than our membership in the councils of churches. We are, after all, members of the councils. Church union has eluded us, except of course for the Union of 1850 which was actually more of an adoption than a union. Our denominational policy statement, "The Unity We Seek to Manifest," reads in part, "Therefore, trusting in the Holy Spirit for guidance, we shall be...prepared to merge with any church when it is clearly the will of God..." That last phrase, "when it is clearly the will of God," signals our extra measure of caution about church union. Yet, perhaps unwittingly, it radicalizes the policy statement. For us Reformed, the will of God is not something to be observed at a distance in which we passively acquiesce when we can no longer escape it. We seek it; we search it out with a passion. As we discover the will of God, we strive to do the will of God in order that in our doing what we know, we may learn what we do not know.

Fulfilling Our Ecumenical Vocation through Dialogue

How does it help us to see all of our ecumenical commitments as natural outgrowths of being Reformed? It legitimates them. The chief value of such legitimation is that it would set us free to tackle the real issues about our ecumenical commitments. It would give us an agreed common basis for dialogue about our ecumenical relations—that basis being at the very heart of our own tradition—and thus able to withstand the storms.

Not that we need more discussions and debates and arguments about ecumenical relations. We need different debates. Often stimulated by efforts to decrease the number of our ecumenical relationships, occasionally controversy is sparked by attempts to increase them. Rarely, if ever, do we risk deepening our relationships. Our ecumenical commitments being tenuous, and to some degree usually at risk, it seems best not to rock the boat lest what we have be thrown overboard. As a result, we seem to keep repeating the same debates. We seem to remain forever stuck on first principles—on the fact of participation rather than on the nature and meaning of participation.

If all were agreed that to be Reformed is to be ecumenical then we would be free to separate ecumenical issues from ecumenical symbols. For example, nearly always our debates about the symbol of our membership in the councils have arisen from expressions of disagreement with stances taken by one or another council on certain issues. Yet, those issues often do not even reach the floor for debate. What should be no more than a disagreement about an issue becomes instead a struggle to reject or retain a relationship—surely one of the most painful of struggles. No wonder we try to deaden the pain of those perennial overtures by treating their reception, and their rejection, with a dose of cynicism—on both sides. That cynicism corrodes not only our ecumenical relationships, but those within the denomination as well.

If we were together persuaded that to be Reformed is to be ecumenical, then those symbols of our ecumenical commitment, membership in the councils, would not be immediately at issue. We could then perhaps focus on the issues raised and examine them with the thoroughness they deserve without their almost inevitably being eclipsed by debate about the symbols.

Such open discussion would help the whole church become involved in the quest for unity, thus strengthening immeasurably the hands and voices of our representatives in ecumenical assemblies. It would also make possible more open debate on the symbols themselves, such as that found in the January 1990 issue of *Perspectives* with its frank discussion of the problems as well as the potentials of the organizations through which we attempt to fulfill our ecumenical vocation. If our ecumenical relationships were affirmed as part of our being Reformed and all were evaluated in that light, we would have some hope that our search for the renewal, reformation, and reunion of the whole church would draw together our denomination as well, rather than divide us as it has so often done in the past.

As I have already suggested, a conviction that to be Reformed is to be ecumenical will also strengthen our basis for dialogue within ecumenical organizations. Often, too often, resolutions of the really difficult church-dividing issues in the ecumenical movement are rejected or, what is worse, deflected from decision because they are not sufficiently in harmony with one or another tradition—i.e., not sufficiently Lutheran or Anglican or Reformed or whatever else. I am persuaded that the issues of order and ministry on which the movement has now run aground will never be settled that way, no matter how long the traditions engage one another. We need to focus on the dynamics of the great tradition, rather than on the deposits of the various traditions. We will come together only as we together address the world, as we together seek to confess the faith, as we together rediscover the dynamic of the tradition, as we together listen to what the Holy Spirit is giving us to say and calling us to do. Such dialogue will necessarily include the witness and testimony of those who have listened to the Spirit in centuries past. Further, we will need especially to test whether the Spirit to whom we are listening is the same Spirit whose testimony we find in the scriptures. All this we will need to do in community—tending carefully to the order of the community so that it may be seen as sign, instrument, and foretaste of the vision of God's future for today's world—which vision we shall then have the credentials to preach.

That task of discernment and testimony is an exciting challenge and a wonderful vocation. Proof of the strength of such witness can be seen in its practice in many places, most familiar to us perhaps in South Africa. For many years now, our sisters and brothers there, and in many other places too, have been calling the whole church to join in thus confessing the faith. It is a call at once ecumenical, Reformed, and evangelical. We should join it with our whole hearts.

Conclusion

I have tried to show that we can be Reformed only if we are truly ecumenical and that the more ecumenical we are, the more Reformed we can become. That calling is not ours alone. It may be said of all the traditions that they can be true to themselves—to their own deepest natures—only as they are drawn into the whole Christian community. To be specific and to begin at home:

Only by confessing the faith with the whole community can the Reformation churches seek the renewal of the whole church and thus be truly reformed.

Only by seeking the Spirit with the whole community can the Orthodox churches receive the whole tradition and thus be truly orthodox.

Only by being open to the whole community can the Roman Catholic church be fully inclusive and thus be truly catholic.

Only by witnessing with the whole community can Evangelicals testify to the fullness of Christ and thus be truly evangelical.

Only by watching and waiting with the whole community can Pentecostals receive all the gifts of the Spirit and thus be truly pentecostal.

Only when we can be true to our particular traditions within the whole community will we be drawn together in the great tradition and be united in Christ. For us then, to be Reformed in the ecumenical movement is to have the best of both worlds; indeed to discover that they are one world.

When submitting this Western Seminary lecture for publication, I passed along the information that the *Christian Century* was seeking respondents to my article on the NCC, which it planned to publish in mid-1990 with the understanding that I would then reply to the responses. The editors of *Perspectives* decided to follow a similar approach. They requested and received responses from Eugene Heideman, secretary for program for the RCA; Charles Van Engen, associate professor of theology of mission at Fuller Seminary; and Clarence Boomsma, administrative secretary of the Interchurch Relations Committee of the Christian Reformed church.

The Heideman response helpfully developed and complemented my thesis. The Van Engen response reiterated a number of traditional concerns in ecumenical-evangelical relations. Clarence Boomsma, however, raised fundamental issues about being Reformed and ecumenical which called for further reflection, particularly on the central issue of the relationship between Word and Spirit. The part of my reply which addresses that issue is therefore reproduced below.

A Reply to Clarence Boomsma

That takes us to Clarence Boomsma's challenge to what I have written. Can any fail to note his loving longing for unity? Even if they do not know the strong testimony of his life and ministry in its service. Right to the heart of the matter he goes, therefore, in a spirit of unfailing (and nearly irresistible) grace.

Nevertheless, demur I must from his statement of the relationship of Word and Spirit. I have long struggled with what I have come to think of as the fundamental irony of the Reformed tradition: While insisting that the Word of God written has been given to us by the Spirit, we have often made the Spirit captive to that Word. And this in the face of the scripture's own clear testimony that the Spirit cannot be bound. We can transcend the irony if we affirm that even as the Canons of Dordt cannot bind the Word of God, so the canon of scripture cannot bind the Spirit of God. This affirmation diminishes not one whit the role of the scripture as the uniquely authoritative record of the Spirit's teaching, as an unfailing school for our spirits as we struggle to be faithful and as the definitive standard for testing the spirits and discerning the Spirit of God. Sustained by the scriptures as the fountainhead of the tradition, and nurtured in the communion of those who have lived and died within it, we dare with them to follow into the future that one Spirit who confesses that Jesus is Lord. Thus is the church reformed *by* the Spirit of God and *according* to the Word of God.

It is I think that very Spirit who is often being sought "when our Reformed members turn to evangelism." I agree with Dr. Boomsma that they do not usually do so in order to "jettison the *content* of our theological tradition" (emphasis added), but precisely because they are seeking what he calls "new dimensions of spirituality" and what I envisioned as new forms of the tradition. Nor do I in the least feel that the confessions are "far afield in articulating the gospel." It is the *form* I wish to free so that we all can incorporate (and *reform*) those new dimensions within our communities rather than freezing out people and forcing them to look elsewhere—often for warmth!

The pain over RCA-CRC separation expressed and obviously personally felt by my respondent, I do not know firsthand as profoundly as he. But I share it, and I agree that precipitous unity is unlikely in the extreme. Nevertheless, there may be "danger that we will 'short-circuit the search'" by seeking unity confessionally rather than ecumenically. Signs of that danger abound in both the principle and the practice of the relationships between our two churches. There is even a trace of it in Dr. Boomsma's quotation from the Ecumenical Charter of the CRC.

As for his gracious invitation to suggest "a more meaningful agenda" for our two churches, he has I think himself put his finger not only on the heart of my article but also on the heart of the relationship between our two churches—and on the heart of the struggles within each of them: The relationship between the Spirit of God and the scriptures of the church.

Tackling that subject together would I think help us both and each, as Dr. Boomsma's response has enlivened and broadened this conversation. It would involve us as well in a debate central to the whole ecumenical movement and also critical for the relationship to it of Evangelicals. That debate will likely be rekindled by the Assembly of the World Council of Churches at Canberra, Australia, in February 1991, the theme of which focuses on the Holy Spirit.

Joining that larger debate together would surely enlighten our own, perhaps serve the larger movement, and likely help clarify theologically our relationship to that movement. If that relationship is to be reformed, we will need to be something other than either conservative or liberal. Both those approaches describe relationships to the spirit of the times and therefore by definition are at least incipiently, and perhaps inherently, heretical. Our search is for the Spirit of God. Our task is neither to preserve the past nor to endorse the present, but to discern God's future given by the Spirit in both the past and the present; and then by a further gift of grace to embody that future in the church and act it out in the world.

An Open Ending

Intercessions offered at the Second World Consultation on National Councils of Churches, The Ecumenical Center, Geneva, Switzerland, October 22, 1986

"The most ecumenical meeting ever held was probably that of 120 representatives of some 70 national councils of churches," is the way Ruth Sovik, deputy general secretary of the WCC, described this consultation in the preface to the volume reporting its procedings (*Instruments of Unity*, Geneva: WCC, 1988). An arguable point I suppose, but a fitting backdrop for these intercessions in which I led the consultation on its third day and which I now enlist to conclude these testimonies.

For open hearts to hear and to know the burdens and concerns we bring to this meeting, both those which we carry in our own hearts and which we struggle to speak from the hearts of others,

We cry to you O Lord.

For new eyes to see and voices to celebrate the wealth of human love and grace, gifts and wisdom, gathered here from around the world,

We cry to you O Lord.

For the churches and councils which we here represent and for our colleagues there and in other places, that they and we may be strong in our faith and faithful in our ecumenical vocation,

We cry to you O Lord.

For the World Council of Churches which brings us together in this meeting and binds us together in our common vocation seeking the unity of the churches, the healing of the nations, and the renewal of creation,

We cry to you O Lord.

For all those who work in this house, who have planned this meeting, whose loving and patient care sustains us in our days here together, and whose presence here inspires us in all our days as a visible symbol of the whole people of God gathered from many lands, praising you in many tongues, offering up the riches of many cultures,

We cry to you O Lord.

For all those sisters and brothers of other faiths with whom we are already united in the struggle for peace and justice, that together we may find ways to still the strife that too often springs from the divisions in and among our faith communities and that we may each and all be instruments of healing in the world,

We cry to you O Lord.

For the well being of all those who suffer from hunger, from ravages of war, the rumors of war, powerlessness, or any other of the untold and unnamed forms of injustice in our modern world,

We cry to you O Lord.

For the repentance of those who arrogate to themselves the power which you have entrusted to all the peoples of the world,

We cry to you O Lord.

For your church in all lands and places and among all peoples that we may always be found faithful,

We cry to you O Lord.

Index

Acts 2, 163-166
America, United States of
  celebration of, 52
  ecumenical criticism of, 113-
    114, 131-133
  fear in, 26-27, 49-50
  freedom in, 26
  mission in, 126-134
  Ronald Reagan's attack on,
    87-88
  violation of its heritage, 20-21
Apartheid
  as status confessionus, 304
  theological roots of, 63-64
Arms race
  as spiritual struggle, 49-50
  destruction of
    economic systems, 49
    environment, 49
    history, 49
    political systems, 49
  effect on children, 121-122
  U.S. and Soviet role in, 47
  (see also Disarmament)

Banning, nature of, 61
Bread for the World,
    importance of, 7

Brouwer, Edward John, 53-54

Cape Breton, 299-300
Children, destruction of in the
    USA, 121-122
Christian Reformed Church,
    relationships with the
    RCA, 258-263, 296
Church order, 274-282
Church, purpose of, 67-70, 72,
    82-84 (see also Church,
    unity of)
Church unity, 204-210
  as an article of faith, 72-76
  need for commitment to, 161-
    162
Churches, relationship with as
    NCC general secretary,
    199-200
Civil disobedience
  in the U.S. Capitol, 89-90
  jailed for, 90-91
  principles of, 91-92
Communication
  in denominational and ecu-
    menical life, 247-255
  quality of, 114-115

Communism and anti-
    communism, 40-41
Community
  as a sign of justice, 173-174
  encounter among, 288-289
  importance of, 184-186
  renewal of, 218
Competence, importance of,
    112-113
Controversy
  as RCA general secretary, 6
  over councils of churches,
    152-154
Councils of Churches
  as centers of conflict, 152-154
  nature of, 315-316
  signs of God's purpose, 72,
    153-154
  tensions with member
    churches, 143-146
  vehicles for sharing
    resources, 172-173
Credibility of ecumenical
    organizations
  importance of, 104
  nature of, 104-115
Cultural barriers, crossing them
    as a form of renewal, 236-
    140
Cultural engagement, as a way
    to renewal, 218-219

Denominational identity
  renewal of, 219-220
  of the RCA, 268
Denominational office location,
    211-214
Dialogue, ecumenical
  approach to, 37-38
  call for openness in, 41
  complicated by governmental
    relations, 7, 43-45, 47-48

nature of, 317-319

Disarmament
  advocacy for at Reagan-
    Gorbachev summits, 79-84,
    97-100
  choose life statement, 9-13
  discussion with Soviet Church
    leaders, 7
  progress in, 101-102
  urgency of, 31-32, 43-51
Diversity, and unity, 305
Divestiture, 68
Divisions, in the church and in
    the world, 153
Drafting of ecumenical
    documents
  early experience with, 7-8
  nature of, 5
  Soviet approach, 4

Ecumenical commitment,
    development of, 148-151,
    256-257
Ecumenical formation, 283-290,
    301-307
Ecumenical renewal
  of the mainline churches,
    215-222
  of the movement itself, 234-
    235
El Salvador
  suffering of, 17-21
  victim of East-West tension,
    14
Eloff Commission, Government
    of South Africa
  formation and work of, 56-57,
    61-62
  testimony before, 56-78
Ephesians 2, 204-210
  essence of the gospel, 71-72

Evangelicals, 316-317

Formation, 177-186 (See also
    Ecumenical Formation)
Freedom of religion, as the
    "first freedom," 33-35

Genesis 11, and apartheid, 67
Genesis 28, 211-214

Hiroshima and Nagasaki, 48

Image of God in various races,
    73
Inclusiveness, 110, 160-161
Institute on Religion and
    Democracy, nature of and
    dialogue with, 36-42

Jews
    freedom for Soviet, 93-96
    working relationships with,
        94-95, 291-293
John 17:20-26, 106
Justice
    in the witness of the churches
        in the U.S., 130-131
    trelationship to peace, 158-159

King, Martin Luther Jr., 133
Kingdom of God, 270-272
Korean War, 53-54

Leadership, primary task of, xv
Libya, bombing of, 79-84
Life, given in Christ, 155-162
Linkage, between disarmament
    and human rights, 93-96,
    97

Marple, Dorothy, 198, 203
Maryknoll sisters, 17

Militarization, 49
Mission, renewal of, 220-221
Motivation for testimony, xvii

National Council of Churches
    future of, 137-140
    relationship with the Evan-
        gelical Lutheran Church
        in America, 197-203
    (see also Councils of
        Churches)
National security, as fuel for
    the arms race, 11
Naude, Beyers, 61-63
Neff, Robert, 177-179
Niebuhr, Reinhold, on
    America, 131-132

Orthodoxy in America, 129

Peace, and the Christmas
    promise, 31-32
Politics and prophecy, 29-30
    (see also Religion in Public
        Life)
    relationship of, 29-30
Prayer, its importance in the
    ecumenical movement,
    142
Presbyterian Church in the
    USA, ecumenical
    significance of office
    transfer, 211-214

Reformed Church in America,
    appreciation for, 272-273,
    294-299
Religion in public life, 123-124
Religious right
    crusading mentality of, 29
    media and, 28
    rise of, 28

Renewal
  need for and impediments to
    220-222
  patterns of, xviii
  (see also Ecumenical
    Renewal)
Resources (see Sharing of)
Roman Catholic Church in the
    ecumenical movement,
    187-196
Russia
  devotion to Motherland, 24
  (see also Soviet Union)
Russian Orthodox Church
  millennial greeting, 116-120
  role in Soviet society, 24

Sharing of resources
  a Biblical study, 163-166
  principles of, 167-176
Solidarity, importance of, xv, 19
South Africa, visit to, 56
South African churches,
    relationships with, 67-69
South African Council of
    Churches, government
    charges against, 56-58
Soviet churches
  first encounter with, 6
  importance of personal
    relationships with leaders,
    8, 102-103
  (see also Russian Orthodox
    Church)
  prayers with, 79-80, 97-100
  relationship with, 98-99
  relationships with through the
    NCCCUSA, 118-120
Soviet threat, awareness of, 15
Soviet Union
  American peoples' openness
    to, 46

authoritarianism in, 25, 26
commemoration of WW II
    in, 23-24
first visit and impressions of,
    22-27
superficial commitment to
    communism, 24
Staff, role in ecumenical
    organizations, 140, 144-145
Stransky, Thomas, 189

Theological method, general
    patterns, xvii
Tradition, 268-270, 286-288 (see
    also Theological Method)
Travel, reentry from, 25-26

U.S. government, criticism of,
    34-35
Unity (see also Church Unity),
    an affirmation of, 241-243

Williamsburg Charter, 123-125
World Alliance of Reformed
    Churches, 314-315
World Council of Churches
  and the heritage of Calvin,
    244-246
  the Vancouver Assembly,
    155-162
  why work for, 147-151
Worship
  as source of renewal, 225-231
  importance of in ecumenical
    movement, 140, 145
  its ecumenical renewal, 217-
    218
Writing
  importance of, xv, xvii
  motivation for, xv, xvii